SNOW ON THE ATLANTIC

ABOUT THE AUTHOR AND TRANSLATOR

Nacho Carretero is an investigative journalist with the Spanish newspaper *El Español*. His reporting has taken him to countries ranging from the Philippines to Rwanda, and he has previously written for *El País*, *El Mundo* and many other publications. The original Spanish edition of *Snow on the Atlantic* has become a bestseller in Spain, as well as a popular TV series on Antena 3.

Thomas Bunstead is a writer and translator based in East Sussex, England. He has translated some of the leading Spanish-language writers working today, including Agustín Fernández Mallo, Enrique Vila-Matas and Juan Villoro, and his own writing has appeared in publications such as *>kill author*, *Paris Review Daily*, and *The TLS*. He is an editor at the literary translation journal *In Other Words*. @thom_bunn

SNOW ON THE ATLANTIC

HOW COCAINE CAME TO EUROPE

NACHO CARRETERO

TRANSLATED BY THOMAS BUNSTEAD

ZED

Snow on the Atlantic was first published in English in 2018 by
Zed Books Ltd, The Foundry, 17 Oval Way, London SE11 5RR, UK.

www.zedbooks.net

Originally published in Spanish by Libros del K.O. in 2015.

This translation is published with arrangement of Oh!Books Agencia
Literaria.

English language translation © Thomas Bunstead 2018.

Typeset in Haarlemmer and Trade Gothic
by Swales & Willis Ltd, Exeter, Devon
Cover design by Steve Leard
Cover photo © Tetra Images/Getty

A catalogue record for this book is available from the British Library

Printed and bound by CPI Group (UK) Ltd, Croydon, CR0 4YY

ISBN 978–1–78699–302–1 pb
ISBN 978–1–78699–303–8 pdf
ISBN 978–1–78699–304–5 epub
ISBN 978–1–78699–305–2 mobi

For Antón: welcome.

For Paloma: thank you.

CONTENTS

CONTENTS

'Make a record of it all. Some day, some bastard is going to stand up and say none of this ever happened.'

Dwight D. Eisenhower, after the liberation of Auschwitz

INTRODUCTION

Old people in *a raia*[1] still tell the tale.

There was an old man who crossed the border between Galicia in Spain and Portugal every day on his bicycle, always with a bag over his shoulder. Each time, the border guards would stop him and ask what was in the bag. Ever accommodating, the man opened it and let them look for themselves. 'Just coal,' he would chirp. The border guards, though irritated, let him through. On the other side, the same scene: the Portuguese border guards (known locally as *guardinhas*) would search the bag before allowing him to cycle on. A scene that played out again and again over the years, to the continued annoyance of the border guards; every time he came along, not only would they not find any contraband, it meant getting coal dust all over their uniforms. Like the Edgar Allan Poe short story in which police ransack a house for a letter that was in front of them the moment they walked through the door, the secret of this *raia* man was in plain sight all along.

He was a bicycle smuggler.

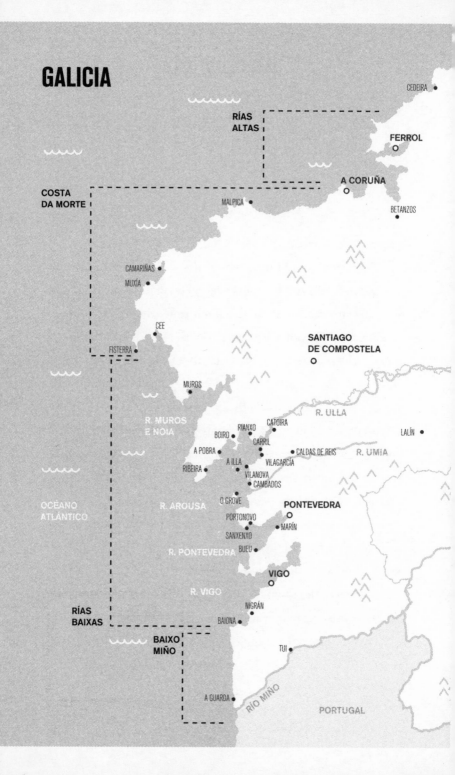

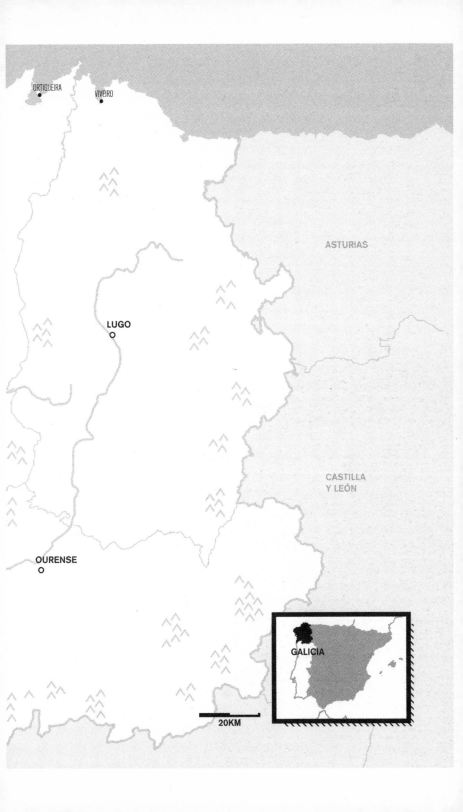

ORTIGUEIRA

VIVEIRO

ASTURIAS

LUGO

CASTILLA
Y LEÓN

OURENSE

GALICIA

20KM

BY LAND, SEA AND *RÍA*

'From the Romans to the Prestige oil spill: everything
sinks off this coast.'

THE SEA: COSTA DA MORTE LEGENDS

It seemed hard to believe when we did the measurements at school: Galicia has 930 miles of coast. More than Andalusia, more than all of the Balearic Islands put together. Zoom in and the shoreline reveals an aversion to straight lines; it comprises an uncompromising welter of recesses and tiny bays, ideal for entering and leaving unseen. The succession of shelves and rocks that skirt it could almost have been designed for ships to run aground on. One of its stretches is called Costa da Morte[1] – the Coast of Death. And it is on the Costa da Morte that this story begins.

There was a time when the only interaction between the villages and towns in the area – most of them nestled away, sheltered from the scouring Atlantic winds – took the form of rivalries between the fishermen's guilds. The remoteness of Galicia brought about a unique accent that other Spaniards often struggle to understand. The jewel in the crown is Cape Finisterre – the end of the world as far as the Romans were concerned; to the Greeks the point from which Charon the ferryman set off across the Styx; and the place where the

Christian Camino de Santiago begins. For most visitors today, it is simply a charming promontory jutting into the ocean. And, it just so happens, a nice steep headland for bringing in contraband.

The people of Costa da Morte, which runs roughly from the city of Coruña to a little way past Finisterre, have always depended on the sea for their livelihood. On fishing and on trade, but also on passing merchant vessels; they would not always wait to get their hands on the cargo at the principal ports of Corme, Laxe, Muxía or Camariñas, often choosing to go out raiding instead. Or they could just keep an eye out for any wreckage that might wash ashore.

Any attempt to count the ships that have sunk off Galicia is itself destined to flounder. There have been 927 documented cases since the Middle Ages – 'If only,' locals say to that. A researcher named Rafael Lema has written a meticulous compilation of these stories entitled *Costa da Morte, un país de sueños y naufragios* (Coast of Death: Country of Dreams and Shipwrecks), which summarises some of the most surprising incidents.

At the end of the nineteenth century, the English merchant vessel *Chamois* ran aground near Laxe. According to local fable, a fisherman went to the aid of the crew, calling out when he drew close to see if the captain wanted assistance. The captain, thinking he was being asked the ship's name, answered '*Chamois*,' and a wondrous linguistic short circuit resulted: the fisherman understood him to be saying that the ship's cargo was cattle (*bois* in Galician) and hurried back to land to tell his compatriots. In no time at all they had sailed out in their hundreds, armed to the teeth – to the horror of the bedraggled Englishmen.

Around the same time there was the *Priam*: when it ran aground, the gold and silver watches that spilled onto the beach were gone within a matter of hours. A grand piano also washed up, and the locals, mistaking it for another chest, hacked it to pieces. They had never laid eyes on such a thing before.

The popular story of the *Compostelano* does not strictly concern a shipwreck. She manoeuvred expertly to enter the River Laxe and, coming to landfall, ran into a sandbank off Cabana beach. When the locals went down to take a look, they are said to have found a cat on board, but no sign of any crew.

One of the worst tragedies took place in 1890, when the English vessel *Serpent* went down off Camariñas and its crew of 500 perished. Their graves can be found in the nearby English Cemetery, positioned scenically between beach and cliff. Twenty years earlier the *Captain* had sunk off Finisterre, and no fewer than 400 men lost their lives.

The horror of shipwrecks did not always take the shape of drowned men. In 1905, the *Palermo*, its hold full of accordions, sunk near Muxía. The onshore breeze was said to carry chilling, ghostly strains that night.

In 1927, the *Nil* beached near Camelle, its hold full of sewing machines, fabrics, carpets and wagon parts. The first thing the ship owners did was to employ some local people to guard the cargo. Little good that did: others came and stripped the vessel in a matter of days. The *Nil* also happened to be carrying boxes of condensed milk. According to the accounts, the locals had never seen condensed milk before, and mistook it for paint. When they took it home and began daubing it on their houses, an infestation of flies followed that was of biblical proportions.

The instances outside living memory also include the staggering 1596 case of the Spanish Armada: 25 vessels sunk, at a cost of more than 1,700 lives. Reports at the time paint the direst of pictures, with bursts of lightning illuminating a watery scene littered with corpses, shattered pieces of ships and men crying out as the waves claimed them.

The sailors on the *Revendal*, *Irish Hood* and *Wolf of Strong* – the three English ships to be wrecked off the Costa da Morte in the nineteenth century – were found mutilated on the beaches. Their fates were sealed by local *raqueiros*, land pirates who made it their job to throw ships off course before going aboard. They would light pyres or hang torches from beacons placed at strategic points along the clifftops. When the ships ran aground, they rowed out and slaughtered the crews. Most of the victims were Englishmen, and it was not long before word reached those shores. At the turn of the twentieth century, the writer Annette Meakin, a friend of Queen Victoria Eugenie, horrified at the accounts, came up with the striking appellation of the Coast of Death. It stuck. British newspapers were soon running articles about the dreaded area, and it was from there that the Madrid press got hold of the story, and, back-translating to *Costa da Morte*, began peddling the title too. Westminster soon sent requests to Spain asking the authorities to take measures against 'these pirate mafias'.

'There was never a mafia,' says Rafael Lema. In his opinion, these were isolated incidents, and the stuff of local legend was just that: 'There is nothing in the records to suggest the existence of any pirate organisation that systematically went around plundering ships.' Although the tales of shipwrecks are open to debate, they still give a sense of a society and an economy taking shape over several centuries on the basis of easily available, and usually not paid-for, cargo.

THE LAND: *A RAIA SECA*, BLACK-MARKET BEGINNINGS

While ships were being plundered on the Costa da Morte – or *allegedly* being plundered – those inland were quick to take advantage. Here the facts are not open to debate or mythologising: from medicine to hard currency, comestibles to electrical appliances, and from consignments of metal to weaponry and immigrants, over time all manner of merchandise has found its way through *a raia seca* (the dry strip/border), as the areas of land that join Galicia and Portugal are known.

The Luso-Hispanic border at these latitudes is famously diffuse. Very old cultural and linguistic overlaps exist between the countries, and there is no clear geographical dividing line. As recently at the nineteenth century some of the inhabitants in the remote villages between Verín and Chaves did not know which country they were citizens of. Nor did they care very much. The most extreme example of this kind of statelessness was in an area called Couto Mixto.

Santiago, Meaus and Rubiás were the three villages that made up Couto Mixto, a remote and mountainous triangle covering an area of 20 square miles. This desolate area was declared a 'murderers' corner' in the Middle Ages, the same status given to a number of regions that were either situated in remote borderlands or decimated by plague or war and then repopulated with freed prisoners. Some 1,000 people installed themselves in Couto Mixto in the eleventh century, and in time it began to operate as an autonomous zone. Both the Earldom of Portugal and the Kingdom of Galicia renounced any claim to it, leaving the people there in territorial limbo.

When Galicia was annexed by the kingdoms of León and Castile at the turn of the twelfth century, Couto Mixto's peculiar lack of definition became starker still. From the thirteenth century onwards, with no Portuguese or Spanish kingdoms laying claim to the area, the inhabitants effectively began functioning as independent subjects: they elected their own representatives, paid no taxes and were exempt from conscription. With no official treaties concerning the area, all sides accepted its de facto self-sovereignty. And so Couto Mixto also became a free-trade zone, untouched by the fledgling Spanish Guardia Civil and the Portuguese Guarda de Finanzas alike. The so-called 'special route' that bisected it was a smugglers' paradise.

This geopolitical limbo carried on until 1864, when Spain and Portugal signed a boundary agreement as part of the Treaty of Lisbon: the border that was established, from the mouth of the River Miño to that of the River Caya in Guadiana, lay not on one side or the other of Couto Mixto but down the middle of it. It spelled the end of this Galician Andorra, whose independence had lasted eight centuries and was the subject of a film by Rodolfo González Veloso called *Rayanos: The Last of the Free Galicians.*

The treaty marked the line that today – in official terms – still separates the Spanish province of Ourense from Portugal. Families were split in two, though many ignored the decree and simply went on observing the same property boundaries as always. In some places neighbours would have yearly meetings to decide on the new boundaries, according to crop demands or new constructions that had been built. So while the authorities enforced one border, the locals operated according to their own agreements. Following the Civil War (1936–39), the border was manned, putting an end to its hitherto permeability and officially making illegal the import and export of all goods. Shepherds were the only people permitted to cross without registering at the border posts. Some, once they had crossed *a raia*, did not come back.

The newly rigid border also marked the clear inequalities between the peoples on either side: in post-war Spain, rural areas such as Galicia were plunged into poverty, while in Portugal the standard of living was relatively high. Not only did Galicians have to make do without medicines and petrol, there was a shortage of foodstuffs, electricity and machine parts. Coffee and lighters became luxury commodities. The locals, looking out by the light of their oil lamps, could see, a short distance away, the Portuguese homes lit by electric bulbs. This was the context for the first ever concerted smuggling efforts: a consequence of the inequalities between the areas on either side of the border.

There was bootleg food and bootleg medicine, bootleg machinery, mechanical parts and weapons. Those bringing the goods charged 49 pesetas for a bundle of food, and 300 pesetas for metals or tools – roughly what an average Galician could earn in a month.

Part of the reason why goods could move across *a raia seca* with such ease was the complicity of the Guardia Civil. There was nothing abnormal about the sight of smugglers and *guardias* sharing a tumbler of wine over a game of dominos in the local tavern. The authorities benefited from the arrangement, a marriage of convenience that has carried on into recent times when the area has become a hotspot for tobacco and drug smuggling.

Such activities would halt only during visits of officials from Madrid. The trains that went back and forth between Spain and Portugal began running at their allotted speeds, and not at the usual 5mph that allowed handovers to take place. When the *Madrileños* were around, people would remove the white handkerchiefs from their windows: the coast was no longer clear. There would be a hiatus of a few days, after which, with the officials safely back in the Spanish capital, the locals could once more obtain penicillin (which the Portuguese brought in from Brazil), as well as coffee, ham, salt cod and cooking oil. English headscarves even made it across the border, destined to be worn by ladies in the Galician market towns of Ourense and Vigo. Clearly, far from being looked down upon, smuggling was an activity to which respect was attached – prestige, even. In the post-war depression that gripped Galicia, contraband was also a means of survival.

During World War Two the area became an international source of tungsten, a metal crucial in the building of German armaments. The specialist miners of tungsten in *a raia* went on to sell it, at times for prices matching that of gold, to 'the blondies', as the Nazi envoys were known. Before the war, tungsten was worth 13 pesetas per kilo, but so great was the demand from the Third Reich that the price shot up to 300 pesetas per kilo. Dozens of Ourense families became rich during those years. This localised boom provided the material for a novel, *Febre* (Fever), by Galician writer Héctor Carré: the Galician border is depicted as a kind of El Dorado, with tungsten miners competing for the spoils. Indeed, at the same time as the Nazis were in the area, resistance fighters who still opposed Franco were hiding out in the Galician hills; they were another source of income for the locals, who sold them contraband Portuguese provisions. There has lately been a resurgence of interest in that singular time, with the Galician Council and the Tourist Institute in Porto working together to uncover the tungsten-smuggling routes – a venture that is to be commended, especially in a place like Galicia where forgetting is what people do best.

THE RIVER: *A RAIA MOLLADA*, THE EMBRYO

While the Ourensanos used mountain trails to transport goods, in Pontevedra they had water: *a raia mollada* (the wet strip), as the estuary is known. Miles wide in places, with many small islands and coastal paths, it forms the Spain–Portugal border at the point where the River Miño meets the sea.

During the post-war years, hundreds of local families – more or less anyone with access to a shore boat – developed an interest in smuggling. They would unload goods from ships and load them onto vehicles for distribution inland. Sound familiar? *A raia mollada* was the embryo for all the drug trafficking in latter-day Galicia. These ur-smugglers laid the foundations – the infrastructure and the black-market culture – for what would go on to be an attractive window display when the Latin American drug cartels came looking for a route into Europe. You can just imagine how it looked to the narcos: everything they needed was in position, and had been for years. And this was the place they chose. To this day, Galicians remain their business partners of choice.

It wasn't always so cinematic. Or violent. It wasn't even immoral. In the lower reaches of the Miño, smuggling emerged as an echo of post-war hardships, as it had done inland. When a rationing system is in force, and yet all kinds of medicines and foodstuffs can be obtained a few miles away, just over the border, contraband becomes a necessity. So it is defined by Praxíteles González Martínez in his book *Yo también fui contrabandista en el estuario del Miño* (I Too Was a Smuggler on the Miño Estuary), a first-person testimony that opens a window onto the Galician border areas in the 1940s. 'People were starving,' writes González, 'and cast envious glances across the border. There, a stone's throw away, was Portugal, with its little white houses, its automobiles and its electricity. Meanwhile, we burned tallow candles to read our books at night and you'd be lucky if you knew anyone who owned a bicycle.' The differences González describes are between one group of people who were starving, and another enjoying the spoils of their African colonies.

Women were the first to take part in smuggling in an organised way. They were responsible for looking after the cattle, which they grazed on the estuary islets, and it was easy for them to use the herds to transport goods such as sugar, rice, oil and soap. In time they began to move coffee, matches and fabrics in their kilos. Out of necessity, the first, rudimentary collectives sprang up, as the women devised warning systems for any time the authorities showed up.

Many Galicians had emigrated to Castile and Catalonia to work as seasonal fruit pickers, and the contraband boom enabled them to come home. Soon men began taking the place of the women at the head of the new collectives. As the amount of goods grew, so did the complexity of the logistics – soon boats and horses were needed. There was a tuberculosis epidemic at the time, so penicillin became a money-spinner. Profit and demand.

From the beginning, the relationship with the Guardia Civil was good. Those in the pay of the government were as hard up as everyone else, and it was almost always them who proposed the pacts. When agreements could not be reached, they would arrest a few smugglers and fine them twice the value of any goods confiscated. In other words, if the goods were of no use, no fine. When the smugglers saw the *guardias* coming, they threw packages overboard or destroyed merchandise (a number of hasty avian bloodbaths were carried out by certain chicken smugglers during this time). A harbinger, in every respect, of the staple image of drug runners throwing packages off the back of speedboats later in the century.

The 1950s saw a gear change when non-essentials began to be smuggled. The Spanish economy wasn't struggling so badly now, while Portugal moved into a phase of depression, and goods began to move in both directions: items such as car parts, copper, scrap metal, tin, wire, rubber, salt cod, octopus, raisins and tobacco. The runners came to be known as *freteiros* or freighters (*frete* being Portuguese for freight), and they earned 200 pesetas for every run they did. To avoid misunderstandings – and to ensure they weren't being cheated – the bosses would wait just over the border. A *freteiro* would hand over the goods in exchange for an aluminium token, which could later be cashed in. Contraband reached such levels of social acceptability that these tokens went on to have monetary value in several towns on both sides of the border, to the tune of 200 pesetas or 100 escudos. Many businesses were only too happy to take them.

Sometimes the freight was human. With the colonial wars in Angola and Mozambique, the Portuguese economy went into decline at the start of the 1960s, and great numbers of Portuguese tried to escape the country, some because of the increasing privations and others to avoid conscription. The Galician contrabandists were part of a new human-trafficking network, of which the River Miño was an important staging post. They charged 600 pesetas per person. A small fortune.

The Galicians got them upriver and into safe houses, and after that into trucks and wagons bound for France. There were cases of conmen passing themselves off as contrabandists and taking emigrants only as far as Asturias in Spain or the Basque Country, before taking off with the money. Isolated cases such as these aside, accounts suggest that the stowaways were well looked after, with the contrabandists even supplying doctors if any of their charges fell ill.

At first people were trafficked with relative ease and at a steady rate, but when the authorities reacted, the operation had to be refined. They would be stowed inside empty petrol tankers, beneath the rear beds of trucks or in the trunks of cars.

One of the contrabandists involved in trafficking these Portuguese emigrants went by the nickname Lito. He remembers transporting a family of four once, and the father spending the entire trip drinking. 'He was petrified,' says Lito.

The man came up to him at the prow of the boat and asked if he had to take his hat off when he stepped on Spanish soil. Lito remembers him singing a song, in a sort of half-Portuguese, half-Galician tongue: '*Bailemos xuntos, sobre as ondiñas do mar | para lhe cortar os collóns a Franco e a cabeza a Salazar*' ('On the waves of the sea, we dance together | and we cut off Franco's balls, and the head of Salazar'). At one point, he fell flat on his face in some mud; it was not the easiest run Lito ever made.

The contraband networks flourished. They spread into new areas, moving up from the estuary and into the land crossings between Vigo and northern Portugal. Scrap metal became the primary commodity; initially, it too could be moved quite openly, but again, once the authorities became more vigilant, the runners had to up their game. For example, the ready young men of Vigo fashioned waistcoats out of scrap metal, which they would put on beneath their jackets, and leg warmers out of tyre rubber. Praxíteles González paints a picture of the youth of the day, with an extra 10 kilos on chest and back and a further 20 on their legs, walking painfully slowly along the streets of Vigo – 'Like robots but in slow motion.' When a bus broke down approaching the border, the driver had no idea it was because so many of the passengers were carrying 30 or 40 kilos of contraband.

For the Guardia Civil or the Portuguese *guardinhas* a posting in Baixo Miño was better than winning the lottery. There is a story of a young Portuguese officer who was sent to the Galician border, where his father, a famously upright man who had managed to avoid all ties with the contrabandists, had held the same post previously. A very awkward situation for both sides. When the son arrived to take up the post – with his father's renown preceding him – he worried that the contrabandists would think he was cut from the same cloth. Worried, that is, about not getting his share. On his first day in the job the young man addressed the question head-on, going from house to house in the villages and towns on the border and leaving the black marketeers in no doubt: no, he wasn't like his father. He liked money as much as any man. And he intended to get paid.

SMOKE

'Go to Madrid, Mariano, get yourself a wife, have some kids, and while you're at it, learn Galician.'

MARLBORO CELTA

There is a story about the Vigo football team, Celta Vigo, playing a big match at their home stadium, the Balaídos, at the beginning of the 1960s. The club president, Celso Lorenzo Villa – a Republican ex-pilot and contrabandist – came and did fly-pasts during the match. People say he flew so low that the jet propellers ruffled the players' hair.

It was in this decade, the 1960s, that the contrabandists came to understand where the real money was: in moving tobacco from Portugal. Nothing, except petrol, was as profitable. The criminal networks underwent a structural change: the small-time and middling black marketeers making way for wholesalers who came to monopolise the market. From smallholdings to plantations; and from independent contrabandists to fully hierarchical organisations, with a *capo* at the head.

Celso Lorenzo Villa was one of the first big Galician tobacco *capos*. A respected man in Baixo Miño, rich, popular and well connected, and president, no less, of Real Club Celta de Vigo. He took over the club in 1959 and had plans to take the recently relegated team back to the higher echelons of national competition. He rarely made an appearance in the Balaídos directors' box, but his board members did. Among them was one Venancio González or 'Capitán Veneno' ('Captain Venom'), who, in his playing days in the 1940s, made a name for himself with his scything tackles – on teammates and opposition alike – on the right wing. There was a story about him snatching an umbrella from a fan who had been shouting insults during a match and using it to batter the man. Twenty years later, as the club moved into its so-called 'Marlboro Celta' phase, 'Captain Venom' was helping to run things.

The Celta of Celso Lorenzo Villa travelled to away stadiums in a state-of-the-art Dodge bus with the club's name and shield painted on the sides: a gift from the Havana Galician Centre. Inside, as well as players and trainers, there would always be a few crates of Marlboro cigarettes, and these would be sold to fans during games.

Celso Lorenzo was married to the daughter of a Guardia Civil sergeant. When the family went to Mass on Sundays, they drove there in a beige Jaguar.

The *capos* of the 1960s employed hundreds of people; altogether, the organisations provided work for thousands in Baixo Miño and Vigo (in more recent times this has spread to the Rías Baixas and Costa da Morte too). They bought their suits in Madrid and Barcelona, drove the best cars, put on the best dinners, paid for local churches and street parties alike, and were always surrounded by beautiful women. And, most importantly, the bosses of these tobacco-smuggling organisations rubbed shoulders with politicians, mayors, bankers and impresarios of all kinds.

The climate was one of tolerance, and the authorities, politicians included, were part of it. Far from being seen as crooks, the contrabandists enjoyed the complete and unreserved support of all. To move contraband was a sought-after job, a profession to be proud of. There is a story in Tui, a town situated between Vigo and the Portugal border, about the wife of a contrabandist who went to register the birth of a son. The administrator at the counter asked the usual questions, and when it came to 'Father's profession' the women had no hesitation in giving 'smuggler' as her answer.

In an almost imperceptible way, this toxic mixture of popular admiration and political complicity helped lay the foundations for what, decades later, would degenerate into a criminal complex of mafia-like proportions.

The media began to take notice of this illicit industry and to talk about the potential pitfalls, but nobody was listening. Long after the die had been cast, the Guardia Civil carried out the odd symbolic raid, playing to the gallery mainly, including one in Coruña: all the contrabandists got off scot-free, but the authorities also got their photo opportunity – standing with the consignment of seized tobacco. Everyone was happy, and an important precedent had been set.

'CONTRABANDISTS ARE THE MOST HONOURABLE PEOPLE AROUND'

Manuel Díaz González was known as 'Speedy' for the pace at which he crossed the Portugal border from A Guarda, the town where he went on to become mayor. Or so said Manuel Fraga, president of the right-leaning Alianza Popular (AP) party, the major opposition party in the 1980s. The journalist Elisa Lois, in an article for *El País*, claimed that Don Manuel had once said to the president of the Galician Comunidad Autónoma (Regional Council), Alberto Núñez Feijóo: 'Know why they used to call the mayor of A Guarda "Speedy"? Because of how quickly he made himself scarce when the Guardia Civil showed up asking about Portuguese contraband!' Fraga was annoyed after some photographs appeared in the press showing Feijóo enjoying the sun aboard the yacht of Marcial Dorado, a legendary trafficker from the island town of Arousa. More about that relationship, and those photos, shortly.

Manuel Díaz was one of those wholesalers who turned into the respected and admired tobacco *capos* of the 1960s and 1970s. A man with no schooling except as a black marketeer, revered by his neighbours, he paid for all the street parties in A Guarda, provided local families with employment and even ran the town football team, Club Sporting Guardés. A Galician-style godfather in every respect, he went on to be appointed mayor by the AP rank and file in 1987.

Four years before being appointed mayor, Speedy had served a sentence in Madrid's Carabanchel prison. He was one of 92 charged in the so-called 'macro-indictment' of November 1984, when a series of raids against contrabandists ultimately led to zero convictions – due solely to institutional negligence. He spent a very short time in the hands of the authorities, as did all the Galicia *capos* taken in these raids. (Before crossing the Galicia border, he actually threw himself from the Guardia Civil Vauxhall Opel in which he was being taken to Madrid, and got away from the officers on foot, only to be taken in again a short while later.) Carabanchel only served to increase his fame, since he spent his time there buying the other prisoners food and blankets, along with anything else they might need.

He always maintained that he gave up his contraband activities upon election. That year, 1987, by which time he was already a town councillor, he gave an interview to the local newspaper, *Faro de Vigo*. It is priceless. Among other things, Manuel Díaz explains that Fraga had been wrong about his nickname: 'I've been called that since I was a child. And I wear it as proudly as my given name.' He mounts a passionate defence of contrabandists, among whose number, perhaps by accident, he names himself: 'A contrabandist's word is gold. It's the same as a handshake between the guy selling the cow and the buyer. You don't need papers, signatures, all that.

And that's what you get with Manuel Díaz!' The final line in the interview, which formed the headline, would go down in history: 'Contrabandists are the most honourable people around.' These were his words – and now they were in print. Manuel Díaz, aka Speedy, died two years later, and among the thousands to attend the funeral – many of them high-ranking politicians and Galician business leaders – was Don Manuel Fraga, recently appointed president of the Galician Regional Council. His was a headline with which the Galician authorities clearly could not have agreed more.

BATEA WINSTONS

One day in the summer of 1982, there was shootout at the Parador de Cambados.[1] Gunshots were heard, the sound of people running, cars speeding off, and then silence. The police came and investigated the episode but came to no conclusions – at least not publicly. 'A spat over some contraband,' people in the area said. It later came out that a number of tobacco *capos* had met at the *parador* that day. According to local journalists, it was a meeting to discuss the direction the business should go in. During a tense lull in proceedings, Vicente 'Terito' Otero took out his gun and shot at Laureano Oubiña. A shootout ensued, but nobody was hurt. Some versions claim that Terito had his gun knocked from his hand, and the bullet hit a third man in the foot. Some also hold that contraband wasn't the reason for the argument, but sums to be donated to the AP for the forthcoming elections. Apart from the fact that shots were fired, the event remains shrouded in mystery.

The alleged gunman, Vicente Otero – also known as both Terito and Don Vicente – was another member of Celso Lorenzo's Marlboro Celta board of directors, and a visible leader of the new crop of contrabandists that brought the business from Baixo Miño up to the Rías Baixas. Raised in a black-market environment, he was only too happy to let people know about his status as a self-made man. He liked to think of himself as elegant, he was always impeccably, if not very tastefully, turned out, and he dyed his hair to hide the grey streaks. His connections came from the contraband networks of the 1960s, from which he emerged as an above-board businessman with his company Transportes Otero – whose fleet of trucks was omnipresent on the motorways of the Cantabria coast and northern Spain in those days – as often as not, of course, filled with crates of blond American tobacco.

Tobacco made a millionaire of Terito. He acquired numerous companies, both as investments and as ways of laundering money. The renowned spa in Mondariz was owned by him, as was, in effect, the whole of the Cambados seaport. He was the first Latin American-style cacique of the *ría*. He was generous with his donations to the town council and the regional government, employed local people, organised town parties and religious pilgrimages, and, above all, ensured that AP won all the local votes, helping it dominate Arousa and the surrounding areas.

Don Vicente was a party activist all his life, and a personal friend of Manuel Fraga. They professed a mutual friendship – neither has ever denied these ties. Fraga was well looked-after whenever he visited Arousa: long dinners would be held, with copious amounts of fresh seafood on offer, either in the Cambados Parador or in one of Don Vicente's restaurants in the A Toxa casino complex, his home away from home.

There would be great fanfare every time the AP leader came to town, and the feeling was mutual; this was shown when the party awarded Don Vicente their gold medallion. After all, he guaranteed support in a region where AP, and its latter-day incarnation, the Partido Popular (PP), has at times enjoyed as much as 70 per cent of the vote.

It is common knowledge in Galicia – and even more common knowledge among the journalists whose patch is the Rías Baixas – that Don Vicente was awarded the gold medallion for the alleged millions he poured into the party coffers, as well as for his work securing votes. Here, his generosity strengthened the ties between the AP and the contrabandists. As Perfecto Conde says in his book *La conexión gallega* (The Galician Connection): 'I have no proof of this financing, but then again no one ever took a lawsuit out against me when I wrote about it.'

Don Vicente's right-hand man was José Ramón 'the Kid' Barral, a native of Ribadumia, which is a mile or so inland from Cambados, reachable along the River Umia. He spent his early days working abroad in the automotive industries, including in Switzerland and Germany, before returning to Galicia and, as a relatively wealthy man, becoming involved in a number of business ventures, for example setting up a kiwi plantation, something never before seen in these climes. It wasn't long before he worked out where the real money was and went into contraband. 'When the Kid moved, not even the wind knew about it,' as Perfecto Conde puts it. 'He'd have three patrol boats, each with 1,800 crates inside, which he'd move upriver, till he was almost in front of his house. All the trails and paths that led to the Umia would have been shut down before the job, a bit like Franco when he went salmon fishing.' The Kid was ambitious, and was one of the first to create links between the Galician clans and the international contraband mafia. All his operations were carried out from his mansion at the foot of the beach in Vilanova de Arousa.

The Kid was a party activist like his mentor – though in his case it went beyond donations: in 1983, the AP membership elected him, by an overwhelming majority, mayor of Ribadumia. At that point he said he would cut his ties with contraband, and was given the party's blessing. Not everyone's, though. A certain Mariano Rajoy was then head of the Pontevedra council, and he took considerable exception to the proximity of the likes of the Kid and Don Vicente. Rajoy confronted Fraga about his relationship with these criminals. Fraga did not warm to this line of questioning, and his comeback has gone down in Galician folklore: 'Go to Madrid, Mariano, get yourself a wife, have some kids, and while you're at it, learn Galician.' Clearly, Rajoy was forgetting the local dialect. He was ahead of his time in his principled stance.

When the Kid claimed that a new page had been turned, it wasn't the whole truth. Throughout his time as mayor of Ribadumia he kept his fingers in certain pies. And he was mayor for a considerable amount of time: he was a town councillor for the AP/PP for 18 years altogether, elected with outright majority after outright majority, until 2001. That was the year when he was caught, along with his brother, overseeing the delivery of 400,000 packets of Magnum cigarettes in Vigo. 'I have been honourable and honest in all my public dealings,' he said in his resignation statement. 'This mistake is a private matter. I ask for your forgiveness. I am stepping down so that the name of Ribadumia will not be associated with criminal activities.'

The proceedings following that bust, and on the grounds of alleged tax evasion in the Virgin Islands, are still pending.

PESETA CONNECTION

Galician contraband made its first quantum leap at the beginning of the 1980s, when *capos* such as Don Vicente and 'the Kid' Barral decided to stop using Portuguese suppliers. This was the point when the trafficking centre shifted definitively from the border and up into the Rías Baixas.

They started buying directly from the manufacturers: US multinationals. It was Patrick Laurent, Director of European Commerce for R. J. Reynolds Tobacco Company, who came up with the idea: why not take any excess in production or any faulty lots and siphon them off into international smuggling networks? Philip Morris International Inc. did the same. The goods were deployed by road from Basel and Antwerp, and by sea from Greece and Italy, with supply ships making stops all along the European coastline, Galicia included. So the tobacco multinationals had three new partners, each formidable in its own right: the Greek crime groups, the Camorra in Italy, and the Galician clans. Annual meetings took place in Monte Carlo, during the Grand Prix: decisions were taken concerning this knotted maze of contraband,

and spoils were shared. There was more than enough to go around.

Thanks to decades of black-market experience, it was not long before the Galician clans became trusted players in the tobacco networks, and this rainy and windswept coastal region became the most important drop-off point in the world of European contraband. Container ships docked in Galician ports in their hundreds, each bearing the same amount of cigarettes as it would take dozens of trucks to transport. Adjudicators estimated that, at the beginning of the 1980s, Galicia was the entry point for a third of all illegal tobacco in Europe. Spanish treasury statistics said that the state was prevented from levying 10,000 million pesetas a year – €60 million in today's money. A study of Galician tobacconists found that, in 1980–82, their sales were down by 850 million pesetas (€5 million) a year.

The tobacco clans began seeking safe havens for their money, with Switzerland the preferred destination. The man responsible for taking the money out of Arousa was a Basque Frenchman named Joseph Arrieta. He would load bundles of money into the boot of his car and drive to Switzerland in a single go, no stopping. Arrieta initially worked alone, but ended up hiring a fleet of cars and bringing in his brother and a number of friends. So great were the amounts of money, and such was the hurry to get it away, that they ended up referring to the amounts by weight: 'I'm bringing three kilos', 'You owe me 300 grams', etc.

The *capos* helped Arrieta with the necessary bribes to Spanish and French customs officials, and the money made it through with ease. Arriving in Geneva, he would leave the car parked near the airport, across the road from a row of banks. An employee of the bank would come out, take the bags from the car, and replace them with others containing the gold bullion destined for Galicia. The contrabandists would squirrel this away or invest it in jewellery to be traded on the black market. This money-laundering process would go on to be dubbed the Peseta Connection.

Arrieta claimed he walked away when he saw that the amounts of money were too great to come solely from tobacco. In a single year at the end of the 1980s, for example, suitcases containing a total of 22,000 million pesetas (or €133 million) crossed the continent in the boot of his car: the apparent combined profits of all the Galician clans. Arrieta knew this could only mean drugs, and it was at that point, he says, that he decided to go to the authorities. Sudden attack of conscience aside, what is certain is that he got into contact with a French magistrate by the name of Germain Sengelin who had been looking into the flow of money between Arousa and Geneva, on the basis of a tip-off from Edmond Eichenberg, a Swiss contrabandist married to a woman from Coruña. Eichenberg is said to have given testimony inside a pickup truck parked on the French–Swiss border: he was sitting in the back, in Switzerland, and the magistrate was in the front, in France.

When Magistrate Sengelin asked Arrieta why he had not gone to the Spanish authorities, he said that, from the Pyrenees down, there was not a man he trusted. In fact, Sengelin did pass his findings to the Spanish authorities – everything he knew about the Peseta Connection. And guess what came of it? Nothing. These dealings continued well into the era of drug trafficking and nobody lifted a finger – either out of indolence or because the Spanish legislative system, which was still making the transition from Franco's dictatorship to democracy, was still in its infancy when it came to addressing money laundering.

In reality, the Peseta Connection was just one junction in a far knottier matrix. Geneva, the money-laundering focal point for criminals across Europe, was the hub. The Arousa contrabandists used the same channels as ETA, the Camorra, the Sicilian Mafia and North African gunrunners. It was in this overlap that the Galicians first came into contact with drugs gangs. The way ahead began to reveal itself.

'A BOOTLEGGER, LIKE MY PAPA'

The modus operandi of the Galician clans was almost exactly the same as that of the drug runners they would one day morph into: the supply ships – known as the 'Mamas' – would wait in international waters, and the speedboats would go out to them, unload the goods and bring them ashore. The clan's boats were always state of the art, with engines and modifications the authorities could only dream of. The convoluted labyrinth that was the coast around Arousa did the rest. These tiny coves and bays were the backdrop for numberless drop-offs, at times in broad daylight. Once ashore, the consignments would be stored in factory premises, churches and often just people's houses, in exchange for generous donations to parish coffers and household grocery funds. From there, the goods would be distributed through a wide variety of establishments (even tobacco stands) or small local organisations. Tobacco would be hidden in the sea itself on occasion, on the underside of '*bateas*', the floating wooden platforms, with ropes that drop into the water, on which mussels were grown. This practice led to the coining of the term '*batea* Winstons'.

The money was good, and you were paid on the spot. Every drop-off, which would never take more than a couple of hours, presented the irresistible opportunity of quick cash. How to remonstrate with such public-spiritedness?

'When the speedboats came in with the tobacco, the lights in town would drop three times,' says 'Manuel', a resident of Vilanova de Arousa who preferred not to be named. ('Not because I was involved or anything …') 'They'd throw the switches at the power station, and that way the guys in the speedboats knew the coast was clear, or it was part of a code telling them where the drop-off point was.' The memories of Manuel give a good sense of the reach of the contrabandists:

> The money was pretty decent. I remember a couple of kids, schoolmates of my son, around 1980 this would have been. One worked as a waiter, getting paid a pittance, and the other, he'd go and do a drop-off and earn the same in one night as his friend would in a month. The one who worked as a waiter told me what a loser he felt when his friend pulled up outside in his Golf GTI.

A local magistrate I spoke to, who again asked to remain anonymous, and who was involved in trying to prosecute contrabandists at the time, had the following to say: 'From a sociological perspective, it was a phenomenon. All of Arousa, and large parts of the Rías Baixas, viewed illicit tobacco as a motor for economic growth. It provided employment for huge numbers of people. People were grateful for the cash, and simply preferred not to think beyond that.'

Everybody knew it was wrong, in other words, but nobody said a word.

Julio Fariñas, a journalist for *La Voz de Galicia*, puts it better: 'So great were the levels of contraband coming through Arousa, the real question was, who *wasn't* involved. It was a way of life.' There is a Mark Twain quotation that would fit such a setting perfectly: 'I once sent a dozen of my friends a telegram saying "flee at once – all is discovered." They all left town immediately.'

This lack of opposition is crucial to understanding a situation that might now seem difficult to believe. The thing was, by the letter of the law, smuggling wasn't a serious offence until 1982. You would only get a caution if caught, and the Guardia Civil focused on other things. Before 1978, smuggling was seen as purely an economic issue, and, as such, the attorney general, via the Customs Surveillance Service (SVA), was in charge of sniffing out the problem. Only in isolated cases could offenders be sent to prison, but even this power was restricted with the arrival of democracy: the separation of powers ushered in by the new constitution meant that the government no longer had the right to restrict people's liberties. So a smuggler could be caught, red-handed, right in the middle of a drop-off, and all he or she would get was a fine – one that customarily went astray in the bureaucratic labyrinth. And if the fine did reach its intended target, the contrabandist, whose possessions would all be registered in other people's names anyway, would simply declare bankruptcy. This was the situation – which had a kind of balance to it – between 1978 and 1982. But then 1983 was a watershed, at least on paper, when laws came in stipulating harsh punishments.

The idea of tobacco as an economic motor was ruining the entire region. The defrauding of the state, and later the European Economic Community (EEC), saw dozens of sectors wither. The mindset was that the region would be worthless if it weren't for American tobacco, and other industries were effectively shelved. Not only did taxes go unpaid in their millions, the idea became ingrained that there was no alternative to contraband, and this prevented people from exploiting the area's many obvious resources, tourism included. The River Arousa, for example, produces more mussels in a year than the rest of Europe put together. Tobacco smuggling had one thing in common with trawl fishing: it flattened everything in its path, and the consequences were immediate.

Another factor explaining the positive view of contraband was the lack of violence between the clans – one thing the locals could be truly thankful for. Conflicts were occasional and usually small-scale, especially when compared with what came with the arrival of drug trafficking in later years: full-blown shootouts, kidnappings and extortion. The raw materials were there for all in the early 1980s, and people mostly rubbed along quite well. Sometimes threats would be issued and there was the isolated assault, but everyone knew that any dead bodies would mean an end to the good times. This included the Guardia Civil, who were so integral to the situation. As when most of the contraband had been coming from Portugal, without the involvement of the authorities nothing would have been possible.

There was an added issue, and for some this was the most serious: the illegality of the principal industry in the Rías Baixas necessarily entailed a criminal culture. It became normal to think and talk about evading the authorities, to respect a community leader such as a *capo* who had nothing to do with lawful state apparatus, and to earn fast money. A scenario was being fashioned in which it was more or less the norm to break the law. It was just the way things were.

Manuel, the Vilanova resident, worked in public administration at the time, and says he 'can't remember a week when our man didn't come by and drop off 200s or 400s of Winstons. We'd buy them from him and sell them in the office. A member of the public would come in to sign something or other, and buy a few packs on the side.' He laughs at the memory. 'We were smugglers too, in a way!' His wife, Elisa, worked as an estate agent: 'It was my job to take clients around the properties,' she says.

> I remember showing people around sometimes, and you'd open a door, and the room would be piled high with Winstons. And no one batted an eyelid. I'd say, 'Okay, let's just pull this lot out so you can get a proper idea of how big the room is.' It just didn't register!

'But, I mean,' Manuel says, 'if when you went in the shop, and they'd ask you, outright, whether you wanted normal, or contraband ...'

In July 1981 some bad weather hit the *rías*, at a very inopportune moment for certain contrabandists. An important drop-off was expected in Cambados, but it was hazardous even to step outside. The powerboats had to stay put for a full three days, and the 'Mama' ship had to sit waiting. The storm abated on the festival of the Virgen del Carmen, tradition-ally seen as the queen of the seas and a guardian to fishermen everywhere – a day of great importance all along the Galician seaboard: all watercraft would go out in procession, brimming with flowers and sounding their horns. But the 'Mama' ship still needed unloading, so the contrabandists went to the priest to see if the festivities could be postponed – they needed ships and men for the job. The request was granted, and the proces-sion was held the following day – some of the ships reportedly still full of cigarette crates. It was a record year for donations in the parish.

There is another anecdote exemplifying the extent to which tobacco smuggling had become part of the fabric of *ría* life: when a child was interviewed on Televisión de Galicia in 1981 (TVG). In a live link to the studio in Vilagarcía, a reporter was going around asking youngsters what they wanted to be when they grew up. The last of these interviewees didn't think twice as he took the microphone in hand: 'A bootlegger, like my papa.'

THE SMOKE LORDS

In 1983, the priest in Illa de Arousa, a picturesque island positioned in a particularly wide portion of the *ría*, found a hole in the church roof. He went straight to the richest and most powerful man in the area, Marcial Dorado, also known as 'Island Marcial': the formidable contrabandist whose fame was later to extend beyond Galicia when photographs emerged of him on a yacht with Alberto Núñez Feijóo, president of the Galician Regional Council. The priest asked for a donation and Marcial obliged: leaky roof fixed. The next year another hole appeared and again the priest went to the master on the island, but this time in vain. Marcial had put away his wallet. A number of months later the SVA intercepted one of his boats, carrying a stash of tobacco. The contrabandist is reported to have seen the situation quite clearly: 'This is what I get for saying no to the priest.'

Marcial Dorado Baúlde ran one of the three primary clans in the *rías*. The likes of Don Vicente and 'the Kid' Barral had paved the way for a new generation of contrabandists, who, younger and more ambitious, assumed control from the 1980s onwards. Don Vicente carried on as the symbolic patriarch, but these new groups moved to a different beat. They were well-structured organisations, led by *capos* with great energy and global ambitions. In the space of a few short years they would reign supreme in Spanish tobacco smuggling and, for periods, across the whole of Europe.

They were the ones to put the finishing touches to the mafia image. They were the so-called *señores do fume* ('smoke lords'): splashy, arrogant millionaires, caciques with connections in all echelons of society. When they came into the casinos, everyone wanted to shake their hands; they washed down their *fruits de mer* with the best Albariño wines and drove the kind of cars you only saw on television. They were not all the same: some, for instance, developed social pretensions and sent their children to the best foreign schools; others, though vastly rich, were still essentially thugs who did nothing to soften their image and only hoped their offspring would follow in their footsteps.

Marcial Dorado was in the former group. His clan, known simply as Marcial's Gang, was the most powerful of all. In a business sense, Dorado was Don Vicente's descendant – in a blood sense too, some claimed, so alike were the pair – and he learned at the older man's knee until striking out on his own. Marcial quickly established a direct line to Patrick Laurent, the great contraband *capo*, and the relationship became close-knit, with the Galician making regular visits to Geneva and Basel. His closest associates were Juan Manuel Lorenzo Lorenzo and Manuel Suárez Nieto.[2] Though a difficult thing to quantify, all evidence suggests that Marcial's Gang rose to become the most powerful tobacco smugglers in Europe. Their network of contacts and their overall control of the Galician *rías* were unrivalled. Manuel Prado López was their man in charge of bribes, and his efficiency was doubtless part of the reason why Marcial came through countless scrapes with the authorities unscathed.[3] Marcial's Gang had infiltrated the Guardia Civil, the SVA, Vigo airport (a radio call would be made any time a police helicopter went out), and numerous banks – one in Ponte Caldelas in particular which always had large quantities of US dollars ready and available for its best clients.

'Butcher Sito' (not to be confused with 'Miñanco Sito') was the nickname of José Ramón Barreiro Fontán, the second most powerful smuggler on the *ría*. His centre of operations was Vilagarcía, a couple of miles from Marcial's island. Ricardo Camba was Sito's second in command, and they too had direct dealings with European contrabandists. Sito was known for his temper; he didn't tend to count to 10. He died in an unexplained car accident in 1985, an event that generated a predictable array of theories, from vengeance killing to suicide. Butcher Sito seems to have been the inspiration for the character of Mariscal in Manuel Rivas's *All Is Silence*, which takes place in this very Galician milieu of smuggling and drug trafficking. Rivas, then working as a journalist, met Sito in the winter of 1983 in the hotel where the *capo*, at that point a fugitive, had holed up. When Rivas tried asking a few questions, Sito picked him up by the throat and told him he would be better off going back to wherever he had come from, unless he wanted to end up at the bottom of a ravine. Had his car not veered off the road, Sito would seem to have been tailor-made for the move to drug trafficking. He clearly had the requisite talents.

R.O.S. Ltd was the pretentious name chosen by the third Arousan smuggling gang. At its head were Ramiro Martínez Señoráns, Olegario Falcón Piñeiro and José Ramón Prado Bugallo, the last better known as 'Miñanco Sito'. This trio did not seem to like the name, and, in their statement to Judge Ramiro, claimed it was a police invention. All the evidence suggests that they were R.O.S., however, and they functioned much like a company, with a complex infrastructure based in Cambados that included accounts ledgers, subcontractors, an array of smoke-screen companies and sophisticated satellite radio equipment for operating ships and trucks. The courts found that the gang had long been in contact with a certain 'Tonino', to whom they would send the distribution money. To begin with there was the idea that Tonino was Antonio Bardelino, head of a branch of the Neapolitan Camorra, who years later went on to be tried as part of the so-called Pizza Connection. In fact, it turned out to be a man named Antonio Esposito, an Italian smuggling counterpart of Patrick Laurent – and also a member of the Camorra. The business figures presented in the hearings were, for the time, almost beyond belief. Between July and December 1983, the R.O.S. group was said to have avoided paying taxes of 1,500 million pesetas, or €10.1 million – and we ought to assume corresponding amounts over the preceding three decades. Not all of the gang's account books were found, so the real figures must have been higher still.

In total, according to the investigations, these three groups had deposited a little over €21.5 million into different accounts in the second half of 1983 alone. All the banks in Arousa would roll out the red carpet when one of the *capos* showed up. Branches in Vilanova, Vilagarcía and Cambados – the managers of which were later prosecuted – had ready cash, in a variety of currencies, permanently on hand. In the 1980s and 1990s, Enrique León was a police officer and later commissioner in Vilagarcía, and, as he explains:

> I remember one family, here in Vilagarcía, who in six months in 1983 deposited 3,000 million pesetas into bank accounts. When the attorney general's office checked the bank's accounts, it found this one registered in the name of a mentally handicapped boy. We went and spoke to the boy and, such was his condition, he didn't know what a current account was.

The three groups cooperated. Showdowns were avoided. Miñanco Sito and Marcial Dorado flew to Geneva together a dozen times. When the judge asked Miñanco Sito about these trips, he said it was by chance that he and Marcial always ended up in adjacent seats. Over the years, Miñanco Sito would come to resemble a Colombian narco, a mini Pablo Escobar of the *ría*: he dressed like them, acted like them, and in the end was working for them.

The antithesis of Miñanco Sito was Laureano Oubiña Piñeiro. He was the best example of the second kind of Galician contrabandist, who, though virtually illiterate, had accounts with unending zeros at the end. Oubiña's gang based their operations between Vilagarcía and Vilanova, where Oubiña bought the emblematic Pazo Baión estate. In general, Oubiña was more discreet in his dealings, and avoiding the gaze of the authorities enabled his gang to expand, going on to become one of the main drug-trafficking organisations in Europe.

In the winter of 1983, a Guardia Civil boat was out patrolling the dock at Ribeira, on the north bank of the River Arousa, when they spotted something moving in the water: a person. Coming nearer, they found it was one of their colleagues, and he was in the advanced stages of hypothermia. They hauled him out, and at first he claimed to have fallen in, but later the truth emerged: a discussion with Manuel 'Sparrowhawk' Carballo had turned into an argument, and Carballo had ended up pushing him in. It turned out that the officer had been asking for his cut, an everyday request, but on this occasion it had ended in a fight and him nearly drowning.

Carballo wasn't usually given to violence; on the contrary, he was known for his cool head, as well as his keen eye for maximising profits. He would later make the move to drug trafficking, bringing members of his family with him, but his was a gory legacy: his son 'Danielito' Carballo Conde was shot in the head in a pub in Vilagarcía, his sister Carmen Carballo was left a quadriplegic after a revenge hit, and his cousin Luis Jueguen just managed to dodge Colombian bullets in a gunfight in Benavente.

Falconetti was the nickname given to Luis Falcón Pérez, apparently after the dangerous and eccentric character in the 1970s US miniseries *Rich Man, Poor Man*. He started out as a stevedore, unloading consignments for Don Vicente, and went on to become one of the most powerful men on the *ría*.

Based in Vilagarcía, he was among the more violent *capos*, and had no compunction about taking on the authorities. He was always said to be armed, and went around Arousa in a car with tinted windows, though at the time nobody knew why. There is a story about him visiting the mayor of Vilanova, José Vázquez, to discuss a land boundary issue. When the politician proved uncooperative, Falconetti took out his gun and placed it on the table: 'Did you know it only costs a million pesetas to bring a hitman over from Portugal these days?' He showed more subtlety at other times, and made full use of his contacts as an AP member (yes, another one). He managed to persuade the Vilagarcía authorities sign off a bingo building in 1984, the first seen in the region, in spite of the municipal secretary's complaints about the 'obviously below-board' nature of the project. The Socialist Party (PSOE) also made their disapproval known, but none of the objections amounted to anything, and they were soon forgotten. The mayor of Vilagarcía at the time, another AP member, was one José Luis Rivera Mallo – who later went on to become a senator and the president of a commission appointed to look into drug use. Falconetti did go to jail in the end, in 1987, for a consignment of hashish he had tried to bring in at Vilagarcía. A stone's throw from the bingo building, as it happens.

Luis Falcón worked closely with a man called Jacinto Santos Viñas, another who would end up in the Galician drug-trafficking hall of fame. In the early days he worked for Falcón, transporting tobacco in the ports of Coruña and Ferrol, pulling his small tugboat in between the steamers and freighters to unload crates of Winstons. His career came to an end years later with a pair of sales: the sale of his tugboat in South Africa, and him being sold to the Guardia Civil by a Moroccan contact. Santos Viñas, as we will soon see, went on to smuggle hashish and cocaine, founding his own family clan and using a Turkish oyster-importing company as a smokescreen.

To the north, on Costa da Morte, the Lulú gang were predominant – they were possibly the most efficient and durable Galician smuggling faction of all. Suffice to say they are still active to this day. 'Nobody moves a thing on the Costa da Morte without their say so,' according to one veteran Guardia Civil.

Then there was the Charlín family. Their patriarchs, the two oldest brothers Manuel and José Luis Charlín Gama, started out as scrap-metal smugglers, but with the arrival of tobacco a criminal saga began that is still playing out today. 'The Old Man', as Manuel is known, and his brothers had poor beginnings, and were said to stage fist fights as children in the winter to stave off hunger. This perhaps had something to do with their attitude as smugglers in later years: impulsive, violent, never standing on ceremony, they acted as though they had nothing to lose. Particularly memorable was the treatment of Celestino Suances, a go-between smuggler in Valladolid who owed them money – 7 million pesetas (€42,000), to be precise. José Luis Charlín sent one of his associates, José Luis Orbáiz Picos, to recover the debt. (Orbáiz Picos was a former Guardia Civil who hung up his tricorn to become a drug runner instead, with his son following in his footsteps.) He was met in the city by a group of local Guardia Civil, who gave him a beating and sent him on his way. A number of months later someone came to the Charlíns and said that Suances had been seen in Arousa, in the Frankfurt restaurant (the names given to bars and restaurants by returning Galician emigrants merit a book in themselves), which was owned by Don Vicente and where Suances often bought seafood. Two of the brothers, Aurelio and José Luis, went down and dragged him out, before driving him to the Charpo canning factory, which they owned. They were met there by Manuel Charlín and Orbáiz, and together they beat Suances to within an inch of his life before placing him in a cold storage unit and handing him a phone, suggesting he rang his wife and told her to wire the money. Incredibly, Suances managed to escape by dismantling the ventilation unit and climbing out. On his return to Valladolid he went to the police, and the Old Man was obliged to go and spend a few months in Belgium.

The Cambados magistrate at the time, a man named José Luis Seoane Spiegelberg, investigated the case. 'We took Suances back to the factory to reconstruct what had happened for us. He suddenly managed to forget everything.' The affair annoyed Spiegelberg so much that, rather than just filling in the forms, he took the unheard-of decision to follow it up and to make an effort to dismantle the trafficking networks in Galicia once and for all. A plan was hatched that would lead to the raids of December 1983 and the 'macro-indictment' that followed them in November 1984, the first concerted operation the Galician smugglers had ever faced.

WHEN THE PRESIDENT OF THE GALICIAN REGIONAL COUNCIL MET THE *CAPOS*

In 1983 Magistrate Spiegelberg dismantled the police head-quarters in a place called O Grove and arranged the arrest of four further officers in Sanxenxo. It went more or less as follows: a young officer from Segovia was sent to work in O Grove, not the brightest recruit but with a recommendation from the sergeant in Segovia. At the end of his first month, when he went to pick up his pay cheque, he was given an additional 15,000 pesetas and a few Winstons 200s cartons. When he asked why, his superior officer shrugged: 'That's how it works here. We get given 1,000 pesetas for every bundle that makes it through, and some cigarettes for ourselves too.' The young officer accepted the bonus. A number of months later the sergeant who had given him his recommendation came to visit, and asked how things were going. So the young man told him: 'Couldn't be better. We get our normal wages, plus a bonus, plus free cigarettes.' This innocent admission turned out to be the starting point for Spiegelberg's investigations.

Fourteen officers were accused of embezzlement, perverting the course of justice, simulating crimes, accepting bribes, contraband charges and falsifying documents. On the night before the trial, the captain general in Coruña tried to step in on the basis that these were agents of the Military Institute and so they ought to be given a military trial. Spiegelberg put his foot down, and the matter went to the Supreme Court, where it was ruled that it was indeed a police matter. They were processed in civil courts five years later.

A veteran of the Policía Nacional, a wry smile on his face, recalls a tip-off in Vilagarcía that same year about a pickup truck full to the roof with crates of cigarettes. The informer asked that they wait before intercepting the vehicle, so the criminals wouldn't know he was the source, and the police obliged, following in an unmarked car until Lalín, Pontevedra, before moving in. The smugglers got out of the vehicle looking remarkably calm – smiling even – but when the police officers showed their badge, their faces dropped. 'Shit!' they said. 'You aren't Guardia Civil.'

'Really,' said the veteran, 'the Guardia Civil were completely corrupt.' There is a whole chapter in Perfecto Conde's book about smuggling bribes accepted by Guardia Civil, as revealed in the clan's account books. They were listed as just one more expense, under the heading 'incentives'. These, and countless other cases of corruption, were what Laureano Oubiña meant when he said, 'Without their help we could have done nothing …'

Spiegelberg says it wasn't until he set up wiretaps on the clans' phones that the dimensions of the business became clear. The Suances/Charlín episode led investigators to roll up their sleeves: phone lines were tapped and individuals placed under surveillance. Spiegelberg remembers listening in on a conversation between two *capos* following the imprisonment of the crew of a Greek supply ship seized by the SVA. When one asked if the Greek sailors knew what they were supposed to say, the other told him not to worry: the interpreters had been bought.

The authorities were a long way behind the clans, and the reason was simple: the contraband law was not passed until 1982 – Organic Law 7/82. Only then did the courts have proper weapons to use against smugglers: contraband was elevated from a minor to a major offence, and punishment was no longer tied to the amount of merchandise seized; hefty fines could now be imposed regardless. The outlook changed – on paper, at least. There was still some way to go before lawmakers could match the power of the clans.

After a few months' work, Spiegelberg gathered his findings and decided that large-scale raids were needed. This was the 'macro-indictment' of November 1984. He had the support of Virginio Fuentes, the socialist governor of Ponte-vedra and one of the few in Galician politics to dare to raise his voice against the smugglers. Fuentes, in fact, did so on the bidding of Felipe González, leader of the PSOE and prime minister from 1982 to 1996, who sensed a potential vote-winner in taking a stand against smuggling. This was a considerable miscalculation. It seems that they were ignorant in Madrid of the unfailing support enjoyed by the contrabandists. Attitudes in Galicia were quite unaffected by these socialist moves.

Such was the reach of the clans, they would get advance warning of any raids. They also found out who the authorities had in their sights, and those in question fled to Portugal in November 1983, a month before the planned raids. Marcial Dorado, Butcher Sito and their men crossed the border, as did Ramiro Martínez and Olegario Falcón of the R.O.S. Miñanco Sito, cocksure as ever, ignored the warnings and stayed; he was arrested coming out of a café in Cambados. Superintendent Enrique León was the man who took him in, and, as he recalls:

> We were out trying to find him, and suddenly I saw him leaving a café. I went over and came up alongside him. I said in a calm voice: 'Are you Miñanco Sito?' 'Yes,' he said, turning to face me. 'What about it?' 'Oh nothing,' I said, and put my hand on his arm. 'Gotcha.'

The fleeing *capos* and gang members stayed in hotels run by their Portuguese counterparts, old business partners they had long since eclipsed. Marcial and his men installed themselves in some luxury suites in a medieval country house in A Boega, near Vilanova da Cerveira on the far side of the Río Miño. Butcher Sito opted for Monte Faro, taking up residence in a converted monastery – this was the scene of his run-in with the writer Manuel Rivas. In the article Rivas went on to publish in *El País*, he said that the Butcher was unhappy about what he called the 'shit-stirring' media. Ramiro Martínez and Olegario Falcón hid away in a place called Lanhleas, spending Christmas there with their families.

The rest stayed on. The indictment did not include Don Vicente, 'the Kid' Barral, Oubiña, Falconetti, Manuel Carballo or either of the Charlíns. This made people in Arousa think these men were untouchable, an idea immortalised in a song: 'You forgot about Don Vicente and the Kid, yes you did / For Carballo and Falcón, no trouble, because they paid you double.' The bust began to resemble an attempt to knock over a horse by throwing figs at it. All smuggling operations continued unabated. In the same year, the Greek freighter *Christina* was impounded, and with it the largest tobacco shipment ever seized in European waters. The record was broken within months, after the *Tessar* and the *Cedar*, also Greek vessels (when the court interpreters were paid off), were taken, with the frigate *Andalucía* firing a shot across their bows during the operation. But journalists specialising in the trafficking networks, like Elisa Lios of *El Correo Gallego* and Manuel Rivas himself, recall that, even with the investigations ongoing, it was business as usual, with drop-offs taking place almost daily.

Meanwhile, the exiles in Portugal carried on running their businesses from there. They made the occasional incursion into Galicia, but spent most of 1984 in their Portuguese lodgings. On 6 July, a strange and unprecedented event took place at the A Boeza country house. The president of the Galician Regional Council at the time, Xerardo Fernández Albor, stopped in to see Marcial and, apparently, the rest of the émigré *capos*. Stories abound about this meeting: some say that it was the contrabandists who, though they did not have an appointment, approached the president and stole five minutes of his time; others that it was a fully scheduled meeting. On one thing everyone agrees: that Albor said it would be in the *capos*' best interests to come back and give themselves up. They said the authorities were persecuting them 'unfairly'. The news later got out and, following questions from the PSOE, Albor had to explain himself before the Galician parliament. He apologised, maintaining that he had not known the exiles would be there that day.

Perhaps coincidentally, perhaps not, Spiegelberg was removed from the investigation and sent to Cantabria. The same happened to Virginio Fuentes, the socialist governor, who was sent to Albacete; a number of months later he was quoted as saying that he wanted nothing more to do with Galician contraband. Finally, Perfecto Conde has written about a telephone conversation the police intercepted between Celestino Ayala, a smuggler from A Pobra do Caramiñal, and Manuel Prado, Marcial's henchman. They discussed the authorities' actions, the attempted busts and Marcial's exile. At one point, Ayala is said to have made the following comment: 'They're going to carry on fucking with us for another year, but don't worry, because then Fraga is coming in.'

Elisa Lois wrote in *El País* in 2013: 'If the tobacco smugglers had been in favour of Manuel Fraga and his politics before the attempts of 1983, their support grew stronger thereafter. Mind you, the smugglers' donations to the electoral campaigns remained just as hush-hush as the times and places of contraband drop-offs.' And, in case we forget, it was at this time that the AP appointed 'the Kid' Barral as mayor of Ribadumia, a position he would hold for a further 18 years.

It seems Albor's words did not fall on deaf ears: the first to hand himself in, in November 1984, was Marcial. After discussions with his lawyer, Alfonso Barcala, he went to Madrid alone and made himself known to the authorities. The others soon followed. He, Ramiro, Olegario and Butcher Sito were put in Carabanchel prison but released after only a few weeks, having paid bonds of 20 million pesetas (€120,000). The *capos* had redoubtable legal teams – the likes of José María Rodríguez Hermida and the combustible Pablo Vioque. Vioque would later go to jail on cocaine-trafficking charges, but not before being elected as president of the Chamber of Commerce in Vilagarcía by the AP. He is a character we will be coming back to.

There are photographs from this time, famous in Spain, of lawyers from Vilagarcía and Cambados handing out cash in the ports, while the sailors from impounded ships made an orderly queue. It was bail money. No detail was spared by the clans.

In all, 93 smugglers were arrested and made to await trial. But, *misterios de España*, the court dates were delayed and delayed. When proceedings were finally ready to begin, in 1993, the attorney general's office realised that the laws had changed since Spain's 1986 accession to the EEC, which meant that the cases were unprosecutable. Some 600 years of proposed jail time, and 1.47 billion pesetas in fines (over €800 million), came to nothing.

After that lesson in impunity, the tobacco-trafficking business boomed, in the face of unmitigated governmental and judicial passivity. The amount of contraband flowing in reached unprecedented volumes. More clans sprang up, they bought faster speedboats, and they went about making new contacts. The Galicians took control. That brief stay for some of the *capos* in Carabanchel also proved decisive: a number of Colombian narcos happened to be imprisoned there at the same time.

THE GREAT LEAP

'Why drive a car down to Andalusia for weed when you can bring a fishing boat-load straight from Morocco?'

WE HAD NO IDEA

Enrique León was a police officer in Vilagarcía de Arousa at the time. He and his team had been taking on the tobacco smugglers for years, a struggle in which they had consistently come a distant second. 'One Friday we were given the go-ahead to set up a wiretap,' he says in his deep, clear voice. He does not remember the exact year – 1985 or 1986, he says.

> We were after some of the leading tobacco guys. On the Monday we sat down to have a listen and, my god, the first conversation we tune into, we hear some Colombian speaking. 'Colombians?' I remember thinking to myself. It was a Colombian and one of the main Galician guys. Then he handed over to another Colombian, and they spoke for a bit, then a third Colombian came on. Two filters before you could speak to the final guy – though at that point we had no idea who it actually was.

León was late to the party. Léon, the rest of the police, the Guardia Civil, the Regional Council, the government – things were in full swing before any of them showed up. The Colombian voice they did not recognise belonged to José Nelson Matta Ballesteros, head of the Ochoa clan and one of the leaders of the Medellín cartel. By picking up the phone that Monday morning in the Rías Baixas, León had stumbled upon the world's third most-wanted drugs trafficker.

At a time when Spain was still taking its first baby steps as a democracy, its politicians and law enforcement agencies had little grasp of the drugs that had begun circulating among young people. And still less the international gangs bringing in these substances. The Arousa journalist Felipe Suárez, in his book *La Operación Nécora +*, talks about the long-haired youths who would congregate at Vilagarcia's Bar Peñon to play cards and smoke joints. He interviewed someone called Chema, one of these *ría* hippies, who said: 'After a match I would smoke a spliff, no worries from anyone. I remember Sergeant Gabeiro saying I should just smoke tobacco, saying I shouldn't mess around with this other stuff. "Don't worry," I'd say to him. "It's Dutch tobacco, it just takes a bit of getting used to."'

This was crucial in the impending 'great leap'. Despite what many believe, it wasn't that the *capos* came and offered hashish and cocaine to a bunch of wet-behind-the-ears striplings, ruining them in the process. No. The local traffickers, already hardwired to smell a business opportunity, identified precisely that in the pungent substances being smoked by their children and their children's friends – just as they had before with petrol, scrap metal and tobacco. Only then did they begin doing their homework, before assuming control of a business that would act like an epidemic on a generation of young people.

'The older guys didn't want to take the step,' says José Antonio Vázquez Taín, who would go on to become a scourge of drug traffickers at the beginning of the twenty-first century. 'They had their tobacco business all lined up; they were millionaires already. They didn't want to take risks – this was unknown territory. It was the younger ones who spotted it – the potential for even less effort and even bigger returns.' It was the sons of Manuel Charlín Gama, to be precise, who first lifted the lid on this particular Pandora's box.

* * *

Tati, Dámaso, Rivero de Aguilar: these are some of the names of the first group of Vilagarcía hippies – they wore their hair long, they were enamoured with Woodstock. And on a trip to England in 1975 they discovered the joys of hashish. They returned again and again, always bringing a little back with them to help wile away the summer. It was not long before the hippies had new cohorts, and together they created a movement that paved the way for the Galician *movida*, centred mainly on the city of Vigo. Locals such as Chenano, Chiruca, Maribel, Tarano, Chis 'the Cripple' and Chema became legendary for the hash they brought from England, their discussions of photography, art and the peace movement, and the orgies they put on. Consummate hippies.

Ángel Facal was the first to start transporting hashish in a systematic way. He and Tati would drive to Morocco and come back with three or four kilos in the boot. It wasn't long before they stopped needing to cross the Strait of Gibraltar, as other dealers had begun bringing the goods to Madrid or Seville. Hashish became easier to source with every passing year, and their own market swelled: not just their friends in Vilagarcía but the youth of Vigo and Santiago de Compostela too, who soon cottoned on to the cut prices in Arousa. As in the rest of Spain, marijuana became very popular. Business was so good that Chis 'the Cripple' and Chema bought a place in Sanxenxo, at that point a high-end tourist spot for Madrileños, and started a bar. They called it Siete Colinas and brought in Ángel 'the Cripple' and 'Deaf' Suso to work with them. After closing they would go drinking in Portonovo, then down to the beach at sunrise – no obligations but making sure they ate something before opening the bar again that evening.

It was during those summers, smoking their way through their hangovers as the 1980s rose on the horizon, that Adelaida, one of the girls in the group, fell in love with Chis. Her father, like so many of his generation, was a smuggler. At the time, nothing to write home about, but from our current perspective, an important seed: her father was none other than Manuel Charlín Gama, and it was through this relationship – about which Manuel had his reservations, even at one point threatening Chis because he started seeing Adelaida before she turned 18 – that Manuel's sons, Adelaida's brothers, joined the group. They were working full time for their father. After just two weeks of Chis et al.'s parties they saw what a waste of time the *batea* Winstons were. They went to their father, put forward the idea … and the rest is history.

THE PIONEERS

Manuel Charlín Gama has the honour of having been the first Galician smuggler to bring a shipment of drugs up the *ría*. The facts surrounding this are flimsy – there are no certifiable statements and no evidence – but in the lore of the Rías Baixas it is an indisputable truth. Any *guardia* or police officer will say the same: the Old Man went first. What had been a hobby for Chis, Chema and the rest, entailing, at most, a trip to Seville every now and then to stuff a couple of kilos into the boot of a car, the smugglers turned into big business. Why drive a car down to Andalusia for weed when you can bring a fishing boat-load straight in from Morocco? The *capos* were in the game.

How they generated the contacts to make the shift from tobacco to drugs has never been clear. But we do know they didn't find it very hard. 'The infrastructure was already there, from tobacco,' says Magistrate Taín. 'This made everything easier and gave their new suppliers confidence. Socially, there weren't really any obstacles: there was a feeling of impunity, permissiveness, social acceptance. It took people a few years to understand what drugs were, what they signified, and meanwhile the *capos* could carry on doing what they liked.' The third pole was the legal backwardness, plus the lack of interest in remedying it. The Galician Regional Council was ill equipped to take on mafia-like gangs that, lest we forget, were also often generous party donors. And the government itself had more important things to think about than the problems in this far-flung corner of Spain – the 99 murders perpetrated by ETA in 1980, for instance, or the 1,000 people joining dole queues daily across the country. And, of course, the law was in the clans' favour: narcotic substances were not yet regulated, and were punishable on the same level as tobacco. Less work, much more money and the same level of risk. How could they say no?

It seems likely that the Galician *capos* first made contact with international drug-trafficking gangs via money-laundering channels. The Charlíns' first move was to get in touch with some Moroccans they used for sending money to Switzerland. As Félix García, current head of the Galician Anti-Drugs and Organised Crime Unit (UDYCO), explains: 'They began with a few small trial runs, and it went well. They probably couldn't believe how easy it was. The network the Galicians had created was unique in Europe.' These trial runs were followed by some full-scale consignments, and from that day on the young hippies of Galicia would never have to leave town again to buy their joints.

Laureano Oubiña was next in. His accountant at the time was a Moroccan named Dris Taija who was later murdered in Fuengirola in 1990. Taija made the case for trying some hashish runs, using the same mantra: less work, more money, same risks. Apparently Oubiña took some convincing. He had cut his teeth in scrap metal, petrol and tobacco, and was unsure about this new substance that people had told him was dangerous. Oubiña asked his wife's advice, and she too had misgivings. This profound period of soul searching complete, Oubiña – who has never been convicted of cocaine trafficking – decided to make the leap by offering to help a Moroccan organisation introduce their merchandise into the *rías*. This too went well. So well that he went straight in with a Pakistani group that was well established in the world of large-scale hashish trafficking. The efficiency of these Galician gentlemen put smiles on the faces of narcos the world over.

Oubiña would go on to say:

> If I have ever been involved in smuggling hashish it is because I always thought it would be legalised at some point, both in Spain and throughout the rest of the world. The difference between hashish and other substances is that it is a soft drug, and as far as I know no one has ever died from taking it.

So apparently serious were the Oubiñas in this way of thinking that they even approached the well-known Spanish writer Antonio Escohotado, author of *A General History of Drugs*. Escohotado says that:

> When [Oubiña] was being indicted, his family asked me to write something for them on the history, effects and current-day usage of hashish, which I was only too happy

to do. I even agreed to be questioned as part of the trial, but at that point Oubiña happened to fire his lawyer – Ruiz Giménez – and as far as I can remember, I was never called to the stand.

The final piece in the clans' financial edifice was on the other side of the Atlantic in Panama. This small Central American country, not so much a tax haven as a tax heaven, was the home away from home for the Colombian cartels, and it was here that the Galicians began investing in companies as a way of laundering Swiss bullion. As would later be revealed, almost all of the *capos'* assets were held by Panamanian companies with obscure and difficult-to-trace paperwork. One of the fixtures here was the head of R.O.S., Miñanco Sito. Always impeccably turned out, his moustache always carefully trimmed, the Escobar of the Ría had a soft spot for the Caribbean, and for its women in particular. He was still married to his first wife, Rosa Pouso, at the time, with whom he'd had two daughters. But his many trips to Panama led him into the arms of the woman who would be his next wife, Odalys Rivera (the surname is Galician), niece of the Minister of Justice in General Noriega's government, which assumed power in 1984. Odalys would bear him a further daughter. 'She was the one who introduced him to cocaine,' according to one veteran *guardia*. 'She knew the Colombian cartels that were installed in Panama and she made the introductions. So it began.' At Sito's side was José Manuel Padín Gestoso, better known as Manolo the Catalan, and it later came to light that he also spent a great deal of time in the country. He was present at early meetings with the Medellín cartel, along with the Honduran Ramón Matta Ballesteros, who was one of Pablo Escobar's underlings and an intermediary for the Colombian and Mexican cartels: it was him who ordered the killing in 1984 of the DEA agent Enrique 'Kiki' Camarena. The pair met in Panama and travelled to Costa Rica together, where they agreed to test the water with some low-key shipments. In Galicia, the Colombians found the perfect gateway into Europe: infrastructure, people who knew the territory, all but absent police force and legislative system, and Spanish-speaking to boot. The Colombian cartels were by now under the heel of the DEA, and business was suffering as a result. So they were only too happy to find a dependable connection in this new market. Arousa turned out to be just the lifeline they had been looking for.

The successful trial shipments underwent a brief pause in April 1984 when the Colombian Minister of Justice Rodrigo Lara Bonilla was murdered after the aggressive stance he had taken against the cartels. He was gunned down from a motorbike in his Mercedes on the north side of Bogotá. His bodyguards raced after Escobar's hitmen, who lost control of the bike in the chase. One died in the crash and the other was arrested and given an 11-month prison sentence. President Belisario Betancur took the murder badly, and declared war on the narcos soon afterwards. Pablo Escobar fled to Nicaragua and his second and third in command, Jorge Luis Ochoa Vásquez and José Nelson Matta Ballesteros, went to Madrid. With them came the boss of the Cali cartel, Gilberto Rodríguez Orejuela.

They did not choose Spain by chance. The recent meetings with the Galicians had left them in no doubt as to the best place to focus their attentions. Matta Ballesteros set up in Coruña, in an enormous apartment overlooking Orzán beach. This was to be the Medellín cartel's local headquarters for money laundering and all dealings with the Galicians. The brother, Ramón Matta, stayed at arm's length but effectively still ran everything over the phone. It must have been one of these conversations that Inspector Enrique León listened in on. While the authorities were still chasing tobacco deals, the cartel had installed itself in Galicia.

Ochoa Vásquez and Rodríguez Orejuela stayed in Madrid to begin consolidating the bridge between Spain and Colombia, and started laundering the huge amounts of cash they had brought with them. Ochoa changed his name almost upon arrival, and had extensive plastic surgery on his face as well. The DEA had pulled out all the stops in their search for him. Orejuela, although he did not change his appearance, did have fake documentation, and together the pair began looking for businesses to invest in. They based themselves in an upmarket villa in Pozuelo de Alarcón, an outlying suburb of the Spanish capital. They employed the services of some prestigious Spanish lawyers, but ultimately drew too much attention to themselves: people couldn't fail to notice such huge amounts of money appearing in the area in such a short space of time. On 15 November 1984, the police stormed the villa and took the pair in. Orejuela had an account book that specified transactions worth millions – cocaine millions. Prime Minister Felipe González got a call from the USA with an urgent extradition request.

The Colombian *capos* went on to spend two years in Spanish jails; this presumably did not come up in the conversation with Ronald Reagan. While their extraditions were being negotiated, Ochoa and Orejuela would get to know the prisons of Santa María Puerto in Cádiz and Carabanchel in Madrid. And, by a staggering coincidence, a number of the Galician smugglers were inside at the same time, following the 1984 'macro-indictment'. They had all the time in the world to share confidences, and to deepen the relationships initiated in Panama. Other Galician *capos* followed suit, and, in passageways and cells, the new ties between Galicia and Colombia were formed. It is said in Arousa – quite rightly – that the origins of the Galician drug-trafficking phenomenon lie in Carabanchel.

The Galician *capos*, well served by their legal teams, were soon released. The Colombians stayed on until 1986 and finally succeeded in avoiding extradition to the US, where 10- or 15-year sentences awaited. To the surprise of the Americans, they were returned to Colombia, where after just a few months they had their freedom. Orejuela's oldest son, Fernando Rodríguez Mondragón, later wrote a book, *El hijo del ajedrecista* (The Chess Player's Son), in which he says: 'It costs us $20m to get out of Spain, and of that, $5m went to Felipe González … His negotiators said there was an election coming up and they needed the money. This was the reason we were able to push the deal through.' The book describes the arrival of the money on Pablo Escobar's private jet, with an extra $10 million for the Audiencia Nacional, the High Court in Spain with jurisdiction over international crimes. These claims remain unsubstantiated, as do others in Mondragón's book, such as the fact that Orejuela also hit it off in

Carabanchel with one of ETA's explosives experts, whom he took with him to Colombia. True or not, it was in 1986 that the Medellín cartel's phase of narco-terrorism began, and from then on bombings became an almost daily occurrence in the country.

José Nelson Matta Ballesteros, meanwhile, managed to avoid the attentions of the Coruña authorities. He was able to carry on working on shipments and money laundering. Perfecto Conde says the Colombians poured millions into the city, and the Coruñese were only too grateful. Automóviles Louzao, a car dealership, was the first to benefit from these injections of liquidity; one of the city's biggest businesses, it had been close to going under. Some of the companies whose cars Louzao sold weren't happy about these new Colombian associates – the likes of BMW, which ended up cutting its ties with the dealership.

Aparcamiento Orzán, the construction company that built the car parks for the town square and the present-day university hospital in Pontevedra, was also showered with narco dollars. The scandal came out in *El País* in 1988. There was a photo of Matta Ballesteros walking his dog in the town square in Ponte-vedra, with the headline: 'Family of cocaine baron making large investments in Spain.' The article included the names of companies and politicians who had taken money from the cartels. Among them was the ex-mayor Francisco Vázquez, a fixture on the Coruñese political scene, once elected to the town council without having even campaigned. Vázquez, who had expedited the permits for the Aparcamiento Orzán jobs, was incensed, and made a complaint against *El País*:

This is nothing but an attack on the good name of Coruña, just as we are beginning to prosper as a city. Just as things are beginning to move, and there is investment and urban development, just as a push has begun that has meant we may have new car parks, palaces for congress, shopping centres …

This statement happened to be the last anyone heard of him in public. The district governor Ramón Berra also spoke out, claiming that Matta Ballesteros was 'clean' and quoting a police report to that effect. Antolín Presedo, PSOE secretary general, said that he viewed the *El País* article as 'paper-thin polemic'.

In other words, *El País* uncovered a whole web of Medellín money, and no one knew a thing about it. Just as well that John Lawn, Director of the DEA, stood up at an anti-drugs summit in Rome nine months later and delivered the following statement:

It is our belief that the main entry point for cocaine into Europe is the Iberian Peninsula. We also know that the extremely powerful Medellín cartel and the Ochoa family are in direct contact with Spanish entities, with whom they share culture and a language. We know that Ochoa lived in Spain for a period of time. This leads us to believe that cocaine first came to Europe via Spain. And that the Ochoa family were responsible, using Matta Ballesteros as their on-the-ground person.

Lawn explained, simply, that cocaine was first exported to Europe in any quantity thanks to the relationship between the cartels and the Galician clans. And that, in the meantime, the authorities, businesses and politicians in Spain had been whistling and looking at the sky. So despairing had the DEA become of the passivity of the Iberians that apparently they had been the ones to pass the information on Matta Ballesteros to *El País* – to provoke a reaction. While the authorities held open their suitcases for the piles of bribe money, the coast remained clear for the Galician *capos*. Their golden age had begun. The time of snow on the Atlantic.

GALICIAN MAFIA

'Nobody understood it: how could Old Man Charlín afford to sell king crabs for next to nothing?'

THE COLOMBIAN FRIEND

At the beginning of the 1990s, the Colombian Hugo Patiño Rojas was involved in running Cali cartel operations in Galicia. 'And still was until recently,' says one *guardia*: 'I think he's back in Colombia now, but I couldn't tell you for sure.' In those days he had an apartment on the outskirts of Coruña overlooking Santa Cristina beach. The Cali cartel – like all the other Colombian cartels – had set up an outpost in Spain, and he was their man in Iberia. In 1992 Patiño closed a deal with José 'the Dog' Santorum Viñas, a *capo* from the Galician municipality of Boiro who is currently serving a prison sentence for smuggling 600 kilos of cocaine. First, the boat dropped off two of José the Dog's men in Colombia – Ignacio Bilbao, who was in charge of the job, and Juan Manuel García Campaña – where they would remain as security until the operation was complete. And it went off without a hitch: the fishing trawler docked in Colombia, the packages were brought on board, the transatlantic return journey was completed, and the merchandise was transported up the *ría* in speedboats. Bilbao and García Campaña were free to go home. On arrival, and thrilled at the success, the latter drank Boiro dry and, for good measure, snorted all that Salnés county had to offer. He got in his car to go home, and, coming into town, came off the road. On impact, he flew out through the windscreen, his body ending up on a first-floor balcony. Death by success.

* * *

Galicia shifted definitively – and smoothly – from hashish to cocaine. The shipments began flooding in; the Colombians and the Moroccans were right to have been confident about the clans. The Galicians became dictionary-definition criminal organisations: carefully run, well connected, and very, very wealthy. As they rose to become the undisputed kings of the *rías*, they also wanted to make sure the whole world knew about it.

The primary link was with the Colombians. Each of the main cartels – Medellín, Cali and Bogotá – sent a number of their top men, men such as Patiño Rojas, to Madrid and Galicia. The money would be laundered in Madrid, collected and sent back to Colombia. The shipments and all transportation issues were controlled from Galicia. Any problems, and the cartel would send one of their hitmen to town. If you heard someone in Arousa speaking with a Colombian accent, you were right to be worried.

A number of the most trusted clan men were sent to Colombia and Panama (where the cartel money was laundered) to oversee their operations there. Manolo the Catalan was among them, and he and the locals got on like a house on fire.

'At the turn of the 1990s, we can start talking about bona fide mafia-like organisations,' says Julio Fariñas. 'It's the only period when we can talk about Galician drug trafficking in such terms. These different organisations were almost always held together by blood ties – like clans. The Galician smallholding mentality was also visible in this: family first. The family backs you no matter what.'

Galicia became – and this is more than just a catchy phrase – Europe's cocaine gateway. The head of the Spanish DEA, George Faz, is on record as saying that nearly 80 per cent of cocaine – blow, nose candy, Bolivian marching powder, whatever anyone wants to call it – to pitch up on the old continent did so through the Galician *rías*.

Although the first contact had been with Pablo Escobar's Medellín cartel, over time it was Cali that became the preferred partner. The boss was Helmer 'Pacho' Herrera Buitrago, and his son ran the Galicia operation, living for a time in Sito Miñanco's home town of Cambados. Both the Colombian authorities and the DEA had Pablo Escobar in their sights at the time, which enabled his Cali counterparts to move ahead.

There were four Galician clans: Sito Miñanco's gang, Laureano Oubiña's gang, the Charlín family, and Marcial Dorado's 'islanders'. A number of smaller groups orbited around them as subcontractors, including that of José the Dog, the Lulús, the Baúlos, the Pulgos, Manuel Carballo's gang, Alfredo Cordero's gang, 'Franky' Sanmillán's boys, the Panarros and Falconetti. Each of whom we will be looking at in closer detail.

Although the clans had origins in distinct geographical areas, they were not territorial. They would bring shipments in wherever they wanted, and there was so much business that no one needed to start any wars. In fact, they would collaborate from time to time, if a shipment were big enough. But even in this period of abundance, the occasional betrayal, swindle or just a misunderstanding meant that scores had to be settled, and the body count slowly started to rise.

The clans were hierarchical, with various levels of command. Famously closed, the authorities had great difficulty infiltrating them. If anything has marked the Galicians apart it is their lack of transparency, their secretiveness and a tendency for extreme suspicion towards anything out of the ordinary – all of which they hold in common with mafia groups, which are also based on family ties and operate according to strict social codes. Their impenetrability was partly why other criminal groups prized them so highly.

The work of the Galician organisations consisted of collecting the cocaine in Colombia, crossing the Atlantic, unloading in Galicia (the most difficult part) and then handing it over to the Colombians to distribute. It might be said they were subcontractors, offering shipment services. But, in reality, this narco bridge between Galicia and Colombia entailed huge risks, each shipment requiring a member of the organisation to accept a one-way ticket to Colombia. If the shipment made it through, the individual would be allowed to return; if not … The main Galician players never tried to play the Colombians, but other smaller groups did. In September 1995, for example, Ignacio Bilbao served as the human security for José the Dog, but the shipment never made it to the Spanish Cali headquarters. His own son had to go to Colombia to collect his body. He was buried at Oza cemetery in Coruña.

The most powerful Galician clans each had their own fleet of fishing boats. Registered under other people's names, naturally. These were almost always fairly old ships, no longer in commercial use. The other groups would use active boats – accession to the EC at the end of the 1980s had been a hammer blow to the local fishing industry, with caps placed on the amounts you were allowed to catch and sell. Driven into unemployment, many sailors tried their luck with other kinds of goods. The risks were high, the potential rewards irresistible. 'Some fishermen alternated between fishing and bringing in drugs shipments,' explains Luis Rubí Blanc, a lawyer and court administrator who years later oversaw the seizure and administration of Laureano Oubiña's Baión country estate. 'The clans had an impressive network among the Galician fleets. But we thought someone was bound to spill the beans at some point. All the fishermen knew what was going on, but none of them ever came to us, not one. Incredible, really.'

A ship owner would receive a call from one of the Galician *capos* with two sets of coordinates – pickup point and drop-off point. The trawler would drop anchor 200 miles offshore in international waters, to be met by speedboats, the fastest means for getting the goods ashore. Once the drugs had been loaded onto the speedboats, the trawler would return, its hold empty, to whichever port it had launched from on its supposed fishing trip.

Compared with tobacco-smuggling jobs, these were quicker and less demanding – fewer packages to be moved. The speedboat would come ashore with one motor running and the young stevedores would start unloading. 'They were absolute beasts when it came to getting packages ashore,' says one *guardia*. 'The speedboat would come onto the beach and everything would be off in no time. Half an hour, 2,000 kilos of cocaine.' The goods would be driven away in cars or pickup trucks.

> Oubiña had four 4x4s, and each could fit 30 packages. That's over 5,000 kilos. They'd load up and drive away with the lights off – at high speeds. No *guardia* had the balls to try to stop them. The only way to do it was to blow out the tyres with spikes. They'd kill you in a race.

He remembers intervening in two drop-offs. 'You move in, and they disappear. Like ghosts. They go up into the hills, and they know the terrain so well, you've got no chance.' Or they might decide to place the packages in one of the many *zulos* – a hiding place, usually obscured using gorse and heather – that pepper the Galician coast. In the hills around Rianxo, in 1990, the Guardia Civil found seven *zulos* in a single month. I spoke to a Vilanova woman called Rosaura, who described a school camping trip on Illa de Arousa. On one of the nights, she said, all the children were inside their tents:

> … and we started to hear noises and see bright lights. The teacher came and told us to stay in our tents. We did – we all knew it was a drop-off anyway. The next day one

of my schoolmates found a *zulo*, and we played a game to see who dared look inside. I guess there must have been packages in it.

Although there are fewer of them now, it is still possible to happen upon these *zulos*. Locals, if they do, prefer not to look too closely. And sometimes people's houses themselves act as *zulos*. 'They offered to build a house for someone in my area,' adds the *guardia*, 'in exchange for hiding merchandise there. And he was hardly going to say no.'

A great deal of care went into choosing the drop-off points. Usually three or four would be established for each operation, and all entrances and exits heavily guarded by local youths. When the speedboat entered the *ría*, the skipper would look out for lights flashing inland. If none were to be seen, it meant something was wrong and they were to proceed to the second location, where, again, no lights meant they should go on to the third or fourth. Nowadays, flashlights have been replaced by 'burners' – mobile phones used once and then thrown away. Call, confirm, ditch the device. The other option was simply to take the merchandise directly into one of the northern Galician ports, several of which, Coruña included, were more or less controlled by the clans. Sometimes the ships would simply dock – no trouble from the authorities – and unload the drugs in fishing crates.

* * *

'The first unload I did was at 3am one morning at Baiona cliffs.' This is Manuel Fernández Padín, a 56-year-old native of Vilanova de Arousa who started working for the Charlíns soon after his thirtieth birthday. A number of years later he picked up the phone and called Judge Garzón, becoming one of the first informants under state protection in post-Franco Spain.

> I was using, I was in a bad way. A lot of partying in Portonovo, drinking, cocaine, LSD … The *rías* are awash with drugs. When I hit rock bottom I went out to try to find work. I was looking for months, but there was nothing. Then I remembered Manolito [Manuel Charlín's son], and I went and asked him. He said he had a tobacco drop-off he could use me on.

Two weeks later Manolito's brother Melchor came and found Padín in a café: 'Go and put on some dark clothes,' he said. 'I'll be back to pick you up tonight.' Melchor pulled up later in his Porsche 911, took Padín for dinner at Los Abertos, a restaurant in Nigrán, and ran through how the unload would work. From there they went to a cove in Baiona to wait in a half-built villa. The speedboats showed up at 3am. 'One of the bosses had a go at us for smoking. An SVA agent might spot them. When we started getting the crates off the speedboats, I realised it wasn't tobacco. It was hashish.' Padín helped bring 2,000 kilos of hashish ashore that night.

> We were bringing it in up this almost vertical slope, and I really wasn't cut out for it: I was overweight, hadn't slept well for a long time and was depressed. After bringing up my first package, I took a fall between some bushes. I hurt my arm pretty badly. I said to myself: you aren't even any good for this.

Nobody noticed Padín's slip, and the drop-off was completed without a hitch.

He did another job a fortnight later. Again he was told to dress in dark clothes, and that this time the drop-off point was at Cape Touriñán in Muxía, in the heart of the Costa da Morte. 'It was the summer of 1989. We went to a hatchery owned by the Charlíns to wait for the boats. This time the Lulús were in on it: they had a shitload of guys out along the nearby roads as lookouts.' When the speedboats came, Padín saw that this time, instead of crates, they were going to be unloading drums.

It was cocaine. 700 kilos or so. El Baúlo was in one of the speedboats – he had brought the ships from Colombia. And there were two Colombians with him. I went and got the Colombians' suitcases for them and took them to the car. They were both pretty quiet, very serious, but not rude or anything. Garzón asked me to name them, but I wouldn't. And I won't tell you now. I'm still afraid to. They were top guys, the Charlíns' contacts with the cartel.

The drums were brought ashore and opened, and the bales of cocaine loaded into a Citroën BX. 'The boot was full, the back-seats were full. The driver was completely squashed in. If the *guardias* had stopped him, they'd have had quite the surprise.' But none did. The getaway was a clean one. And Padín got 500,000 pesetas for his trouble.

Before turning informer, he became Melchor Charlín's right-hand-man. 'We would always keep a bit of coke to sell on ourselves. But Melchor had a rule. He never went through other dealers.'

Padín would load 10 kilos into his car and drive around the region selling.

The rest we kept in a warehouse garage in Caldas de Reis. Everyone was using in those days. Sometimes I'd get a call, and when I showed up for the sale, find someone from my past life – 'You? No way!' Everyone was into it. We sold a lot in Madrid and Andalusia as well. Or people came to Galicia to buy. We were the epicentre, our stuff was across the whole of Spain. Whoever wanted cocaine had to come to Arousa. The Charlíns were no slouches. Melchor's main job was the hashish drop-offs. But he couldn't be at every single one, sometimes other guys ran things. The cocaine drop-offs were run by the Colombians and coordinated by the Old Man's sons. They'd bring young guys with them to do the donkey work.

And were there ever any bust-ups with other organisations?

No, everyone got on fine, but there was a lot of competition. The Charlíns were always going around talking about how much money so-and-so had, and they themselves were obsessed with getting money. They wanted to be the richest. A lot of people envied them. I guess that's why they ended up in jail. You could retire off what you made from one job. But them, they always wanted more.

* * *

After a drop-off, the Galicians would either bring the cocaine to the local cartel contact or transport it to Madrid. The main gangs also had their own fleets of trucks – owned by dummy companies, normally fish and seafood businesses – that would go directly from Arousa to Mercamadrid, the capital's massive wholesale market hall. One such company was the seafood restaurant La Baselle, one of a number owned by the Charlíns. La Baselle dropped their prices to an extraordinary degree, ruining their legal competitors. Nobody understood it: how could Old Man Charlín afford to sell king crabs for next to nothing? Really, though, they did know why. There was a period when the only seafood being bought at Mercamadrid came from the Charlíns. And sometimes these shipments also contained cocaine destined for the cartel's man in Madrid.

Once the cartels were in possession of the cocaine – never before – the Galicians would get their money. Sometimes each side would take half the merchandise, but more often the cartel would take 70 per cent and the clan 30 per cent, or, on a particularly risky operation, the split would be 60/40. The Galicians then tended to sell their portion to the Colombians to sell on, which meant they would receive the whole payment in cash. But a small amount would always stay within the confines of the *ría*, going to dealers who flooded the coastal area with cocaine. During those years, no drug was easier to find. And the prices were low. If in Madrid a single gram was 10,000 pesetas (€60), you would be able to get it for 6,000 pesetas (€35) in Vilagarcía. A little over half the price. A little bit of nose candy wasn't hard to find. Not nearly hard enough.

Once the clan had been paid, next came everyone else involved in the operation: ship owners, sailors, speedboat skippers, the young guys doing the unloads, truck drivers, car drivers, errand boys, etc. A kilo of cocaine went for around 10 million pesetas (€60,000). If one of the clans brought in 1,000 kilos in an operation and took 30 per cent, that would mean close to €20 million each time. 'They bring in wealth,' the locals would say. And what wealth.

The Colombians took care of distribution – all across Spain and to the UK, France, Italy, the Netherlands, Sweden, Poland, Latvia, Estonia and Russia – from little Arousa to the farthest reaches of the continent. Never has any Galician export done so well. Not even the seafood.

The modus operandi would vary, and if the coast was under close surveillance at a particular time, or the authorities seemed particularly wary, the narcos would change tack. It was at this time that the phenomenon of drug mules reached Spanish shores: individuals who would swallow cocaine in thick wraps or balloons, which would be excreted once the person had entered the country. There are no reliable statistics for the amount being brought into Spain by drug mules; the security forces did not yet know about the method, and there was nothing in place in airports to prevent it. Madrid Barajas and Santiago Lavacolla were the main airports to which the mules flew. Felipe Suárez tells us about a flight leaving Vilaxoán – near Vilagarcía – with four illiterate locals on board. They were bound for Brazil, and one of the Galician *capos* was with them. These individuals were shown a good time in Rio de Janeiro, and later each had to insert 30 kilos of cocaine in pellets into his or her rectum. They flew to Italy then took a boat from there back to Vilagarcía, where they made immediate trips to the toilets. Each of them had been promised 2 million pesetas, but they received only half that. One man threatened to go to the police, and was later found semi-conscious after a beating. Needless to say, he didn't go to the police.

Hiding drugs was no easy task, and surreal accidents were not infrequent. Such as when valises stuffed full of money were found in local reservoirs, or when a pile of cash was consumed in a hayloft fire. One night, in a place called Carril, a low-grade dealer called Romualdo, one of the Charlíns' underlings, hid two kilos of hashish in his barn. He came out the next morning to find his pig had eaten it all – the creature lay dead among the hens. Romualdo and his wife went to prison, and the story of the pig who OD'd filled a two-page spread in the local paper. Romualdo became a local celebrity. One day, his son was in a car accident – he crashed into the Audi of Manolo the Catalan, of all people. The young man, petrified, went to try to make amends. Nothing he could say seemed to work – Manolo was very unhappy about the dent. So then he tried it: 'Come on, though! I'm Romualdo's son, the guy whose pig died from eating hashish.'

AROUSA: NARCOLAND

In the famous clam-picking town of Carril, just along from Vilagarcía on the *ría*, everyone knew when a drop-off had gone well for Otero Garrigue: he would come walking into town, one foot in the road, the other up on the pavement. A veteran police officer laughs at the memory: 'He always came along like that when he was in a good mood.'

Garrigue never made it big in the world of drug trafficking. This eccentric celebratory walk was a small-scale version of the mafia-like conspicuousness that reared up on Galician shores in the 1980s and 1990s. Business was going well, next came the extravagance. According to one *guardia* present during this first golden age: 'They started buying big houses and mansions and driving around in flash cars. They'd made it, and now they wanted to make sure everyone knew.' Fernando Alonso, manager of the Galician Anti-Drug Trafficking Foundation, also remembers what it was like: 'They did what the hell they wanted. The big traffickers, the middle-grade ones, the lesser guys. They all started going around like Sicilian *capos*. Arousa almost turned into Sicily then. I've got nothing against Sicily, but that was the way we were headed. Without a doubt.'

'First stop for all the *capos* was a mansion,' explains the UDYCO's Félix García. 'That was mandatory. And for the younger guys, a fast car.' The Charlíns bought Vista Real, a seventeenth-century country house in Vilanova de Arousa. Laureano Oubiña, not wishing to be left behind, bought the country estate in Baión, gazumping Old Man Charlín in the sale. This medieval property had been renovated at the turn of the century, and the grounds included 300 hectares of Albariño grape vineyards.

As is the way with any nouveau riche set, they had to have the biggest and best of everything. Oubiña had the French windows taken out and replaced with tacky new multicoloured panes. Next he sent for marble busts of himself and his wife. Then he wanted a stone refrigerator installed; he wanted it to match everything else on the estate, but the technicians said this was not viable. Oubiña spent years trying to have his stone refrigerator put in.

Marcial Dorado, who, in those days, to the best of anyone's information, was still smuggling tobacco, built a huge mansion in Illa de Arousa, in which he had a gigantic Buddha statue installed. And in the living room's glass roof, a swimming pool. Sito Miñanco, meanwhile, was more interested in cars: he bought three Corvettes and needed no excuse to take them out for a spin.

The ostentatiousness of the narcos gave birth to various legends. Like the one about the system of tunnels Oubiña dug beneath his estate, or the compartments inside the beams of the house for hiding wads of money. People in Vilanova still talk about the morning they awoke to find money floating in the reservoir after one of the *capos*, drug agents at the door, threw a fortune down the toilet.

'They were obsessed with nice things. They hoovered up assets with absolute impunity,' explains Fernando Alonso. 'All kinds of things: houses, cars, small boats, big boats, yachts, businesses, apartments, land ...' And the young men working for them were just as keen to flaunt it: after a successful shipment, it would be straight to the BMW or Mercedes dealership. It was in those years that Vilanova came to be known as 'Vila-Merc'.

And they were no strangers to the high life. The clan bosses were known for their love of fine dining. They would eat epic seafood meals, which was partly down to the fact that all the seafood companies belonged to them: the best catches would go straight to their tables, to be washed down by the best Albariño vintages. They would be given their own private room in the casino at A Toxa. Felipe Suárez, a local journalist, counted 107 visits by Sito Miñanco to the casino in a period of 20 months. And the parties, often attended by high-ranking officers from the Guardia Civil, were never-ending. Nobody liked to miss out on the *capos'* soirées: not police officers, not politicians. They even had parties in the Vilagarcía Chamber of Commerce. All very cinematic, but also just the way things were.

Local journalists also had their fun. Particularly the sports journalists and any others not involved in investigating the clans' activities. Sito Miñanco often invited them along – he was a great lover of football, and an even greater dinner host. There is an article by Manuel Jabois, 'The Crushed Legs of the Crab', describing a dinner attended by many leading Galician journalists.[1] Very good wine, champagnes, the best seafood the *ría* had to offer, and, for the after-dinner entertainment, some high-end prostitutes. As Jabois says: 'The *capo* didn't mind travelling the length and breadth of various continents if it meant being on time for a date with a 19-year-old Cambados girl.'

The *capos* loved call girls, but they also loved rubbing shoulders with the rich and famous. The singer Isabel Pantoja, a superstar in the world of 1980s *copla* music – a sort of Spanish folk-pop – sang at one of Sito Miñanco's Cambados dinners, and even Julio Iglesias had an indirect brush with the clans: his former manager, Rodríguez Galvís, was investigated for allegedly acting as a go-between in some cocaine shipments. Both Galvís and Iglesias were regularly seen in A Toxa casino. The businessman Carlos Goyanes, a fixture at A-list parties of the era, was charged as part of Operation Nécora. He was accused of distributing Galicia-bought cocaine at parties in Ibiza and Marbella – parties that the Galician *capos* themselves attended. He faced an eight-year sentence but was ultimately found not guilty.

'Picture a redneck, any country bumpkin, and then picture them with lots of money,' says one observer of the Galician *capos*. 'Tacky in the extreme. Shirts unbuttoned to show off their gold chains, and hands and wrists dripping in jewellery.' Their riches could do nothing to hide their lack of cultivation. Hence the kitschiness of the whole thing. They would all own seafood places, or a scrapyard, or a bar or two, or livestock –

they had to, in order to have something to show the authorities, and for money-laundering purposes. It meant that such images as a farmer with a Porsche Cayenne parked at the gate were commonplace, or that of the woman, a Rolex on her wrist, serving fried calamari sandwiches in a beach hut. Everyone knew. The state did nothing to prevent a scenario in which some people simply chose drug trafficking as their career, and could coexist alongside people living far more normal lives. The kid finishing his shift at the grocers and hopping into his sports car? Only in the Rías Baixas.

They were never short of crucifixes or statues of the Virgen del Carmen, patron saint of sailors. Most of the *capos* would risk their lives at sea at some point. The Carmen would be stamped on the speedboats and on buildings that had been inspected by the authorities. And on Virgen del Carmen day, when all the local vessels would parade the docks decked with flowers, the boats leading the processions were not the property of the local councils. They belonged to the narcos.

The clans had their own codes and mafia-like practices, much of them far shabbier than anything you are likely to see in the movies. Something local journalists were forced to endure: 'I came back from picking my son up at school one day,' says one, 'and we found a dead cat hung from its tail on the front door. It was a warning, and there was no mistaking who from.' Another came home to find a funeral wreath: 'My name was spelled out in the floral letters.' These were testing years for any journalist tasked with investigating the clans.

It might seem like a joke, or perhaps just evidence of the lack of attention moviemakers paid to the social reality of the Galician *rías* in those days, but one of the films that best captures the golden years of drug trafficking in the area is the comedy *Airbag*. The tone is funny and absurd, but the Galician *capo* played by Paco Rabal is also fairly true to life in his dealings with Portuguese traffickers: he has his own chauffeur, jewellery aplenty, violent tendencies, young ladies constantly hanging off his arm – and he's always welcome at the casino. He is a friend and benefactor to politicians. Though a parody, the film has a streak of truth to it, one that most people probably did not believe at the time. In one scene Rabal threatens some other characters, who, surrounded by his gun-toting under-lings, try to cool him down: 'You can't shoot!' they say. 'Look at all these witnesses.' The *capo*, taking a look around, replies: 'But they live in this city, and the city is mine. And, by the way, so are the judges.'

Which is the way it was. Out-and-out impunity. People in the *rías* accepted, tolerated and even admired them. The same unending mantra – 'They bring wealth' – as had been heard since the days of Marlboro Celta. Condescension and acquiescence blended into one. 'Better to be working for the clans than to go out stealing,' people would say. 'Young men have got to do something with their time.' The line between criminality and social acceptability was diffuse, and the philanthropy of the *capos* made it more so. Just as the tobacco smugglers had done since the 1950s, the narcos financed all kinds of social initiatives and charities. Church coffers were always full, street parties and processions were grand affairs, and even the football teams and sports grounds were there by the grace of the narcos. They controlled everything.

'The social acceptance was based in the tobacco years,' explains Julio Fariñas. 'The tolerance had become entrenched. People had learned to live with activities that were manifestly illegal, which made fertile ground for unabated drug trafficking. People didn't want to know, they prefer to look the other way – just as it's always been in Galicia.'

All Is Silence was the title chosen by Galician novelist Manuel Rivas for one of his books, suggesting that there is something in the very mindset that is propitious to drug trafficking. A Galician *omertà*, custom, mania or cultural ballast that means people do not stick their noses where they are not wanted. '*Alá cada quen.*' 'To each their own' – even the narcos.

'And in any case, what could they have done?' says Enrique León. 'Who was going to go and inform on the *capos*, really? No one wanted the bother, just as much as no one had the balls. It makes sense.' Enrique has hit on a keynote in this sociological symphony: nobody did anything because the state, the authorities, all the institutions whose job it really was also did nothing. In the face of the passivity, one might almost say absence, of the state, how can you ask individuals to step up? The Guardia Civil were viewed as even less trustworthy than the narcos, the police were under-resourced, the judges shrugged their shoulders, the Regional Council had other things on its plate and Madrid – everyone knew Madrid would do nothing. There simply was not anyone *to* stop Sito in his Chevrolets. 'The city is mine,' as Paco Rabal said.

It was no coincidence that Galicia, and not Asturias or Cantabria, became such a cocaine gateway. As we've seen, there were numerous very real enabling factors. And some very real guilty parties too, numbed to the day-to-day reality by money, power – or, indeed, a lack of resources. 'The Galician government,' explains Fernando Alonso, 'spent many a year refusing to recognise the existence of organised drug trafficking. It isn't so much that they weren't fighting it, they actually claimed it didn't exist.' And so back to the parallels with Sicily, where the mafia did as they pleased because, according to officialdom in Rome, they were a figment of somebody's imagination. Alonso again: 'Every year they spent denying the truth, the clans gained another five years' advantage in terms of organisation and strength. It was this passivity, this state of denial, that allowed them to establish themselves. It was this negligence that allowed them to grow.'

'It was a disgrace,' writes Felipe Suárez in his book *La Operación Nécora* +. 'For six long years, nobody in this country lifted a finger to deal with this social evil.' Just look at what happened to the last people to try to do anything about it: Magistrate Seoane Spiegelberg and governor Virginio Fuentes, sent to Santander and Albacete respectively. The PSOE saw that taking on the clans was no vote-winner – something the PP had known for years. Not just that. A high-level Galician judge, who preferred not to be named, put it more clearly: 'In Galicia there has never been a political party that has not received funding from the narcos. Not one.'

If Miñanco was going around Vilagarcía with two Caribbean girls in the back seat of his convertible Chevrolet, with cocaine being unloaded on the beach nearby, it was because everyone was happy about it. Or, at least, that they did not mind.

THE *CAPOS*

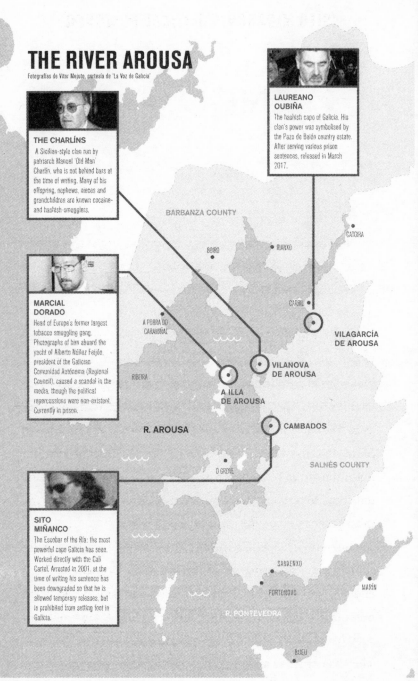

THE RIVER AROUSA

Fotografías de Vítor Mejuto, cortesía de 'La Voz de Galicia'

LAUREANO OUBIÑA

The hashish capo of Galicia. His clan's power was symbolised by the Pazo de Baión country estate. After serving various prison sentences, released in March 2017.

THE CHARLÍNS

A Sicilian-style clan run by patriarch Manuel 'Old Man' Charlín, who is not behind bars at the time of writing. Many of his offspring, nephews, nieces and grandchildren are known cocaine- and hashish-smugglers.

MARCIAL DORADO

Head of Europe's former largest tobacco smuggling gang. Photographs of him aboard the yacht of Alberto Núñez Feijóo, president of the Galician Comunidad Autónoma (Regional Council), caused a scandal in the media, though the political repercussions were non-existent. Currently in prison.

SITO MIÑANCO

The Escobar of the Ría: the most powerful capo Galicia has seen. Worked directly with the Cali Cartel. Arrested in 2001, at the time of writing his sentence has been downgraded so that he is allowed temporary releases, but is prohibited from setting foot in Galicia.

BARBANZA COUNTY

CATOIRA

BOIRO

RIANXO

CARRIL

A POBRA DO CARAMIÑAL

VILAGARCÍA DE AROUSA

RIBEIRA

VILANOVA DE AROUSA

A ILLA DE AROUSA

R. AROUSA

CAMBADOS

SALNÉS COUNTY

O GROVE

SANXENXO

MARÍN

PORTONOVO

R. PONTEVEDRA

BUEU

'SITO MIÑANCO, POLITICAL PRISONER'

'It's a good thing I don't believe in violence. If I did, you'd all be dead.' (Sito Miñanco, speaking to the Operation Nécora magistrates)

In 2000, the Coruña band Os Papaqueixos released what would be their biggest hit, 'Teknotrafikante'. The song, a blend of ska and Galician folk, is rough and ready, but its lyrics have entered the imaginary of the Galician underground. 'Sito Miñanco, political prisoner!' goes one. Another: 'Lots of Sintasol, Lots of Sintasol. How many lines is that?'[1] These are not intended to glorify Miñanco, but as parodies. And yet he did come to be well respected. Venerated, even. Certainly the most powerful *capo* the *rías* have ever known.

Born in 1955 in Cambados, José Ramón Prado Bugallo came from a seafaring family known as the Miñancos. They endured the same hard times as everyone, and he grew up missing more school classes than he attended. He would go shell fishing with his father, though they didn't have a licence. They were furtive and did not play by the rules: they used the so-called 'can' technique, a kind of illegal trawl fishing that devastates the ecosystem. It was in those days that his long-running relationship with the marine authorities began. Very soon, fed up of fishing nets and fines, he got a job working as a messenger and dogsbody on a speedboat. At first, a few odd jobs, but then, once his prodigious boat-piloting skills became apparent, the tobacco clans employed him to work on some drop-offs. He was appointed a skipper in Don Vicente's gang and became a *ría* legend in his speedboat, *Rayo de Luna* (Moonbeam), slaloming between *bateas* and coming ashore with the motor still running. When he struck out on his own, setting up the infamous R.O.S., he had a new speedboat built, lighter and faster, and named it *Sipra II* – the same name he would end up giving to a number of his dummy businesses. R.O.S. hit the ground running and by the early 1980s had become one of the most powerful drug-trafficking organisations in Europe.

Other narcos respected Miñanco because of his origins on the *ría*. He commanded great loyalty. He knew the sea, knew what it was to skipper a speedboat and to risk one's life in a chase. 'The bastard showed up at the port one day with terrible sunburn,' recalls one police officer. 'We said, "What's happening, Sito? Been out for a pickup?" He just said, "Not guilty, man."' He could navigate the *rías* blindfold, and had a natural way with people; polite and respectful, he wasn't at all given to violence. He had a reputation for only working with serious professionals, and for surrounding himself with people who admired him. The families of his business contacts never wanted for anything: if they went to court, Sito would take care of the legal costs and appoint a lawyer himself. And if one of his men disappeared or went to jail, the family would receive a monthly pension, and the children's studies would be paid for. He looked after his own, in other words. Hence his success.

His first wife was a woman named Rosa Pouso, and they had two daughters together. The marriage did not last long, however. If there was one thing that could unsettle his focus it was women. Alejandrina was one of his most well-known girlfriends. He also took up with a girl in Arousa, aged 19 when he started seeing her, and had a regular squeeze in Barcelona. There were even rumours that he had relations with the daughter of a PSOE politician in Arousa who was prominent in denouncing drug trafficking and led protests against the *capos* – and ended up receiving death threats from Sito's people.

It was in Panama that he made the leap to drug trafficking, working with the Cali cartel. There they knew him as 'the Galicia millionaire'. Sito would collect his luggage in the diplomatic area at the Panamanian airport and was known as a high-roller at the Marriott casino. He even had his Mercedes shipped over from Cambados just to be able to drive it on the streets of Panama City. He bought an opulent apartment in the upper-class neighbourhood of Punta Paitilla, and Odalys Rivera – niece to one of General Noriega's ministers and a hostess in said diplomatic area at the airport – moved in with him. They married and had a daughter, and Odalys went on to run his drug operations when he was behind bars.

Towards the end of the 1980s, Sito was everywhere and nowhere. Officially a resident of Antwerp and Panama, he would appear from time to time in Cambados, where he kept a mansion. Just in case, he permanently rented two suites at the Rías Bajas Hotel in Pontevedra, where they still talk about the parties he threw. He had a number of apartments in Madrid, plus a villa in the outlying suburb of Pozuelo de Alarcón that he saw as his safehouse; only his most trusted henchmen knew about it. Police records show that between 1989 and 1990 he made at least two visits apiece to the US, Venezuela, Costa Rica, Peru, the Dominican Republic and Chile, and many more to Panama, Colombia, Belgium and the Netherlands. After an arrest warrant in the mid-1990s, issued by Judge Garzón, he became even more mobile; he entered the lists of the DEA and Interpol, and suddenly half the Spanish police force prioritised his arrest. Sito would show up in Cambados every now and again, spend a night with one of his women and then disappear back to Colombia, Panama or wherever it happened to be. To people in Arousa he was an out-and-out untouchable.

Another weakness was cars: as well as the Chevrolets, he drove a Ferrari Testarossa, a Toyota Supra, two Mercedes and a BMW. One of his men, Santiago García Pasín, had the sole job of building hidden compartments into his vehicles for hiding cash or small amounts of drugs.

The reason why Sito could live the high life was because he had an empire. The Arousan narco organisation, probably the most powerful Galicia has ever known, counted among its ranks not just pilots and sailors but a constellation of lawyers, civil servants, journalists, counterfeiters, politicians, and officers in the Guardia Civil, the Policía Nacional and the SVA – followed, unfortunately, by a depressing 'etcetera'. A big payroll. Should any of his moles abuse his confidence or try to double-cross him, Sito had no compunction about outing them in the media. On 31 December 1989, he was entering Arousa on one of his speedboats when a navy patrol under Sergeant Marcos Corral ordered him to stop. Corral and his men searched the boat: it was brimming with crates of cigarettes. According to Sito, Corral requisitioned a few of these and went away. Sick of such 'abuses', Sito sent a letter to Radio Arousa, which they read out on air – to much controversy:

> It ought to be known that Sergeant Corral has his own clients and that, of course, this isn't the first time he has carried out such a manoeuvre ... At the end of the day, they are far shadier than any one of us. When justice is done to us, it is our hope that justice also be done with these sewer rats.

Also on the payroll was José Manuel Rodríguez Núñez, an employee at the Pontevedra telephone exchange who informed Sito's gangs whenever a wiretap was set up. If he knew he was being listened to, Sito liked inventing red-herring jobs.

The organisation had five speedboats, five trucks, five tugboats and even two cargo ships and a couple of yachts. An intricate web of businesses surrounded it, five of which were based in Panama. One was called Pontevedra-Panamá Investments (not suspicious at all), and its president was named as Sito's cousin, Manuel López Bugallo. Another was the shipyard the gang used to carry out repairs on all the vessels, and which the cartels ended up using as well to work on any boats bound for Florida. Sito had countless business interests in Spain, always run via intermediaries.

Numerous smaller clans orbited Sito, helping in the execution of jobs and with contacts. One was Os Peixeiros, or the Fishermen, run by José Manuel Chaves Corbacho, who would end up dead after falling out with Manuel Ozores Parracho in 1991 in Caldas de Reis. Years after that, in 2006, Chaves Corbacho's son ran over Ozores Parracho in Vilanova, not long after the latter had come out of prison. The police never believed this could really have been an accident, but charges were never brought.

Another long-time collaborator was the Island Group, under Juan Manuel Fernández Costas, or 'Karateka', who in 2012 testified that he derived his wealth from a pedalo company on Nigrán beach. Others included the Panarros, whose boss, José Agra Agra, would end up being recognised and arrested in a Pontevedra café in spite of a disguise of sunglasses, baseball hat and heavy beard. He was convicted for a 2003 operation in which 4,000 kilos of cocaine were brought ashore in two boats. Then there were the Pulgos, a clan headed by a trio of brothers from Boiro. A number of tobacco-smuggling charges have stuck to them, but they have never been convicted of drug trafficking, even though the authorities are well aware of their activities. Sito himself attended one of the brothers' weddings in Padrón in 2000. We will come back to these 'secondary' clans later on, as they are among the many, initially in the shadow of the main players, who would later step up and take control of trafficking in the region.

Sito's gang included Manolo the Catalan and Danielito Carballo, the second of whom would end up with a bullet in the head in 1993. José Alberto Aguín Magdalena, known as Blondie, was seen by the police as the true second in command. Blondie was close to a PP member in Cambados in whose business Sito invested large sums of money. Such coincidences are endless. José Garrido González and Juan Fernández Sineiro completed the top echelon of the organisation, which even had an image consultant, the journalist Pedro Galindo Guerra, a sometime employee of the state-owned Television Española who was later arrested for membership of the group. He was directing the show *Casinos of Spain* at the time.

Sito's clan was a well-oiled machine, running on the all-important fuel of social acceptance. They also understood the system. Even after years of involvement in drug trafficking, they continued bringing tobacco in. A clever ruse, since they could still pretend to be the 'smoke lords' of old, unsullied by drugs connections. And everybody was happy.

And why wouldn't they be. Sito is known to have paid for the hospital visits of various locals who couldn't raise the funds themselves. He even patented certain hare-brained ideas, such as a supposed cure for cancer – no joke. The police recorded a number of conversations with an academic in Hungary, negotiating the patent – this, he said, was what he would retire on.

But one couldn't be a big *capo* without a bit of football thrown in. Club Juventud Cambados is one of Galicia's best-known teams – thanks to Sito. He became president in 1986 when the club was floundering in the Regional Preferente division, the country's fifth tier. Three years later they were in the Segunda B, the third division, and after coming fourth had a playoff for promotion to the Segunda A. Sito put 30 million pesetas (€180,000) into the Juventud coffers at the start of every season, which meant the players were getting better salaries than those at nearby top-flight perennials like Deportivo de La Coruña and Celta de Vigo. The stands were always full, and Sito himself would sometimes make an appearance – mixing with the hoi-polloi for the day. When he was in town, the team would sail to the stadium on board his yacht. There was more than enough room: the vessel, named *Night Mare* and running a Union Jack on the masts, was a 45-footer and had three 2,200-horsepower inboard motors. When Sito turned the motors on, people said they could be heard on the far side of the *ría*.

He paid for everything. He would take Juventud Cambados on pre-season tours in Panama – putting $12,000 in General Noriega's election coffers along the way – or to Costa Rica. The town parties in Cambados would feature the best Bulgarian orchestras. The council did not have to pay a thing, and so grateful were they that, on 7 May 1989, the mayor, Santiago Tirado (PP), named him as a favourite son of Cambados and put a plaque up in his honour. On that day, Tirado fought to get a place in the photo. A year later, in June 1990, once the DEA had announced that Sito was a wanted man, Tirado took part in an anti-drugs march in O Grove, organised by mothers of the lost generation. This time the fight was to get away from there, as the insults rained down.

When Juventud Cambados were promoted to the Segunda B, Sito agreed to take part in an interview on Radio Arousa, but only to answer sports-related questions. He was interviewed by Felipe Suárez, who knew very well about the *capo*'s other involvements. After the show, Suárez took the narco to one side and posed some less comfortable questions. 'I swear on my daughters, who mean more to me than anything in this world, that I have never had anything to do with drugs. And if I'm lying, may I lose my right hand.' Similar scenes played out, sometimes with the added embellishment of tears, whenever the question was put to the *capo*. Even when Judge Garzón issued an arrest warrant in June 1990, Sito tried to keep up the façade. The order was passed to the DEA and Interpol, and within 24 hours Sito was among the most-wanted drug traffickers in the world. And the legend continued to grow: on 24 June he set up a meeting with Colonel Arsenio Ayuso of the Guardia Civil at the Pentax Hotel in Lisbon. Sito arrived surrounded by bodyguards, before repeating his performance, as Ayuso later revealed: '"I have been bringing tobacco in for years," he said. "I hold my hands up to that, everyone knows about it. But I have never in all my days touched a single gram of hashish or cocaine."' They said their goodbyes and Sito vanished once more. Ayuso later learned than Sito had brought a 2.5-ton consignment of cocaine into Arousa that same month.

It would be another year before the *capo* was caught. Operation Andrés (the authorities' code word for Sito) took place on 19 January 1991, again under the direction of Judge Garzón. The police raided the gang's safehouse in Pozuelo de

Alarcón just as a drop-off was taking place – being coordinated from the villa. Sito was standing at a table covered in nautical charts, a satellite phone to his ear. 'Damn,' he is reported to have said, looking up. 'Now you've got me.'

Sito was very, very unhappy. He knew what had gone wrong: the Colombians had given him up. Two members of the Cali cartel, Cristina Osorio and Jorge Isaac Vélez, had been arrested a few weeks earlier in Madrid with 200 kilos of cocaine in the boot of their car. They gave Sito's name up as part of the plea bargain. On 18 January, two days before his arrest, Sito called Fabio Ochoa, one of the Cali chiefs, and the conversation was intercepted by the police.

'Your friends are pissing me off,' said Sito. 'They're messing me about.'

'What's happening?'

'They're messing me about. I can't be holding a truck for three months for them while they go around laughing at me.'

The double-cross was completed by a Lebanese drug trafficker and DEA informant, who went into detail on the drop-off. One of the police officers involved in the operation said Sito was obsessed with overseeing jobs himself: 'He didn't know how to delegate. It's like he wanted to go back to his days on the speedboats.'

Thirteen other gang members were arrested, including José María Díaz Lavilla, who was the son of a High Court judge, and Eugenio Díaz, Don Vicente's son. Also at the Pozuelo villa that day were García Pasín, he of the stash compartments for Sito's cars, a henchman named Machucho and three Caribbean prostitutes.

Of course, that was not the end of Sito's story. Garzón would go on to sentence him three years later, but when the *capo* was later released he would continue to make interesting moves. In reality, in the eyes of many officers, he is still doing so today.

LAUREANO OUBIÑA IN CLOGS

'Look, your lordship, I'm not a trafficker, and even if I was
I wouldn't go round selling the stuff from door to door.'
(Laureano Oubiña)

Laureano Oubiña walked into court for the Operation Nécora
'macro-indictment' wearing clogs. An example, if an extreme
one, of his attempts to put himself across as the illiterate
villager – someone obviously incapable of running a drug-
trafficking organisation. He needn't have bothered. It took
only three questions before he spat the following at the judge:
'I've never invested anything in drugs, or in houses, or country
estates, or whatever the fuck you want to say.'

'He had a short fuse,' says one journalist. 'A real brute.
Zero manners.' And another: 'He had the ability to tear strips
off people, and was only too happy to use it.' According to one
guardia: 'He loved having a go at people. An angry, ignorant
donkey.' Perhaps the clogs weren't needed. He always tried to
pass himself off as a country bumpkin who had been drawn
into a business that then got out of hand. Even in an interview

with *Vanity Fair* in 2011, he refused to blink: 'My hope is that the state will help me rehabilitate, just like they do with drug addicts. Trafficking is a drug in itself, and should be dealt with the same way.'

Oubiña was born in Cambados in 1946 and learned the art of trafficking almost as soon as he could walk. At the age of 15 he was doing deliveries in his parents' grocery van. At 17, although he had barely learned to read or write, he had set up his own black-market group: from the van to a truck and from coffee to *batea* Winstons. He then got married, to Rosa María Carro, who would go on to bear him no fewer than eight children. But in 1983 he fell for his secretary, Esther Lago, and after they married she became the real brains behind the Oubiña organisation.

His relationship with the authorities is a story worth telling. Or enumerating, rather. Rarely did a year pass in which he failed to have a difference of opinion with the local police or Guardia Civil. Those who know him make a clear diagnosis: his temperament has been his downfall. He first appeared in court in 1967, after beating up a local man in Cangados. One year later he was back before the Pontevedra court – having not paid the fine. In 1977 the Guardia Civil proposed sanctions after he was said to have jeered at one of their officers in the street – for what, precisely, it never became clear. In the same year he made an audacious attempt to bribe the commandant in O Grove, and was arrested. Just a year later, he was implicated in tobacco smuggling and all of his properties were raided. The following year he was tried for the alleged bribing of the commandant, but acquitted due to lack of evidence. The case was reopened in 1981 and he went back to prison until 1982. Four days after his release, the judge accused him of belonging to the Servandos tobacco clan. After some time out in 1987, he became involved in large-scale operations once more; he was detained in Girona for trying to bring in 700 crates of tobacco. A year later his house was being searched when he took a potshot at an officer. He was put in prison, where he beat up Ricardo Portabales, an informant for Operation Nécora. Released in 1990, Garzón put him away again after a matter of weeks. The list goes on, and in fact it was in the 1990s that he truly made his mark.

He had two daughters with Esther Lago – Lara and Esther – and the four of them moved in to a villa in A Laxe in 1984. Four years later the hashish *capo* realised his great ambition: buying the country estate in Baión. This would eventually contribute to his downfall. With its 290 hectares of Albariño vineyards, it was acquired via a local collective that had received a loan of 138 million pesetas (€830,000). Something was obviously wrong here: the loan had been made in the name of one Luisa Castela Fernández, a train conductor's widow who rented a house in Cáceres for 200 pesetas a month. Joining the dots, she turned out to be the aunt of Pablo Vioque, Oubiña's former lawyer, a founding member of the AP in Vilagarcía, president of the Chamber of Commerce in Arousa, and a drug trafficker.

The estate itself became Oubiña's main dummy business. The Albariño vineyard was the largest of its kind in southern Galicia. Oubiña set himself up as a major wine producer, and his vintages began gracing the tables of all the best restaurants.

Such displays of wealth would end up costing him. The estate was emblematic of the golden era of Galician drug trafficking. It was the place where mothers of dead drug addicts would gather for demonstrations, and where Garzón's helicopter touched down in Operation Nécora. Oubiña's folly was seized by the authorities in 1995, and he never got it back.

He is the only one of the *ría capos* who, as far as we know, never went into cocaine. Hashish and tobacco, in huge quantities, but nothing else. And although certain police officers refuse to believe it, nothing has ever been proved to the contrary.

His first hashish job was in 1989: 23 drums smuggled in at Baio. He had 16 men on his payroll by this time, all of them working exclusively for him. He also owned a fleet of trawlers for bringing the goods over from Morocco – *Victoria A*, *Estimada*, *Thais*, *Honey Moon*, *Verónica*, *Turia*, *American* and *Katie* were the vessels' names. He also had a speedboat named *Seagull* that flew a Liberian flag.

The clan transported the merchandise by road to Germany, the Netherlands and England, using Oubiña's Penedo and Transgalicia trucking companies. The northern European operations were headed by Vital Nuñez Carvalho, while Manuel López Mozo coordinated all freighting activities. In a 2011 interview, Oubiña stated: 'I would like to be very clear about one thing: I never bought or sold a single gram of hashish. In the three unsuccessful operations I was convicted for, I simply provided transport services, by land and sea.'

As with Sito's gang, Oubiña's was circled by a number of smaller fish. One of the most regular collaborators was Manuel

González Crujeiras, better known as 'Slapdash', a legendary *capo* from Ribeira and perhaps the most significant drug trafficker to have operated in the county of Barbanza, on the far side of the *ría* from Arousa. He oversaw drop-offs, sometimes personally skippering trawlers and speedboats. Over the years he became an expert in narco logistics, and, with the shutdown of Oubiña's organisation, he went into business for himself. He was caught in 2001 aboard a trawler carrying 1,800 tons of cocaine, and in 2011, on his first day of leave from prison, he fled to Colombia.

Surrounding the organisation was a protective financial labyrinth, perhaps the most intricate the attorney general's office has ever encountered in Galicia. This masterpiece of financial engineering was fashioned by an all-star team of lawyers in Panama, who charged exorbitant prices for their services. 'They took him for every peseta they could,' says one *guardia*. 'They charged him ridiculous amounts, but the fact he could hardly read meant they got away with it.' The three largest companies were Ranger Corporation, Fashion Earrings and Norwich Cresti Panamá. In Galicia, one of the primary businesses was the construction company and estate agency Oula Ltd, with 16 country estates and various apartments on its books. None of these were in Oubiña's name. The farce reached such levels that, in the eyes of the government, Oubiña was genuinely poor, with no possessions and no income whatsoever. This method acting was taken to such levels that in 1989 he went to the unemployment office in Cambados to sign on, claiming that he had been fired from his position as an estate agent for Oula Ltd. They refused, and he reported them. The hearing was set for 11 June the following year, 1990, which would turn out to be the day before Operation Nécora took place. Oubiña failed to appear in court.

Oubiña's representative in all his many legal skirmishes was Pablo Vioque, assisted by Francisco Velasco Nieto, another lawyer closely tied to Galician drug trafficking. Another of Oubiña's most trusted men was Antolín Ríos Janeiro, also known as Tolín, who had the job of bringing money back from whichever country a hashish consignment had been taken to.

But Esther Lago, his second wife, was the real lynchpin. 'One smart cookie,' one retired police officer says of her. 'Smart as you like.' Esther died in a car crash in 2001, in Corbillón, on the outskirts of Cambados. It was 2.30am and she had gone out to collect her daughter from a disco. The investigation found that she had fallen asleep at the wheel. She was still alive when the ambulance arrived, but died of heart failure in the hospital. Oubiña was in prison at the time, but was given leave to attend the funeral. 'It was quite a crash,' recalls one officer. 'Head-on into the corner of a house.' A house, improbably enough, that was being used by the anti-drugs squad at the time as its wiretap centre. The boss of one of the largest drug-trafficking organisations had just crashed her car into it.

Oubiña was arrested in 1990 as part of Operation Nécora. They initially went to look for him on the country estate, but he was not living there so they went to his villa in A Laxe. The officers rang the doorbell, and he answered in his pyjamas.

None of the charges stuck, and he carried on running his business throughout the 1990s. Finally behind bars again in

2000, after serving various prison sentences, primarily on money-laundering charges, he was released in March 2017. His son-in-law, David Pérez, has followed in his footsteps. The Oubiñas are still going strong.

THE CHARLÍNS, A CLAN 'À LA SICILIANA'

'Do I own country estates? Gentlemen, bear in mind that in Galicia we call 20 square metres a country estate.'
(Manuel Charlín Gama)

The officer looked in through the window and saw Old Man Charlín sitting in his kitchen in his set of post-war pyjamas. He gave the signal and his colleagues went round and knocked at the door. The lady of the house, Josefa Pomares, answered. Apparently Manolo wasn't at home.

It was 3 November 1995, and on the previous day Judge Garzón had ordered the arrest of the Charlín *capo*, who had been released without bail after Operation Nécora. And so Garzón turned to evidence of a different consignment, and sent a group of officers to bring him in again.

Knowing Josefa was lying, they entered the premises. Charlín was nowhere to be found. Ransacking the villa, they marvelled at all the luxury features, including an enormous indoor gym on the ground floor. After a while one of the officers noticed a mark on a wall: a concealed door that led to a

10 metre square strong room. They tried to prise it open, to no avail, and ended up shouting in that they had found him and there was no way out. Eventually the *capo* opened the door and, still in his pyjamas, gave himself up.

Manuel Charlín Gama was born in Villanova de Arousa in 1932. Famously taciturn, when he does speak, his words often drip with sarcasm – the sign of an innately suspicious character. As a boy he worked with his parents on an almond farm, the proceeds of which the whole family subsisted on. In his youth, having had enough of making do, he set up on his own as a wholesaler of shellfish, shrimp and crab. His approach to business soon became apparent: he was arrested at the age of 26 for blast fishing. Despite this episode, business was good and he went on to build a seafood factory. Into this he began injecting the money he made trafficking Portuguese goods: penicillin, copper, alcohol … And, with the guidance of Don Vicente Otero – who else – he made the move to tobacco. It was during this time that he became acquainted with the authorities. His first proper brush with the law came in 1960 when he was arrested for being at the wheel of a pickup carrying a consignment of Winstons.

The 'Godfather', as people in Vilanova referred to him, is the only Galician drug kingpin who, at the time of writing, is not behind bars. He was also the first to start. His children tipped him off to the potential of drugs, and he did not waste a second. While the Guardia Civil were still getting to grips with tobacco smuggling, he had made the shift to hashish.

As with Sito's visit to Carabanchel, it was jail that prompted Old Man Charlín to go into cocaine. The Celestino Suances assault landed him in Barcelona's Modelo prison, and it was here that Charlín made some important new friends, marking the beginning of a major drug-trafficking career, a long and meandering journey on which his entire family would eventually join him. The Charlíns were a clan in the true sense, with almost all of its members sharing blood ties. Or, to put it another way, most of the Charlíns became drug traffickers. 'And, what is more, with the blessing of the patriarch,' said one journalist I spoke to.

> The Old Man didn't seem to care at all about the wellbeing of his sons or his nephews. He brought them all in – his two brothers, his six sons, two of his grandsons, in-laws, cousins – he put them all in the firing line. One was an addict and, at one point, the Old Man had the idea of putting him in charge of a very risky operation. If it went badly, as he half-expected it would, it would be a weak link out of the way. Business first, always.

This was also certainly the most violent of the Galician clans. They would not hesitate to take revenge for the smallest slight, and left scores of dead bodies in their wake.

José Benito was the most discreet of the Old Man's brothers. He managed to keep clear of the law, with no convictions, not even a single court appearance, until 2000, when SVA officers in Algeciras intercepted 3,000 kilos of hashish arriving from Tangiers. It was being transported on a truck carrying fish oil – the sniffer dog is to be commended for its work. José Benito's wife, María Pilar Paz Santórum, was arrested with him, and their son would also fall foul of the law a few years later. José Benito then awaited a trial that never came: he died of a heart attack in 2007 while driving his car near Vilanova, in a place called As Sinas.

Another of the Old Man's brothers, José Luis Charlín Gama, has the dubious honour of receiving the longest sentence ever given to a drug trafficker in Spain: in 1991 he was given 36 years for trying to smuggle 1,000 kilos of cocaine on board *Rand*, a merchant vessel. In 2002, he made a request to be moved to an open prison, claiming that he had a job offer from a shoemaker in a shopping centre in Las Rozas, Madrid. The prison board was receptive to the idea: 'He has been an exemplary inmate and, at 56 years of age, and after 10 years in prison, has had time to reflect on the fortitude of the rule of law.' But José Luis had not been reflecting: nothing of the kind. It was a matter of weeks before the authorities learned that the job offer was a fabrication.

A daughter of José Luis, Yolanda Charlín, also went to prison for the *Rand* shipment. After her release, she was again put away, this time in 2013, in conjunction with a raid on a Turkish-run heroin lab in Valladolid.

The Old Man's oldest daughter, Josefa Charlín Pomares, was seen as his right-hand woman. She served a sentence from 2001 to 2012 for drug trafficking and money laundering. She led the clan when the Old Man was in prison – at a distance, most of the time. She featured on wanted lists drawn up by Garzón from 1994 onwards, at which point she fled the country. She was on the run for seven years, until the authorities picked her up in Porto, 100 miles from Arousa.

Manolito and Melchor Charlín were next in command. Melchor ran one operation in 1989 in which 4,000 kilos of hashish were brought in at Baiona; when Garzón came after the two brothers, they too disappeared. Melchor went to Chile, where he hid out for five years before being arrested in Rabat, Morocco. Latin America was also Manolito's chosen destination, and, in 1993, with three arrest warrants bearing his name and Interpol searching high and low, he showed up in Illa de Arousa one day, asking about a house that was on the market. Having discussed the price, he disappeared once more, back to Latin America. Incidentally, when Manolito enquired, the vendor said it was not for sale.

Out of all the siblings, Adelaida Charlín was the quietest, the least showy, but we know that in 1991 alone she ran one operation in which 800 kilos of cocaine were smuggled onto the Spanish mainland and coordinated the transport of a further 1,000 kilos. She was brought to trial on both counts, and her nearest and dearest were dragged down with her; her former husband, Antonio Acuña Rial, and her boyfriend at the time, Pasquale Imperator, were convicted as part of the same proceedings.

When the elders were behind bars, and no more siblings remained to take the reins, Óscar and Teresa Charlín assumed control of the clan's finances; the pair later ended up in jail for money laundering and tax evasion as part of an operation known as Repesca (Retrial). The same proceedings saw the conviction of one of Old Man Charlín's granddaughters, Noemí Outón; her sentence was reduced to seven years after she paid a bond of €30,000. She was arrested when the state was auctioning off the clan's assets, and she had the bright idea of offering €800,000 for everything.

The Charlíns worked hand in hand with the Caneos clan, whose boss was Manuel Baúlo Trigo. Either a very audacious man or very thoughtless, he was found to have had his fingers in scores of shipments, always with family members in tow, including his three sons, Daniel, Anselmo and Ramón, and his wife Carballo Jueguen (sister to the *capo* Manuel Carballo), who looked after the clan's accounts.

These two clans were all but a single entity during this time – there was even some interbreeding. Manuel's son Daniel Baúlo and Yolanda Charlín, niece to Old Man Charlín and daughter of José Luis, were an item for a time. This relationship, which was very much love–hate, would end up leaving its mark on both clans. Like any story of passion worthy of the name, it was to end in tragedy.

In October 1989, the Caneos and the Charlíns were still celebrating a successful 600-kilo shipment when another job landed in their laps. Old Man Charlín was in prison at the time, and they had to wait until Christmas for his go-ahead. The fishing vessel *Halcon II* set sail from Santa Cruz de Tenerife on Christmas Day, and was met off Guajira, Colombia, by the Bogotá cartel, their established partners in Latin America. The Galicians received 535 kilos of cocaine, and handed over Daniel Baúlo as security. They set off with the bales attached to the anchor – the closest possible position to the sea, in case the need suddenly arose to jettison. Which, as it turned out, it did. Almost as soon as the *Halcon II* had embarked on the return crossing, it was spotted by a US patrol boat, and the cocaine was dropped into the ocean. The Colombians, unfortunately, did not believe the story, and issued an ultimatum: 60 million pesetas (€360,000), or Daniel Baúlo would be going back to Arousa in a box. Old Man Charlín refused to put up the whole amount, and the hostage's mother turned to her nephew, Danielito Carballo, who was working with Sito Miñanco at the time. The money was finally raised and Baúlo returned in one piece. Then the mutterings began: about the truth or otherwise of the US patrol, about missing bales, about whether someone had in fact kept some of the cargo ... There was already a great deal of mistrust between the two clans, and this only added to it. The issues were long-standing: apart from anything else, the Charlíns owed the Caneos money. The relationship between Daniel Baúlo and Yolanda Charlín was the straw that broke the camel's back: in 1992, Yolanda visited Daniel in prison one day, and brought her current squeeze along with her. Daniel then threatened to give information on the Charlíns, and the clans never worked together again.

Although the *Halcon II* collaboration did not come off, the two clans were indicted together for that shipment and the one on the *Rand*. The Caneos, fed up with overdue payments and dirty tricks in both business and matters of the heart, found themselves with an opportunity to kill two birds with one stone: to reduce their sentences and get back at the Charlíns. Manuel and Daniel – father and son – told Garzón they wanted to cooperate. Two other inmates, Ricardo Portabales and Manuel Fernández Padín, had already expressed a willingness to do the same. Padín talks about bumping into Baúlo in a corridor at the Audiencia Nacional one day: "'Padín, isn't it?" he said to me. "That's right," I said. "Who are you?" They told me they were from Cambados. "Aren't you afraid?" I said. "Afraid of who?" said Manuel. "Not a bit! *Si eles teñen mans, nós temos mans!*"' (If they've got hands, we've got hands.) Very audacious, or very thoughtless: four days later Manuel Baúlo was found murdered in his home.

It happened at 10.15am on 12 September 1994. Baúlo was reading the newspaper in his dining room when three Colombian youths – Luis Aldemir, 20 years old, John Salcedo, 24, and Abel de Jesús Vázquez, 25 – entered the garden. One came and knocked on the door, claiming they were police and had come to search the premises. Carmen opened the door and saw that the young man was carrying a gun. She tried to stop them, but it was too late. Manuel dived for the phone, and it was the last thing he did. They shot him at point-blank range, before turning their guns on Carmen, to stop her cries. They searched the house, hoping to find Daniel, but he was out. Two of his brothers were there, and one succeeded in wounding one of the intruders. The wound slowed up the Colombians, in turn helping the police to find and arrest them before they could leave the country.

Manuel Baúlo died on the spot. Carmen, a bullet lodged in her spine, spent the rest of her life in a wheelchair. The youngest of the intruders confessed to the attack, while the other two have always maintained their innocence.

As far as the police know, the gunmen were sent by the Bogotá cartel, at the request of the Charlíns. The Baúlos' treachery was not something they were prepared to let pass. Proceedings over the *Halcon II* and *Rand* shipments began a few months later. With the key witness out of the way, the leading Charlíns were found not guilty. Not only that: the clan actually managed to implicate Manuel Baúlo. Old Man Charlín testified that there had never been any problems between them. In the end, the dead man took the blame.

Months after that, Carmen Carballo, sitting in her wheel-chair, would reveal that her husband and her son Daniel had been threatened by a Colombian in the port at Cambados; he wanted them to withdraw their statements. Even Danielito, her nephew and an associate of Sito Miñanco, had tried to convince them not to turn informants; there were sure to be consequences. The strange thing about this episode is that Daniel, years later, having avoided the attack by being out that morning, was arrested as part of Operation Destello, along with José Benito Charlín Paz, one of Old Man Charlín's nephews. The Charlíns and the Caneos, together again. Love overcoming hate.

The Charlíns' network of money-laundering businesses was quite extensive. The primary companies were the Charpo canning factory in Vilanova and the aforementioned seafood company, A Baselle, although the list went on: a waste-treat-ment plant, numerous *bateas*, a hatchery, a turbot nursery, a construction company, a wine maker and an agribusiness. The jewel in the crown, however, was the country estate in Vista Real, which they had plumped for after missing out on Baión. They owned a further 29 country estates, a forest and dozens of apartments, as well as a fleet of ships that included four trawlers and six speedboats. Such a fabulous array did not have the effect of making them unlucky, either: altogether, members of the family won the lottery 18 times. 'They would often win, and then make a large investment in something,' says Luis Rubí, the lawyer who investigated their assets. 'In fact, the lottery was one of the things that helped us pick apart all their overlapping interests. Two or three of the winning tickets had been bought in a supermarket on the outskirts of Córdoba. Something obviously didn't add up.'

At the time of writing, a third generation of Charlíns is occupying newspaper columns and appearing in courtrooms. The clan has survived, and continues in its dealings. Old Man Charlín has retired, and watches on from his home in Vilanova. A view of the mountains, the newspapers delivered every day, a nice cup of coffee. Taciturn, suspicious, choosing his words.

MARCIAL DORADO, ON HIS YACHT, WITH THE PRESIDENT

'I couldn't tell you what colour cocaine is, or hash for that matter. I have never laid eyes on either in my life. Nor do I want to.' (Marcial Dorado, interviewed by Felipe Suárez)

'It happened in 2006; we had a tip-off. From a narco who was going to be there. But we never had a chance to get them, and it has never been proved in a court of law.' Another agent who asked not to be named:

> It was on Foz beach in Lugo. Two speedboats came in, one carrying the cocaine bales and the other carrying fuel. The merchandise was unloaded and placed in two 4x4s. 2,000 kilos, minimum. The cars drove to a warehouse nearby, and a red digger was used to take the bales off. Then they left. It went down perfectly. We arrived just after they had moved out – you could still see the marks left by the speed-boats in the sand.

What the agent is describing is one of probably hundreds of drop-offs to have taken place in Galicia that no one has ever heard about. Only when something goes wrong will an operation make the news. The job in question was directed by José Antonio Creo Fernández, a narco who always kept a low profile – so low, he was never heard of again. 'Maybe something was wrong with the goods, maybe he owed someone money. All we know is something must have happened, because he fled to Portugal.' His wife used to go and visit him there, but, a few months before this book was written, he was reported dead. The story remains a mystery, particularly the part with which this agent concludes: José Antonio Creo was not alone in running this operation; Marcial Dorado was with him. 'He was there – my informer saw him. And this is one informer I happen to know we can trust.'

The revelation merits telling: there is a long-standing debate in Galicia about whether Marcial Dorado ever trafficked drugs, or always stuck to tobacco. The authorities have only succeeded in implicating him in one case from 2003, when he was convicted for the sale of a ship called *South Sea*, which was used for a cocaine consignment. At the time of writing, he is serving the sentence arising from that conviction. 'That was a mistake, and they made him pay for it. But he has been treated like a drug trafficker without ever having been one.' So says one veteran *guardia*, convinced that Dorado never graduated from being one of the 'smoke lords'. 'It's my belief that he never went into drug trafficking,' he says. 'He never needed to.' One journalist with intimate knowledge of Dorado's career agrees: 'I don't think he ever went into drugs, no. He tripped up in 2003, and was arrested as an accessory. But all his wealth came from tobacco.' Others are of the view, however, that Dorado was an associate of the cartels, only cleverer about it than the other *capos*. In February 2015, the Audiencia Nacional handed down a six-year sentence for money laundering, after a months-long investigation into his considerable assets. In the court's view: 'Marcial Dorado has been a tobacco smuggler, but it does not necessarily follow that he has not also trafficked in drugs.' The judges considered it proven that the *capo* deposited 106 million Swiss francs (€69 million) into various accounts over the course of the 1990s. Over 50 million of that was deposited as hard currency in Swiss accounts. The court said it was 'impossible that these deposits could have been the profits of tobacco sales only'. Evidence was also submitted of a lumber shipment from Togo in 2000, one of the containers of which was found to hold cocaine. Two of Dorado's businesses were associated with the shipment.

'Dorado is a naturally intelligent guy,' says one police officer. 'He never had an education, but he was extremely canny.' A judgement with which Julio Fariñas concurs: 'A real head for business, any type of business.' This debate is still very much ongoing in Galicia. And these recent revelations only serve to fuel it.

Born in Cambados in 1950, Dorado has always been an Illa de Arousa boy – his family moved there when he was a child. His mother worked as a cleaner in the house of tobacco *capo* Don Vicente – all the leaders of the main clans crossed paths at one time or another with Don Vicente. Out of necessity she sent Marcial and his two brothers to live with Narciso

Suárez, a millionaire Falangist who owned the fleet of speed-boats that connected the Illa with the mainland. Until 1989, when a bridge was built, this was the only way to cross. So it was that Marcial began skippering speedboats from a young age, and his renown quickly grew as one of the fastest on the *ría*. Don Vicente soon brought him into the fold, and within a few years he was moving American tobacco into Arousa. By the end of the 1980s – now with the nickname 'Island Marcial' – he was the number one tobacco smuggler in the Rías Baixas, with an empire that managed to withstand the Peseta Connection investigations. He married María del Carmen Fariña and they had two daughters together, both of whom were sent to school in England. He wanted them to have the best education and to stay clear of his world. He failed on the second count: María Dorado, who went on to become a lawyer, was convicted in the 2015 money-laundering trial. She became part of the clan's management team, of course a family affair. Otilia Ramos, Dorado's partner at the time, went down with her.

Tobacco made Dorado a multimillionaire, but, unlike his contemporaries, he was not interested in flaunting his wealth. The mansion he built in Illa de Arousa was a good metaphor for his character: entirely unprepossessing from the outside, not the kind of place anyone would stop to look at. The interior, however, included a swimming pool with a glass bottom, a wine cellar, a games room, and a tennis court complete with floodlights. Discretion did not signify a lack of funds. Dorado regularly went to the best restaurants, where he ate the best seafood and drank the most expensive wines.

Though well known inside Galicia, the rest of the country first got sight of Dorado in 2013. This was when *El País* published the pictures of Alberto Núñez Feijóo on his yacht, raising the spectre of a Galician narco-politician. The shockwaves were considerable: here was the president of the Regional Council of Galicia enjoying himself on a pleasure boat belonging to one of the top *capos* in the *ría*. The photos were taken in 1995. Feijóo and Dorado, the article explained, met that year when the former was on a posting at the Galician health board. The pair became friends and this promising young politician began visiting the Illa de Arousa mansion on a regular basis for lavish dinners. 'Dorado loved to hobnob,' explains Julio Fariñas. 'Being well connected was an obsession. He had friends in all kinds of places, and the world of politics was no exception.'

The pair went on holiday together, spending time in Cascais, Andorra and Ibiza, where Dorado kept a yacht, as well as at a house in Baiona where Dorado kept another yacht.

After the photos went public, and with all of Galicia in shock, Feijóo was forced to explain himself. He made a statement saying that the relationship had no bearing on his position in public life, and that, while he had been Dorado's guest on occasion, mutual friends had always been present. He was categorical about the lack of economic ties between them, and said he knew nothing of the *capo*'s business dealings. The latter was difficult to swallow, given that, in 1995, Dorado's status inside Galicia was fairly clear and he had twice been to court – once as part of the 1984 'macro-indictment' and once in 1990, when he was charged, but found not guilty, as part of Operation Nécora. Feijóo claimed he had taken the word of mutual friends that Dorado was not involved in smuggling. He also said that he cut all ties in 1997, after the Audiencia Nacional opened an investigation into Dorado's dealings. He was later forced to admit, after a wiretap recording came to light, that the men had kept in contact, if only sporadically, as late as 2003. The matter was more or less forgotten after that, and at the time of writing Feijóo is still president. The political rumour mills even mention him as possible heir to Mariano Rajoy as head of the PP.

In fact, Feijóo had known about the photos since 2004, which was when the police came across them, during a raid on one of Dorado's properties. It would appear that they were passed to a member of the Galician PSOE, who threatened to make them public unless the PP agreed to tone down some of its rhetoric. All's fair.

It did little for Feijóo's public standing when Dorado decided to make a statement from prison: 'He is a good guy, very hard working. I always thought he'd go far, he gave off a sense of integrity and passion for his work. And I can confirm he did not know anything about me being a drug trafficker in the past, present or future.'

This has always been Dorado's mantra. Any time he has the opportunity to speak in public, he uses it to distance himself from drugs. A number of years ago a policeman in Arousa received a phone call from Dorado's wife, asking if he would testify before the Audiencia that her husband had only worked in tobacco. The policeman told her he was sorry, but he had his dignity to think about.

Whatever its business, Dorado's group was extremely powerful, with an infrastructure and wage bill on a par with any of the drug-trafficking clans. One of his most trusted side-kicks was José Luis 'Hawser' Hermida Paz, who occasionally went in with the Charlíns on jobs. 'Hawser' was among those convicted as part of the *Rand* operation: a 14-year stretch.

Another of Dorado's henchmen was Manuel Prado López, who went into drug trafficking when Dorado's gang was dismantled in 2003. Like 'Hawser', he was drawn to the warmth of the Charlíns' hearth, and later became an interme-diary between them and the Bogotá cartel. He was arrested in 2006 as part of Operation Destello, following the case of Daniel Baúlo's 'missing' cocaine bales.

And, of course, Dorado constructed a business fortress around himself. One of the wealthiest smugglers in Galicia, he had bank accounts in Switzerland, Portugal and the Bahamas. He owned several estate agencies and petrol stations, a large vineyard in Portugal, and he went into olive-oil production in Morocco. There was a point when he was running a consor-tium comprising 28 Spanish and foreign companies. Until the attorney general's hammer came down, Dorado owned four country estates in Portugal, six apartments in Galicia, 10 commercial premises in Santiago de Compostela and a factory in Vilanova. Beyond Galicia, there were various properties in Ávila, Madrid, León, Seville and Malaga – a portfolio of over 208 premises. And, as if that were not enough, in 1998 he won the lottery – sheer good luck, of course.

The debate over Dorado's status as tobacco or drug kingpin demonstrates that, until very recently, although they went unnoticed, the tobacco runners were still operating in Galicia. Operating in the shadows of the more conspicuous narcos, dozens of these 'smoke lords' have gone on living extremely well, all thanks to those '*batea* Winstons'.

WHITE TIDE

'Can this really be happening?'

LET US LIVE

It wasn't easy convincing them to form a team. None of the 'airheads' – as they were known in Vilanova – had much time for football. In fact, all they wanted to do was hang out at the park, smoke joints and pour amphetamines down their throats. The only other thing they liked was going into Cambados or Vilagarcía, colonising a bar and getting very drunk. Anything else was a bit too much like hard work. So, in the summer of 1982, it took quite a bit of doing to encourage them to assemble a football team.

The story of the 'Let us Live' football team describes the scars produced by drug trafficking in the youth of the Rías Baixas. What effect might it have on a small area such as this sheltering the busiest cocaine-trafficking organisations in Europe? The answers are to be found in *White Tide*, a 2011 documentary that won a Reina Sofia Prize as a rigorous and forceful anti-drug initiative. It shows how an entire genera-tion – those born in the 1960s – was laid low. The difference between these youths and the pioneers – the likes of the previ-ously discussed Chis, Chema, Tati and Dámaso, who at the beginning of the 1970s opened the Charlíns' eyes to the potential of drugs – was that they did not stop with hashish. Caught between the clans and the cartels, they paid for being in the wrong place at the wrong time. They are referred to locally as a lost generation: hundreds of young people who ended up dead, or marked for life in some way by the successive shockwaves of drug consignments, speedboats, drop-offs, mansions and convertible cars.

It was Manuel Fernández Padín, one of Garzón's informers, who had the idea to set up a football team. He turned 20 in 1982, and was involved with a cultural association called Onuba that ran the Vilanova public parade days and street parties. It also organised a football tournament involving dozens of teams – something the 'airheads' never had time for. Padín's work was cut out for him if he was going to prise his friends from the parks and bars and get them to put boots on. He began by approaching 'Soupy' Nito and Gelucho, the oldest members of the group. The former agreed to take part, but a few days before the tournament he joined another team. The latter also said yes, but only if he could be coach – no matter that he didn't have the first clue about the game. These two were the intermediaries between the group and the local hash, amphetamine and – eventually – heroin dealers. Neither survived to tell the tale.

* * *

'My first memory of drugs is from when I was a kid,' says Veronica, who is from Vilagarcía.

I came back from school one day and saw two kids talking out in the street, and one handed the other these little bags. I thought they had sugar in them. This was out in a main street in Vilagarcía, not some backstreet. Then the next week, there they were again. Sometimes bags of different sizes – smaller, larger – but always the same thing inside. One day I asked my parents: what is that those boys are swapping? Sugar? Obviously, it wasn't sugar.

Veronica lived just off Calle Baldosa, one of the main streets in Vilagarcía leading down to the port. 'It was really bad. Junkies everywhere. You'd go along and they'd just be lying there, out of it.' Another Vilagarcía woman, María, concurs: 'It was symptomatic of what was going on. All the kids became zombies.' The port itself, barely 100 metres away, was awash with young men and women desperate for a fix. During those years the streets of Arousa suffered from constant withdrawal syndrome.

The rest of Spain had similar problems: in a country suddenly awash with heroin, hundreds were the *barrios* and towns that lost youngsters in their dozens. It was the same in Arousa, but, contrary to popular belief, heroin did not come in through Galicia. It could be that the levels of addiction to this substance were higher in Vilagarcía because cocaine was so easy to acquire and because drug taking in general was so socially accepted. It made it more likely for people to get hooked on other things. It should not be forgotten that so many of the young men who worked on the drop-offs, or as errand boys for the clans, were paid in cocaine.

The incidence of AIDS nationwide between 1984 and 1986 – when most cases were due to shared needles – was 105 cases per 100,000 people. In Galicia it was 72 per 100,000, but in counties such as Salnés it went as high as 147 per 100,000.[1] In a 1995 questionnaire, a third of Galician schools admitted that drugs were being sold in their environs, and in that same year alone 53 people died of overdoses. Another questionnaire found that cocaine consumption was higher in Salnés county than in any other area of Spain.

* * *

After convincing Gelucho to come on board, Padín managed to induce one or two more. His brother Rafael was one of the easier catches – he played for Vilanova FC, which had once reached as high as the Third Division. From the beginning, he was the star of the team. Rafael is one of the few in the group still alive, though he has needed a liver transplant.

The rest were not great players. Manolo 'the Baker', almost always stoned any time he stepped foot on a pitch, was captain. He died a number of years later of a heroin overdose. Manolo 'the Clown' played in defence, and was also later to lose a battle with heroin. In goal was Pacheco, who died in a fire caused by a cigarette he was smoking, following years of deep and reclusive alcoholism. José Lorenzo, the striker, is now dead as well: he had an epileptic fit while swimming off a beach, and those who were there describe his dog trying to drag him from the water – an image they will never forget. Adolfo Reigosa and Paulino Bareta were the last to agree to take part. Both were later to die of AIDS. Padín made one last signing before the tournament began, bringing in a friend from outside the group, Jesús María Carnicero. Carnicero and the Padín brothers are the only players from Let us Live still alive.

The name of the team had nothing to do with a poetic cry for help, or a plea from the depths of addiction. It was chosen simply because everyone in the town hated them and they hated everyone back. Let us Live – i.e. leave us in peace, leave us to get high, let us lie here watching life pass by. Only in later years would the name take on a more poetic charge. Most of the group were the children of sailors and labourers. Most had dropped out of school, members of families juggling jobs like everybody else in 1980s Spain. They could have gone to sea with their fathers if they wanted, but – once more – they just couldn't be bothered. For them it was all about drinking, getting high and listening to punk. Their strip for the tournament was emblazoned with an anarchist 'A', as was the pennant they exchanged at the beginning of matches. And, to everyone's surprise, while Gelucho toted a litre bottle of beer on the bench, the team won its first game.

The tournament referee was called Manolo Fariña, and he would solemnly shake the captains' hands – as though this were some important cup final – and proceed, during the match, to blow his whistle for even the most minor infractions. There were games in which people were given red cards before kick-off … And then, to even more raised eyebrows, Let us Live won their second match. Then the third. They were in the final. Their opponents were the tournament favourites, comprised of semi-pros from a number of local clubs, some of the best from across the *ría* area. This was the side to which 'Soupy' Nito had defected, and it was he who swapped pennants at the start; the anarchist 'A' drew a smile. A photo was taken before kick-off – legendary in the town because the disciplinarian Manolo Fariña can be seen actually smiling.

A larger than usual crowd showed up for this game: everyone was fascinated that the 'airheads' had done anything at all, let alone reach a final. And, in another twist, the crowd then got behind them. In that one match, the spectators supported the weak.

Skinny and dishevelled in their anarchist get-up, Let us Live managed to keep a clean sheet for the entire 90 minutes. All of them were caked in dust and sweat by then. And, five minutes before the end, José Lorenzo – the young man who would end up dead in the shallows – scored the winning goal.

The players piled in, celebrating in a way they never thought they would. And at the open-air dance held at the close of the tournament, Gelucho, the trainer who knew nothing about football, lifted the trophy, with all the town folk cheering and clapping.

In years to come these young men would join the long list of the dead: the lost generation of Galicia. They carried on with the amphetamines, the LSD, and with heroin too. A battery most did not survive. They were the first crop of young people in the Rías Baixas, and in Galicia as a whole, to have borne the stigma – something they would always be associated with – of drugs being their way of life.

Let us Live, incidentally, lifted that trophy having not conceded a single goal in the whole tournament.

RISE UP

One morning in 1994, two *guardias* arrived at the entrance to Laureano Oubiña's Baión estate. They had been sent to oversee a crowd of 'Mothers Against Drugs', though they had no orders to break up the protest. They arrived to scenes of men and women (fathers were present too) furiously hammering on the gates, before turning their anger on the officers. After a brief attempt to calm the group, the pair got back in their vehicle and fled. Carmen Avendaño, spokesperson for Asociación Érguete ('Rise Up' in Galician), was there: 'You wouldn't believe how quickly they turned tail and ran. I tried to calm people down, but it was impossible. People thought the *guardias* had come to have a go at them. Temperatures were high that day.'

Érguete was founded by a group of women from Vigo, with the goal of taking a stand against the clans. As they saw it, these people, apparently with complete impunity, were selling the drugs that had been killing their children, and at bargain-basement prices too.

'The *guardias* told us to watch ourselves; there were armed men on the estate. And there were. Esther Lago had a bunch of bodyguards with machine guns. But there was something about that day. People just didn't care.'

The lawyer Luis Rubí, who oversaw the administration of Oubiña's assets after places like the Baión estate were expropriated, also remembers the day: 'It was at the point when the mothers were on the verge of storming the place that the state had to intervene. They were furious at these guys getting away with everything, the fact they were living it up while all these young lads were literally dying before their eyes.'

This demonstration at the entrance to Baión, and many subsequent ones, have gone down as a symbol of Galicia's fight against the narcos: the beginning of the end for a pact of silence so deep-rooted, so entrenched, as to appear ineradicable. Despairing mothers squaring up to *capos* and their armed thugs. Galicia had all the makings of a narco sanctuary, and these were the first people to put their foot down. Along with the Galician Anti-Drugs Foundation (FGCN), Érguete generated the social pressure that finally forced the authorities to act.

There were very few of them to begin with. 'They were out on their own,' says Fernando Alonso, current president of the FGCN. 'You had Felipe Suárez, Minister Alonso, plus three people from Vilagarcía. No one wanted anything to do with it.' Five brave people – brave to the point of foolishness – taking a stand against organisations that had been profiting unhindered since the second half of the 1980s. The first move was to set up a headquarters, which they did in Vilagarcía town centre, its defiant banner visible on a first-floor balcony in Plaza Galicia. It occupies the same premises to this day, and inside, in a small, sun-filled meeting room, Alonso spells out their mission: 'We're here to say, loud and clear: in Galicia, we don't want drugs, and we don't want drug traffickers. And we say it to their faces.'

The difficulty to begin with was that, if you stuck your head above the parapet, it might get lopped off. 'There was a handful to begin with, nobody came out in support. Nobody came to the first few events they put on.' One of these was a 'white flag' festival they copied from an initiative in Sicily, inviting people to come and sign a ledger – in the form of an enormous white flag – stating their opposition to mafia groups. 'And white it stayed during the first few years. Nobody was willing to put their name down.'

It was a hard sell, convincing people to associate themselves with such gestures of defiance. Drug trafficking, as we have seen, was deeply embedded, its reach was enormous, and many people still thought nothing bad was happening. In an area all but abandoned by the government, smugglers were still viewed as generators of jobs and wealth. And then for someone to turn up trying to sling mud at the single local industry that made anyone any money?

'Watch your step.' It wasn't long before the threatening calls began. 'The difficult thing,' says Fernando Alonso, 'is that this meant outing your own neighbours. And taking those first steps, the first time such a thing had ever been done, was hard. It needed even more courage because we were right there, right in amongst it.'

Carmen Avendaño says there were at least three attempts on her life. She describes being out for a drive with her father and finding out – when she was coming down a hill – that her brakes had been cut: 'Realising what was happening, I managed to turn the car into a ditch. When I took it into the mechanics, they said someone must have removed the back left wheel and drained the brake fluid. Since then, I always check my brakes.' Her car was tampered with on two other occasions. 'But they never managed to hurt me. It can't have been their strong point.'

The story of Érguete begins in the working-class barrio of Lavadores, a place that suffered particularly badly in the 1980s drug epidemic. Avendaño was a member of a residents' association whose meetings became dominated by conversations about drugs. 'But it was talked about like a gang issue, in the way we'd talked about criminals – not like a social problem that could end up affecting people's lives.' Things changed when people started describing the addictions their children had succumbed to. In Avendaño's case it was her second-oldest son Jaime; he went on to suffer two embolisms, the consequences of which still affect him today. 'It was then that people started seeing things differently. These kids weren't criminals, they were ill … But the problem was getting the rest of society to see it. Even psychiatrists and psychologists, in those days, refused to admit drug addicts. It really was like starting from nothing.' Echoes of the *guardia* who did not know what was in the joint the young man next to him was smoking. People not only did not know, they did not *want* to know. Not so dissimilar to the rest of Spain, where people were also slow to catch on.

In 1986, the Érguete mothers invited politicians and the local media to a press conference. But straightaway it became clear that it was about more than its vague and generic 'fight against drugs' agenda might have suggested. Avendaño and the rest of the mothers proceeded to read out a list of 38 bars in Vigo where hard drugs were being sold. 'We knew we might be making trouble for ourselves, but these people were flooding the city with drugs. In our view, they had blood on their hands. Our children's blood.' A repeat meeting was held soon after, at which they read out the names of the same bars, only this time some of the landlords were in attendance. 'We knew there were narcos in the room. There were police too, and they were all in cahoots, so we needed to watch ourselves. Because, as well, at that second meeting we read out the names of some narcos. Last names and all.'

Among the names made public that day was that of an ex-soldier who owned a bar in the old town of Vigo, on Calle Herrería. Heroin and weapons were passing through the premises, and prostitutes were also available there. 'All of which we said. The whole nine yards. That really upset the apple cart.' The next day Avendaño had to go to the market, and she took her youngest son with her. To reach the market, they had to park and walk along Calle Herrería. And the bar owner was standing in the doorway, smoking a cigarette. She remembers:

I started shaking. My thoughts were of my boy, that they were going to kill my boy. But I pulled myself together, carried on walking, and looked him in the eye. I held his gaze until we came alongside him and know what he did? He looked down. That was when I knew we'd won.

A year and a half later the ex-soldier and trafficker was shot dead coming out of a strip bar in Portugal.

Érguete's renown grew quickly. The bravery of its members drew people's attention and pricked their social conscience. Local politicians, until now all too accommodating to the drug traffickers, hurried to align themselves with the mothers. The foundation was on the cusp of establishing a number of centres across the province when Avendaño's fourth son, Abel, died of an overdose. 'It was terrible. It destroyed me. I just shut my eyes to the world. I didn't want to believe it. I didn't think I'd come through that. I completely fell apart.' She was close to giving up her firebrand activist work, but the rest of the mothers in the group helped her. 'I remember one of them, Dora, saying we should leave it now, let the judges and the politicians deal with it, that was their job. The thought of that! I said, "No, not a chance. We can't drop it now."'

When we started going to different places along the coast, giving talks and organising meetings, that was when the really serious threats began. All the other women wanted to take the fight to the narcos; I felt a bit more cautious. I knew how badly they could hurt us if they chose to.

Almost nobody came to the first meetings in Arousa. This was virgin territory, an ultra-closed society – like throwing open the door on a decades-old *zulo*. The few to attend, though they stayed quiet during the event, approached Avendaño and the others afterwards to ask, in low, desperate voices, what they could do about their children. Gradually the numbers rose.

Word spread, and the rooms began to fill up. And that was when the clans started taking notice, and they sent people down too, initially to try to sabotage us. They let us talk during the meeting. We'd say: 'We know they're using your children for the drop-offs, and none of you say a word. We also know there's no investment in this area, no business initiatives, and people are dying. And still none of you say a word?' Have you any idea what it means to go to a place like Arousa and say those kind of things? Then the guys sent by the clans would pipe up: what were we going on about? We were just a bunch of crazy old women, everyone knew the drop-offs only involved tobacco, and it was up to *us* to keep our kids out of trouble, we ought to raise them better ... Sometimes we hired security men, but it never came to blows. Because we were women, I think. If we'd have been men, they'd have laid into us, I'm sure.

These interventions soon gave way to open intimidation, with *capos* themselves showing up at meetings. 'Sito came to one,' says Avendaño. 'And Oubiña another. With hitmen at their sides. They made sure people saw them, and they had a good look at us. And that was enough – off they went.'

Rather than backing down, Érguete began organising rallies. They would march through places such as Vilagarcía and Cambados singing anti-narco songs. 'Yes to tobacco; no to drugs,' went one chant. Another: 'Justice for the dead.' 'We're not mad, we're not terrorists; we're mothers, we're realists.' All part of their campaign to harry and ultimately topple the *capos*. Years before 2013, when the '*indignados*' of Spain brought *escraches* into popular usage – marches and gatherings to publicly shame anyone acting above the law, such as those Spanish MPs accused by the Platform of Mortgage Victims (PAH) – the Érguete was holding similar events. Among its first targets was Luis 'Falconetti' Falcón. When the *capo* was taken to the old jail in A Parda, in Pontevedra, on a hash-smuggling charge, Érguete members were there at the gates – chanting and making a commotion. In the end, the social pressure led to Falconetti being transferred to another prison. They began making their presence felt at every hearing, court date or jail transfer involving a narco. A previously unheard-of bravery – born perhaps of maternal suffering – led them to face down the most fearsome drug traffickers in Europe. The reverberations were massive. They awoke Galicia. They made it rise up.

More than their accusers' gender, it was the fact that the eyes of society were on these activities that made the narcos keep their distance. This brought Érguete into contact with some high-level politicians, and the media became interested. These 'mothers against drugs' quickly became an institution on the coast, while the narcos, though far from pleased, chose to keep clear of the fuss. Some people – journalists, certain authorities – viewed the contact between Avendaño and certain politicians with suspicion, particularly because Avendaño was a PSOE member. 'And the PSOE had an interest in all the commotion being made,' says one journalist, 'particularly if they didn't have to make it themselves. Bringing media focus to the drug trafficking meant they could push the line that the Regional Government was being remiss. Her fight was

real; I'm just saying it wasn't without political dimensions.'
Avendaño accepts as much:

> I've come in for criticism, and I hear it, but I had always
> been involved in social action. And always had just as
> much time for people on the left or the right, as long as
> they were honest and had a social conscience. Even Fraga
> I got on with. There was a lot of respect there. The fact is,
> he loved me. He'd call me up and ask me what the next
> move should be!

She first met Fraga in 1988, when he was still a member of the
opposition, though he had already been touted as a possible
future regional president.

> I had a list of 13 points that explained what was going on in
> the *rías*. I asked if we should go through them one by one,
> and he told me just to read the whole lot. As I did so, he sat
> with his hand on his forehead, head bowed. Not moving.
> At the end, he lifted his head and I saw that he was in tears:
> 'And all of this is really going on?' he said.

She says the politicians lacked information and insight. A
debatable point, considering the clear connection between the
political classes and contrabandists of all kinds. Not least the
ties between Fraga himself and tobacco kingpin Don Vicente
Otero, *capo di tutti capi* and enthusiastic PP party member. That
the Galician governing bodies knew nothing seems difficult to
believe, but it is true that they could have underestimated the

situation. Or simply that the clans had grown so powerful, and 'generated enough wealth', that no one felt motivated to stand in their way. As one judge said, all too matter-of-factly: 'There has never been a political party in Galicia that has not taken money from narcos. Not one.'

As Avendaño say:

That's true, but it wasn't the same across the board. The guys at the top didn't know how bad it had become. I know that Mariano Rajoy, when he was part of the Regional Government, tried to take on the narcos. He made his feelings known when people like Barral, Vioque and Don Vicente tried to join the party. And it cost him his job. Later, after he went to Madrid and became Minister for Internal Affairs, I met him when Sito Miñanco was arrested. He said it was the happiest day of his life.

She also says that Fraga, once he became regional president, made resources available to Érguete, regardless of any alleged political affiliations.

A police officer I spoke to expressed other reservations:

Avendaño loved the attention. She liked going on TV. And it was her fame that saved her boys, all of whom had criminal records as long as your arm. I'm not saying her cause wasn't noble, but she also got a lot of credit for other people's work. Sometimes it seemed like she had singlehandedly dealt with the drug-trafficking situation.

Her children's brushes with the law are not Avendaño's favourite topic. She looks at the Dictaphone, takes a deep breath: 'Look, it hardly matters now.' She talks about a two-year sentence her son Abel was given for a crime he committed while deep in the throes of withdrawal symptoms. Abel fled to Portugal and called his mother for help, and she got in touch with a lawyer to help get him a passport. It cost her 150,000 pesetas (about €900), she sent it across the border, and then he, after Avendaño had contacted someone at the Cuban embassy in Spain, flew to Havana with his girlfriend, where there were jobs waiting for the pair. Five months later Avendaño got a call from his son's girlfriend: Abel had been arrested by Interpol. 'It was Charlín's doing. I found out afterwards. He gave information to the Portuguese police. I had to fly to Havana, and we finally managed to get him extradited. I swore that day that for every mark Old Man Charlín made on me, I'd make two on him.' Another deep breath. 'I understand that some people don't like us. But I think the majority can see why we did what we did.'

After Galicia, Érguete went knocking on doors in Madrid. In 1989 the mothers had a meeting with Felipe González, leader of the PSOE and prime minister from 1982 to 1996, and the following year with the leader of the opposition at the time, José María Aznar. 'González said we needed more funding. He was taken aback at all the information we were able to show him.' As well as politicians, they paid visits to judges and public prosecutors, among them Baltasar Garzón and Javier Zaragoza (later to become chief prosecutor at the Audiencia Nacional). Érguete succeeded in bringing people's attention to what until then had been a blind spot in the national discourse. And when Galicia began occupying front pages and TV news shows, the political agenda had to make space for it too. 'I truly believe that, without a social movement, the police and the courts could have done nothing. We would be like Sicily now. It was essential for us to react, to oppose what was going on. And that's exactly what we did.'

Many saw Érguete's actions as the necessary bucket of cold water in the face of a lethargic, status quo-supporting political class that had operated half-passively, half-complicitly for years. Two years after the group's inception, Garzón's Operation Nécora was carried out: the state's first concerted move against the Galician clans. 'Till then the narcos were laughing us off. Calling us hysterical, calling us whores. They didn't take us seriously.'

The 'macro-indictment' took place in Madrid, and members of Érguete had front-row seats. Avendaño was called on to testify in the case against Laureano Oubiña. When she sat down, Old Man Charlín caught her eye. She says he made a very deliberate throat-slitting gesture.

'Almost all of them got off, but it took the wind out of their sails. Till then they thought they couldn't be touched. As for us, we were thrilled.' The pardons were a kick in the face, but they were pleased about the new situation: the *capos* no longer had the invisibility they previously enjoyed, which also meant it would cost them if they did decide to come after any of the Érguete members. The *escraches* became regular events.

Avendaño was also volunteering at A Parda prison at the time, and there she crossed paths with Old Man Charlín one day, who had been convicted soon after Operation Nécora. 'He was walking around like he owned the place. He wasn't really that old, though in the court he had tried to give the impression of being very decrepit. I told him he was a disgrace; I told him where to go. And he just walked away, didn't say a word.' On another occasion, in Vigo airport, she bumped into Esther Lago, Laureano Oubiña's wife:

She was wearing a leopard-print dress, and leopard-print shoes too. She looked like some model. She was there waiting at arrivals, so I went over and gave her both barrels: 'Bitch,' I said. 'Murderer. Where'd you get the money for all your nice clothes?' But she gave as good as she got. Yes, I got an answer that day. And I slapped her.

They realised the attitude had changed. They'd lost people's admiration. It brought them down a peg or two. We were strong, and they knew it. Come the judges, come journalists, that didn't worry them; it was us – those crazy Érguete women, they'd say – it was us who really got to them.

Avendaño remembers the day Old Man Charlín had to climb the prison steps on all fours.

There was a large group of us gathered in A Lama, in Pontevedra. We'd been told Charlín was going to be transferred from Carabanchel, and we got a call when he was coming into town. We put on quite a show, I can tell you. We surrounded the car, we were bashing the sides, the roof. It was out of control. The police put a cordon up, and Charlín dragged himself out of the car, and crawled up the steps to the prison. Or slithered. Like a snake. Like a snake.

The satisfaction of having seen him going into prison like that, it just made all the pain and suffering feel like it had been worth it.

Érguete is still operating today. Its headquarters remain in the Lavadores barrio where it began. Of the founding women, only Avendaño and her friend Dora are still alive, though the latter no longer belongs to the group. Nowadays most of the work consists of helping addicts and others on the margins of society.

On a Televisión de Galicia news report from the late 1980s, a reporter interviewed a mother in Vilagarcía – she was leaning out of a window in her house. In a broken voice, she spoke about her son being a drug addict. An image that captures the generation of Galician mothers who watched their children die in front of them, and then went out to take on the narcos. She says in Galician:

And what do we mothers do? Stand there watching them selling the stuff, taking the stuff. Only a mother like me knows what it is to have drugs inside the home. They all need locking up. They need to be made to pay for what we've been through, all we've suffered through the suffering of our children.

OPERATION NÉCORA

'Nab them in their pyjamas.'

THE PUZZLE

We didn't sleep that day. We were at the Hotel Compostela in Santiago. At 4am I had a shower, got dressed and we headed to the police station. I'll never forget it: hundreds of officers, some in uniform, some in civvies. The place was packed, all the rooms, all the hallways. Nobody saying a word. Everyone just waiting in silence. A sardine tin. We show up, and it's all eyes on us. You could have cut the air with a knife, everyone waiting to hear what we were going to say. Garzón gives me an elbow: 'Look at this lot.'

It was 12 June 1990. Operation Nécora was in motion.

* * *

On a January morning in 1988, the Pontevedra civil governor Jorge Parada Mejuto went to Madrid to present a report. Impelled by the work of Érguete and a number of other organisations, he had set up a meeting with Rafael Vera, the Secretary of State for Security, to whom he explained the same thing Carmen Avendaño would be explaining to the president a number of months later, something that the DEA and Interpol had been talking about for a number of years, and that all Galician politicians already knew very well: that Colombian cocaine was making its way through Galicia, that dozens of very powerful clans existed that organised the drop-offs, and that their infrastructure and networks dated back to the days of tobacco smuggling, the players in which had never been brought to justice.

Vera convened the National Anti-Drugs Commission the following day. Among those attending were high-level representatives from the Policía Nacional, the Guardia Civil, the government, the SVA and the attorney general's office. The basic outline for the so-called Operation Pontevedra – a large-scale investigation that later divided down into various smaller initiatives – was agreed that day. One of these, incidentally, was given the name Operation 'Depends'. A retired *guardia* from Madrid explains that, each time they questioned locals in Galicia, they would always vacillate, always somehow avoid giving proper answers. Hundreds of 'it depends' later, they had a name for the operation.

These early moves led to a few arrests in the opening months of 1989, including those of Laureano Oubiña and Manolito Charlín. But the courts knew they had nothing they could hold the *capos* on. Oubiña, for instance, was charged with kicking an officer during a raid; he would be out within weeks. That same year, after a brief sentence, Manolito coordinated a 4,000-kilo hashish consignment, entering at Baiona.

And all of these governing agencies were still full of the clans' moles. Any measures originating in Madrid would be known about in Galicia days in advance. It was impossible to catch the clans in the act. The only way to alter this dynamic was to plan a massive and coordinated strike, unprecedented in scale. One that would be made possible thanks to the testimonies of two informants: Ricardo Portabales and Manuel Fernández Padín.

* * *

Ricardo Portabales worked for José Paz Carballo, a mid-level smuggler from Rubiáns, Vilagarcía district, who had started out as a cattle trader and later went on, after a period trafficking hashish, to large cocaine consignments. He was responsible for bringing 80 tons of cannabis into Arousa in 1988 and worked the following year on a very lucrative 100-kilo cocaine job in Marín. Portabales said he had become Paz Carballo's right-hand man, a kind of protected apprentice who over time gained his mentor's trust.

Portabales' son later collated and published his father's diaries as a memoir. In it he recalls the first time Paz Carballo took Portabales to a post-consignment counting session. They drove to a lean-to up in the hills above the *ría*, outside which a woman stood guard. She led them into a space with a straw-covered floor; clearing some aside, she stamped her foot twice, and a trapdoor opened onto a cellar below. Paz Carballo's cousin Albino Paz Diz was down there with two other members of the clan, and Portabales describes them as counting the money like bank tellers on fast forward. 'I remember being struck by the sheer amounts of cash, and all the different currencies it came in,' writes Portabales. 'There were US dollars, pesetas, marks, francs, pounds … All in cardboard boxes and sacks. They were counting at a table – you couldn't see the tabletop for notes.' Manolo the Catalan and a bank manager from Arousa were also present. A guard stood outside the door with a walkie-talkie and a shotgun. Paz Carballo and Portabales joined in with the count, which lasted 46 hours, during which time they took short breaks to eat, and snorted cocaine to stay awake. Discrepancies in the numbers meant the count had to be repeated three or four times. In the end there were 1,800 million pesetas (€10 million) in stacks on the table.

Portabales describes his rapid rise: it was a matter of months, he says, before he became an integral member of the clan. He talks about a trip to Colombia in which he was given the unenviable task of complaining to the Cali cartel about the quality of some recent shipments. The journey into the jungle beyond Bogotá included 150 miles in the back of a pickup truck, a further stretch on the back of a donkey and a suffocating night's sleep, before a helicopter ride that brought them out at a mansion situated in dense jungle. There he was received by José Gonzalo Rodríguez Gacha, one of the cartel leaders. Portabales explained the issues they'd been having, and Gacha had the following to say:

> I want you to know that the merchandise I provide is of such high quality that I am prepared to fight for it … You say to me that if your services are not important to me, I should stop using them. But now I'm going to tell you something you don't know: I'm not going to stop using

your services, and you're not going to withdraw them. Because, Alfonso, I know you aren't lying to me, don't I? … I am quite aware that my competitors are trying to steal my clients, and I know some of them have been to see you, offering goods not from these fields, but from Peru, places like that, Bolivia. And that they offered a deal that would be better for you: cheaper merchandise, and a bigger cut for your transporting services. But here's the thing: those bastards aren't going to come stepping on other people's toes any more … Tomorrow, my dear friends, we have a small display lined up, one we are sure you're going to enjoy.

This display took place in a cocaine laboratory in another part of the jungle. 'Now, my friends, I am going to show you what happens to anyone who fails to understand that this is a family, and not a place to collaborate with enemies, to get in bed with those who want to fuck us over.' A man Portabales assumed to be an informer had been spreadeagled and tied to a tree beside the river. He had been badly beaten, but was still breathing.

This treatment is reserved for anyone who puts his or her colleagues' lives in danger. This piece of shit was about to rat on us, all because some gringo at the DEA promised him a few dollars, but nothing gets past us. Anyone who thinks they can snitch and get away with it, we find them – sooner or later we find them. And when we do, they end up telling us all their little secrets.

The man was then tied to a bamboo platform with a hole in it, into which his penis, bleeding from a cut, was introduced. The platform was pushed into the river, and the piranhas did the rest. The man screamed for them to just kill him, Portabales recounts. Then the group returned to the mansion and said their goodbyes. Such moments brought home the true nature of the people the clans were doing business with.

Portabales was taken in during the opening salvos of Operation Pontevedra. He was stopped on the road near Marín, and the police found 38 grams of cocaine, 20 grams of hashish, 64,000 pesetas and a .38 calibre Taurus in the car. After six months in A Parda prison, he took the decision to cooperate. He has always maintained that his conscience was the decisive factor – as well as seeing what prison does to people. Whatever the reason for his change of heart, it changed. He was owed 7 million pesetas (€42,000), and, when he demanded Paz Carballo pay up on a visit, he was told he could have 800,000 pesetas (less than €6,000); the rest had apparently been lost. Nothing like economic disappointment to loosen the tongue: on 22 August 1989, he rang Pontevedra magistrate no. 3, Luciano Varela, and got quite a few things off his chest. The admissions made in that conversation reached the Audiencia Nacional, and the report made its way into the hands of a young judge whose star was rapidly rising after an investigation into ETA. His name was Baltasar Garzón.

Years later, Portabales would claim that the authorities forced him to cooperate, on the one hand threatening a long sentence if he refused, and on the other making offers they later failed to keep. These complaints have proliferated over time, in interviews, on a blog he keeps, even on a Facebook page that his son manages on his behalf. Nobody will ever know the true nature of the small print he signed up to. What is clear, though, is that Portabales came out with these things after his state protection was withdrawn in 2011, when the Spanish stated judged him no longer to be in danger. He seems less convinced, residing nowadays in Portugal and preventing his picture from being circulated in the media. His credibility has diminished gradually over time, partly because of the frequency of his verbal attacks. Some even claim that he made the whole story up, that he is a compulsive liar. But what we know for certain is that, at the time, both Garzón and Javier Zaragoza looked into what this reformed narco had to say, and thought it was watertight.

There were a number of top Galician narcos, Oubiña and Manolito Charlín included, in the same prison as Portabales, and they were less than pleased when they heard what he was up to. At a medical one day, he heard the door shut behind him, and when he went to see who it was, a towel was wrapped around his head. Kicks and punches rained down. He came away from that beating with a broken nose and long-term back problems. They threatened to kill him. Curled up on the floor, he says he recognised the voice of Manolito Charlín and the white ankle boots and black cords of Oubiña.

'He wrote to me in terror,' says Garzón in Pilar Urbano's book *El hombre que veía amanecer* (The Man Who Saw the Sun Rise).

I was already very unsure: an investigation based on the testimony of someone also under investigation is always fragile, frighteningly fragile. So we had the police act on Portabales' information the second he came out with it: a safehouse, a cellar, a *zulo*, a cabin, all these place where documents might be hidden, or weapons, money, or cocaine; a mussel bed, a speedboat making strange manoeuvres, a bar … He gave a lot of credible stuff.

Portabales submitted to Garzón's questioning for eight months. The testimony, flimsy to begin with, gradually became more substantial. And still more so when a second informer came forward: Manuel Fernández Padín.

* * *

Today Padín lives on the outskirts of Madrid – not so easy to find, but not impossible either.

'Yes, I live in fear. I always have,' he says, sitting at a café terrace table, leaning in close, neck tense, eyes staring. It has been a number of years since the state removed his security detail. 'I don't know if they're still planning things, the Charlíns. It makes your head spin just thinking about it. Nowadays the Old Man is still controlling operations, but when it comes time for his grandsons and so on to take over, maybe they'll come for me. They have long memories.'
There was a time when Padín had bodyguards 24/7.

Any time I went to Galicia, they doubled my security. I wasn't allowed to go out at night. On one of the first mornings, I woke up to find my car had been set on fire. My parents' house was constantly being graffitied. I still go back, but it's bad. I have to be on my guard the whole time.

Padín had worked for the Charlíns, helping on at least two drop-offs. The night-time excesses of his earlier life in Pontevedra came back to haunt him in the form of manic depression and psychosis. He quickly tired of the work and decided to go public with what he knew – instead of going to the police, though, he rang up the daytime TV show *Corazonadas*.

We ended up doing an interview, but with my face in shadows and my voice distorted. The day it was on, I went to watch in a bar called Arco de Vella in Vilanova. One of the younger-generation Charlíns came in and sat at the same table. When it started, he began laughing. 'It's you,' he said. I said, 'No, no it isn't.' 'But look at that curly hair,' he said. 'And the legs, and the way he talks. It's you.' And I thought, fuck, I'm done for here.

The Charlíns' punishment took the form of a set-up. A few days after the TV programme had aired, they asked him to run four kilos of cocaine to Pontevedra for them. When he was halfway there, the police pulled him over. 'That fucking TV programme was in my thoughts. Christ was I worried.' But Padín had hidden the cocaine extraordinarily well, and the officer, acting on a tip-off from Old Man Charlín, found nothing. Padín made his way to the drop-off point, a shopping centre in Pontevedra, but found nobody there to meet him. He became extremely nervous, and the situation was not helped by the presence of a security guard who kept on looking at him.

I'd gotten all worked up, and I decided to leave the stuff among some pallets. I dropped it, and the guard went straight over and pulled it out. He notified the Guardia Civil. I even knew this guy – he worked with my brother-in-law as a doorman at Espacio Azul, a nightclub in Barrantes. He later told me he thought the packet was a bomb.

He was arrested and placed in the cells at Pontevedra court. They interrogated him '10 times a day, but I told them nothing, nothing but lies. Then, after a few days, they made me an offer: short jail sentence, protection for my family and a job abroad.' All of which was extremely tempting, but he held out. 'I knew they wouldn't be able to follow through.' He was then sent to prison in Valladolid, where he stayed for three months, after which he went to Madrid's Carabanchel prison, where, knowing that several Charlín members were also inside, he sought protection. It was this stay in Madrid that prompted a change of heart. Especially when Garzón came to see him, accompanied by Portabales. 'I gave my testimony without a lawyer even being there. I told them everything I knew. I'd had enough; I just couldn't take it any more.'

And to Garzón's delight, Padín's information verified the earlier testimony of Portabales.

* * *

In May 1990, Garzón organised a dinner, inviting Javier Zaragoza and a number of politicians high up in government, none of them from Galicia. There he put forward a highly ambitious plan for over 50 simultaneous raids, requiring one of the largest detachments of police officers and *guardias* for a single task since the transition to democracy. The result of months of investigations, fact-finding, informers and wire taps, and initially known as Operation Mago (Wizard), this was the seed of Operation Nécora.

It very nearly failed to get out of the traps. On the eve of the operation, Padín received an unexpected visit from Jorge Argote, the lawyer for the Spanish Home Office in the Anti-Terrorist Liberation Groups (GAL) case,[1] Garzón's other hugely complicated undertaking at the time. According to Padín, Argote came to see him in prison: 'It was out of the blue for me. I'd never even met the man. We sat down and he put a blank cheque in front of me. He said, "Will you help us? All you have to do is tell the truth."' Argote wanted him to go on record to say that all his information to date had been false, in the hope of destroying the investigation, damaging Garzón, and thereby halting the GAL case. 'He told me to name my price. I took the cheque and wrote 20,000 million pesetas [€120 million in 1989]. He looked at it and said I had to be out of my mind. "Okay," I said. "Two hundred million then." We had a deal.' Just when Padín was on the verge of double-crossing Garzón, some important evidence came to light in the GAL case, leading to the arrest of two ETA suspects, José Amedo and Michel Domínguez. 'Suddenly I wasn't useful to them any more. Bang went my way out.'

A number of weeks later, Padín told Garzón what had happened. Far from being annoyed, the judge was depress-ingly unsurprised. 'Sure,' he said. 'They try that kind of thing all the time. Don't worry about it.'

THE BIG ROUNDUP

I speak to Javier Zaragoza in his study at the Audiencia Nacional. Sitting with legs crossed and one arm holding the chair back, he says that even as the officers climbed into the vans that night, they still did not know where they were going. The drivers thought they were headed for Andalusia to take part in a move against Gibraltar hashish smugglers. When they got in, they found envelopes on their seats, and only then did they learn that Galicia was their destination. Such was the secrecy required by Operation Nécora. And yet still the word managed to get out.

In 1988, the retrograde money-laundering laws were reformed, and a clause introduced whereby profits derived from drug trafficking could be investigated. Just like Al Capone, the Galician *capos* were now vulnerable to the taxman. The following year a post was created in Galicia for a public anti-drugs prosecutor, and a decree law soon came into effect for the regulation of speedboat licensing and construction. Then the authorities watched to see what the response would be. And Operation Nécora, the result of months of planning by

Garzón and Zaragoza – guided by the confessions of Portabales and Padín – was the culmination. It was the first concerted
effort by the state to take on Galician drug trafficking.

> Once that pair started to talk, the most surprising thing to
> us was finding out about these clans: very well organised,
> very powerful, and seemingly operating with complete
> freedom. We spent a number of months taking statements,
> investigating, building a case. The extent of the problem in
> Galicia dawned on us. Drug trafficking was deeply rooted,
> and there was widespread social acceptance. You hear the
> phrase quite often: a new Sicily. I don't know if that's quite
> right, but clearly the authorities weren't doing enough.

Once the case was solid enough, Garzón took the decision to
mount a large-scale raid against the main clans. The date was
set for 12 June 1990. And the first of his orders was clear: not
a word to the powers that be in Galicia. Only people in Madrid
knew what was being prepared, and very few of those directly
involved knew the true scale of the operation.

The idea was to hit the *capos*' homes simultaneously. It
would have to be done in the early hours. 'Nab them in their
pyjamas,' says Javier Zaragoza with a smile.

'We flew to Santiago de Compostela the night before, a
normal domestic flight,' he says. Also on the plane, along with
Zaragoza and Garzón, were the chief of the anti-drugs squad,
Alberto García Parras, and the chief commissioner of the
judicial police, Pedro Rodríguez Nicolás. The four ate dinner
together in the Franco area of Santiago, in the old town.

We had chosen Santiago as the centre for operations. At the dinner we fine-tuned certain details, the exact timings, the whos, the hows ... We were still in the restaurant when the sun came up. No sleep that night. We all went and had showers and headed to the police station.

There Zaragoza encountered the scene previously described: hundreds of nervous officers packed together, a dense curtain of cigarette smoke. There were 217 officers in total, and almost all of them in the dark. 'There was a large support unit, and none of them had been told the reason for the call. A lot of very nervous-looking men.' Garzón gave a speech explaining the operation, the police chiefs went into the details with their respective units, and the procession of vans pulled out at 5am, direction Vilagarcía. 'A whole column of vehicles. No sirens, headlights off.' Don Vicente happened to be driving in the opposite direction at the same hour, and came past the line of vans; he was booked on an early flight out of Santiago de Compostela. He later said that, on seeing this deployment of force, he thought they were going to raid some unlicensed shell fishermen. It seems highly unlikely that he really thought this, and in any case he went to see Garzón under his own steam a few days later to tell him – in no uncertain terms – that the 'Oterito' talked about by Portabales wasn't him. He was 'Terito'. Don Vicente would later be acquitted of all charges.

The first to fall was Laureano Oubiña, after one squadron knocked down the door to his villa in A Laxe, Vilagarcía. And indeed he was in his pyjamas (stripy ones) when they placed the handcuffs on him, though he had managed to get as far as his 4x4 and turn the engine on. In Rubiáns, the next town along, José Paz Carballo was taken in, and in Vilanova Manolito and Melchor Charlín, though the Old Man himself would not be arrested for a number of months, when police found him hiding in the *zulo* abutting his personal gym. Also in his pyjamas, incidentally. Those early risers in Arousa who comprehended what was going on began joining together in public places, and a jubilant group of the Érguete women gathered at the police station in Vilagarcía, cheering and clapping. Not everyone came out, it must be said. Many local people stayed inside their homes. In silence.

Marcial Dorado was arrested at his home in Illa de Arousa, though it would be only a matter of days before he was back there. A leading Galician judge claims that Dorado knew about the raid in advance and decided to hand himself in. His legal category went on to change from accused to witness, and he came out of the operation without a blemish. 'Dorado's nobody's fool,' says the judge. 'He went straight to Garzón's office. And got off scot-free.' The matter was taken no further.

The other setback, the most grievous one, was what they found in Cambados. Or rather, what they failed to find. This was Sito Miñanco's base, but the *capo* wasn't there. He apparently fled that same morning, after an eleventh-hour tip-off. His associate Danielito Carballo was there, however, along with Manolo the Catalan and Narciso Fernández.

On the same morning, the high-profile businessmen Carlos Goyanes and Celso Barreiros were arrested in Madrid: from a media perspective, this was the icing on the cake.

Garzón personally spearheaded the move, riding in the helicopter that touched down in the grounds of the Baión estate.
The state had made its move, to general applause and rejoicing
– from the Érguete mothers in particular. By mid-morning 18
arrests had been made, out of a list of 22 targets, though not a
single gram of drugs was found. Over the subsequent months
the number of detainees would rise to 48, paving the way for
a series of trials in the Madrid high courts. The highest-profile
arrest was that, eventually, of Sito at his safehouse in Pozuelo
de Alarcón, after his Cali associates informed on him. His trial
was held separately.

All the big names were down. And in spite of the apparent
success, this brilliantly executed operation was only an opening
flurry: statistics later showed that, by 1990, 18,000 individuals
had been implicated, directly or indirectly, in Galician drug
trafficking. A long road lay ahead – one that is still being travelled to this day.

The *capos* were initially placed in the cells at the old police
station in Vilagarcía – formerly they had been dungeons
– before being transferred to Alcalá Meco prison in Madrid.
'There was very little sleep then either,' says Zaragoza. 'We
spent the whole time taking statements. And crossing our
fingers that the cases weren't going to fall apart, just praying
for no leaks or coordinated countermoves by the respective
defence teams.' But mistakes were made, and serious ones.
One fundamental thing was that the *capos* needed to be kept
cut off, stopped from watching the news on TV, or hearing
the radio or reading any papers. And to be kept ignorant of
the fact the other *capos* had been incarcerated. These were the

instructions given to staff at Alcalá Meco – instructions that were roundly ignored.

A week after the raids, *El País* ran a piece revealing that the *capos'* names had been written on the doors of their respective cells. The first time any of them went out for a shower, they would have seen them. The paper claimed that the *capos* could shout to one another from their cells. Notes were said to have been passed inside books or piles of laundry. They thereby managed to make key points in their statements match, and kept one another updated after each interrogation.

Garzón, enraged, went to the secretary general of national prisons, Antoni Asunción, who ordered an investigation into the goings-on at Alcalá Meco. The sheer reach of the *capos'* tentacles seems to have caught the investigators off guard. The prison rejected *El País'* claims, saying that the *capos'* names had only been hung on their doors for a number of hours, and that the men had never communicated.

The shambles of Alcalá Meco was just one of many hindrances that arose during Garzón's and Zaragoza's preliminary investigations. The defence succeeded in tripping up Portabales, who made a number of contradictory statements. It did not help that he started going on TV talk shows, including one very memorable edition of a programme called *The Lie Detector*. Zaragoza says the statements were 'in general very solid', though Padín's hung together better. He says that too many people were set to be compromised by the findings of Nécora, not least certain politicians in Galicia. 'We came in for a lot of criticism, much of it focused on Portables. But it was the only way for us to run an operation of this kind – Italian-style, you might say. It had to happen like this.'

Pre-trial proceedings were concluded in February 1992, and court proceedings began in July. 'We could have gone on investigating,' says Zaragoza. 'On and on. There was so much information, we had to draw the line somewhere. We could have gone on for years. It was like a deluge.'

The trial, which lasted until July 1994, would see further statements from the *capos*, as well as the indelible image of Oubiña in his clogs, disdainfully batting away answers. 'He wouldn't be bowed,' recalls Zaragoza. 'He didn't give a single straight answer.'

Less brusque, and more outlandish, were the answers given by Manuel Abal Feijóo, a young speedboat skipper who worked for Sito Miñanco. He would go on to become head of the narco carriers who were the twenty-first-century successors to the drug traffickers in the region, but at that time he was just an Arousa upstart who appeared at court in track-suit and trainers. During cross-examination he was shown a photo of himself in Viana do Castelo, Portugal, standing at the helm of a speedboat. He calmly explained the circumstances behind the photo: he assured the judge he had been on holiday with his girlfriend, and she wanted a photo of him in the boat. 'Just like other people get their picture inside a Porsche or at a train window,' he said. In the auditorium, smiles gave way to outright laughter. Abal Feijóo went on to be found not guilty.

The answers given by the *capos*, meanwhile, bordered on the surreal. Particularly their cool when denying great reams of evidence. José Paz Carballo, for example, showed preternatural calm when responding to questions about a 600-mile car journey he had made to Algeciras. He said he had gone down there 'to have a few drinks'. And it went on. At one point Zaragoza asked him why he had a scanner in his car. To which he replied:

> What's a scanner? There's this little gizmo in the car, that much I know, and it goes *beep beep beep* sometimes when you're driving. That's all.
>
> *Zaragoza*: And why is this scanner in your car?
>
> *Paz Carballo*: I don't know. I didn't buy it, my son did. He liked the way it looked.
>
> *Zaragoza*: A pair of walkie-talkies were also found in your home. Can you tell me what they were for?
>
> *Paz Carballo*: My father-in-law and I used to use them when we went to buy livestock in Soutelo and A Estrada.

The sentencings took place in September 1994. Old Man Charlín had been found not guilty a number of months earlier. The outcome of this huge ensemble task was underwhelming in the extreme. Of the 48 cases, only 33 led to jail sentences. Oubiña, Paz Carballo, Alfredo Cordero and Charlín were among the 15 to come away unscathed. Once more there was the sense of the *capos* being above the law, though it did not last long. The shockwaves of Nécora continued to spread in the coming years, up until 2004, by which time practically all of the main players were behind bars. And, Old Man Charlín and Sito Miñanco aside (the latter's prisoner status was downgraded in 2015, so that now he only has to show up at a prison facility at weekends), that is where they remain to this day.

Rulings aside, Nécora did show that the *capos* were not invulnerable. As the sensation of their impunity withered, all of Galicia shook. It was a breath of fresh air. Félix García sums it up: 'Though hundreds more operations were going to be needed, nonetheless it was a watershed. It hit them hard.' The outlook had changed.

THE STRUGGLE CONTINUES

'As long as there was someone there to receive it, the cartels would carry on sending the goods. And there was always someone there to receive it.'

AFTER NÉCORA

'That was the end of all the flashiness,' says one police officer. 'No more blowing a million pesetas on drinks in a night for Laureano Oubiña.' The sentencings of 1994, with all the main *capos* acquitted, were a disappointment, but the proceedings still constituted a clear warning. The clans, hitherto immune, could be got at. It was a shot across the bows.

Discretion became the order of the day: no more driving around in convertibles. Becoming a news item on TV – the main news programme on TVE led with the story of the busts – and the fact that the whole of Spain now knew what they looked like was more than they had bargained for. They understood the magnitude of their excesses, and began pulling back. They became more reserved, more diplomatic.

All of which had a sanitising effect on Galicia. No longer was there a sense of the place as a narco sanctuary, forgotten by the authorities, run by drug lords. Now, if anyone wanted to carry on in this line of work, they tended to watch their step; you couldn't go around brazenly doing as you pleased. It might not seem like much, but it was. Suddenly there was a clear line

between those involved in drug trafficking and those operating within the norms of acceptable society – a line whose
blurriness until then had damaged the whole region.

But otherwise it was business as usual. In some ways things
grew worse: more lanes were added to the Atlantic highway
between the Colombian and Galician seaboards. As long as
there was someone there to receive it, the cartels would carry
on sending the goods. And there was always someone there to
receive it. The cocaine and hashish money in the region did not
suddenly disappear. Silence and complicity continued. 'There
has been a cancer here,' said the mayor of Vilanova at the time,
José Vázquez. 'It continues to metastasise. I don't even think
people are particularly against the traffickers now. The ethical
dimension is gone. Also, people are quick to forget.' Those
who knew the situation at close quarters were pessimistic. And
– as tends to be the way – the pessimists were proved right.

A single year after all the high-profile busts, on 23
February 1991, the SVA impounded *El Bongo*, a fishing vessel
with no national affiliation, after finding 35 bales of cocaine
on board, amounting to 1,200 kilos. At that time, it was the
largest amount ever intercepted on the high seas. Get used to
that phrase, because from this point on it becomes a constant
refrain: drug consignments were part of a tournament in which
no one stayed champion for long. The SVA boarded *El Bongo*
200 miles south of the Canary Islands and were met with a
deplorable scene: the crew, comprising nine Colombians
from the Cali cartel and one Peruvian, had been at anchor
for a month after the vessel's engines had broken down and
were badly malnourished. They had begun helping themselves

to the merchandise to keep hunger at bay. The SVA agents, masquerading as their Galician contacts, were shown straight to the cocaine. The crew were immediately arrested and taken to hospital in Las Palmas.

The commandeering of *El Bongo* fell within Operation Santino and led to dozens more arrests. With Garzón fully occupied with the Nécora proceedings, Santino fell to Judge Carlos Bueren. Although his work acquired nowhere near the acclaim of Garzón's on Nécora, it led to many more prison sentences, put tons of drugs out of circulation, and comprised so many boardings of boats – including the prevention of a brazen attempt by some associates of Sito Miñanco to bring 1,100 kilos of cocaine directly into port at Coruña – and so many busts on land that it would be impossible to describe them all here.

In December 1994, three months after the absolution of the main *capos* in the Nécora proceedings, a trawler named *Alza* was impounded off Finisterre with 10,000 kilos of Moroccan hashish on board. Agents stationed at A Illa de Ons, on the River Pontevedra, had spotted her 15 miles offshore. A seven-hour helicopter chase ensued, at the end of which the narcos resigned themselves to grounding the ship, bringing it in near O Sardiñeiro beach, between Finisterre and Corcubión, and swimming ashore. The locals, thinking them sailors in difficulties, came to their aid. One of the captains, Ramón Cores Caldelas, even managed to get a lift to nearby Muros, and from there he fled to Portugal – with half the Guardia Civil behind him. He was finally caught and imprisoned over the border, though it seems he continued his business dealings from behind bars. He came to a tragic end: in 1998 his body was found with three bullets in it, having also been set on fire, in a ditch in Caldas de Reis, near Vilagarcía. No arrests were made in connection with the case, which centred around debts incurred during Cores Caldelas's time in prison.

A Vilagarcía *capo* named Humberto Rodríguez, who had ties to Sito Miñanco, also fled the scene of the *Alza* pursuit. In fact, though he was never indicted for it, the authorities believed that Miñanco had coordinated the *Alza* consignment from prison. One of his associates, Hernando Gómez Ayala, was caught on a mobile phone in his cell making preparatory calls. Laureano Oubiña had been caught with a laptop in his cell a number of years before. The issue was discussed in parliament, and the Izquierda Unida (United Left) party was excoriating about the apparent ease with which so many Galician narcos were able to communicate with the outside world.

On 8 June 1997, Operation Amanecer (Sunrise) intercepted 3,000 kilos of hashish being brought ashore at Patos beach, Nigrán, a cove on the southern reaches of the Vigo River. A couple of SVA agents spotted a speedboat flying upriver at 6am. The bales of hashish it was carrying turned out to have been collected from a supply ship called the *Wendy*. The SVA agents apprehended the speedboat as it was going back out to collect a further 5,000 kilos.

Operation Amanecer is perhaps the clearest proof that Nécora had failed to prompt any kind of talent drain from the primary local industry, not even with the national media watching the well-established *capos*' every move. The police had been monitoring Oubiña and his associates for a number of months and they knew about this particular consignment ahead of time. Oubiña himself was arrested as he drove towards Vigo, where he was due personally to receive the goods and transfer them into the on-land distribution networks. Apparently, when they put the handcuffs on him, he said, 'My wife is going to kill me.' He was then implicated in a shipment of 15,000 kilos of hashish that had been intercepted in Martorell, inland from Barcelona, a job he had worked on with a Corsican gangster named Jacques Canavaggio.

On the day of Oubiña's arrest, José Manuel 'O Piturro' Vázquez Vázquez, Juan Ramón 'Karateka' Fernández Costas and Juan Mouta Tourís were also taken into custody. We will be coming back to these men, leaders of some of the second-echelon clans, which, while the pressure grew on the established *capos*, seized the opportunity to grow their respective businesses. Along with Oubiña, this trio was taken to Madrid, where the authorities played them 10 hours of intercepted phone calls, code-word riddled conversations about the operation. Their lawyers went so far as to claim that not a single word in these recordings could be connected with the trafficking of drugs.

Within days, and in an almost nostalgic move, the attorney general's office had also found Sito Miñanco's fingerprints on this shipment. Miñanco was then in Alcalá Meco prison, but the investigators found that he had been making phone calls, including one to O Piturro at the same time as the drop-off. As it turned out, Miñanco was found not guilty of any connection and left prison the following year. One retired *guardia* I spoke to was quite convinced of Miñanco's involvement: 'Absolutely, he was behind this one. There's no doubt. He got off on technicalities.' By technicalities he means irregularities in the wiretaps Garzón had ordered. One person who was successfully implicated was Oubiña, who fled the country for Greece when he saw the charges he was facing.

That same year, 1997, José Pérez 'Bighead' Rial collaborated with the Cali cartel on a 3,000-kilo cocaine shipment from Bogotá. The fishing vessel *Segundo Arrogante* was scheduled to launch from Vilagarcía in July to collect the goods. The interesting thing about this case is that the ship's captain was given false information: he thought it was a tobacco shipment. Meeting the Colombian supply ship on the high seas on 7 August, he refused to take the cocaine, but the Colombians quickly won him over. He would have been better off sticking to his guns: the *Segundo Arrogante* was intercepted on its return to Marín, and nearly the entire three tons of cocaine were confiscated. (There was a botched attempt to jettison the cargo when the crew realised they were about to be boarded.) Bighead was married to Paula Charlín at the time, leading some people to surmise that this was another of Old Man Charlín's jobs.

Further proof of the ongoing contraband orgy in the area came with Operation Temple in 1999, in which Spain and various European authorities collaborated. The Spanish seized 14,000 kilos of cocaine on board the ship *Tammsaare*, the second-largest amount ever seized at that time. More than half was destined to be handled by the clan known as the Woodcutters – their boss, Manuel 'Nelo' Lafuente, was a former lumberjack. The rest of the cocaine was to be shared between the Neapolitan Camorra and some Eastern European gangs.

The job had been coordinated by Alfonso 'Antonio' León, the Cali cartel's top man in Spain at the time, and *Tammsaare*'s seizure led to arrests in Madrid, Alicante and the Canary Islands. Fourteen of the Woodcutter clan were arrested in Meis, Pontevedra province. Nelo was given a six-year sentence. His brother José Lafuente would also end up behind bars after tying a debtor to a tree in Meis and showing him that a chainsaw, correctly applied, can be just as effective for separating people's hands from their arms as for chopping wood.

José Manuel Vila Sieira, known as 'the President' because of his time running Sporting Lampón, a football club in Boiro, was another up-and-coming narco involved in the *Tammsaare* shipment. The President's response to incarceration was to turn informer: in exchange for providing Garzón with the whereabouts of a 5,000-kilo stash of cocaine in A Pobra do Caramiñal, he was given a minimum sentence. Strangely, he was arrested in 2009 aboard the fishing vessel *Doña Fortuna*, which had five tons of cocaine on board – strangely, because here was a man who had provided the authorities with information, and yet had then been allowed back in by the cartels. As Vito Corleone said: 'It's not personal. It's strictly business.' Anything went, in other words, as long as the money kept coming.

In 1992, a full two years after Nécora, Robert C. Bonner, Administrator of the DEA at the time, was interviewed about the situation in Galicia. He was less than optimistic: 'The Cali cartel is actively involved in recruiting Spanish citizens to do certain jobs for them, such as piloting boats with large ship-ments of cocaine on board, destined for Galicia and other parts of Europe.' For the head of the DEA to specifically name Galicia did not seem like a good sign. He went on to say that, of the approximately 14 tons of cocaine seized in Europe the previous year, half was seized in Galicia. 'But, according to our calculation, another 100, 200 tons made it through. A third of Cali cartel cocaine is being sent to Europe, and Spain is the principal entry point.'

The Colombian cartels clearly still had a soft spot for the *rías* and, as well as the established players, a new crop of Galician narcos was emerging for them to do business with. With so much attention on the likes of Oubiña, Dorado and the Charlíns, many smaller players were now in a position to make gains.

THE OTHERS

The Lulús

Something about the Costa da Morte wasn't right. So thought Luis Rubí, then SVA director, in 1995. He had come across a group of young brothers who drove around in red Porsches, spent their time having jet-ski races, and lived in enormous mansions with no ostensible source of income that could support such a lifestyle. These brothers were members of the Lulús, the clan that dominated – and still dominates – drug trafficking on this stretch of the coast. Rubí decided to take it up with Fernando García Gesto, the fresh-faced head of the clan – still not yet 30 years old at the time.

When we first spoke, he had been into a bank in Muxía a few days earlier and had changed 600,000 Dutch florins for pesetas. I asked him where it had all come from. 'From deep-sea *longueirón* fishing,' he said. I didn't even know what a *longueirón* was.[1] When I said nothing, he went on: 'And from barnacles. Would you like us to send you some barnacles, sir?'

'They came up with the wildest explanations,' Rubí recalls. 'This bunch of kids, going around changing florins in their millions, driving convertibles … We showed them the teller receipts, it still made no difference. They had an answer for everything.'

The Lulús were one of the clans that had functioned alongside the big-name players in the 1990s but avoided the media spotlight (at least from outside Galicia). But their CVs were easily as impressive as those of Sito or the Charlíns.

In January 1993 they brought 3,300 kilos of hashish in at Muxía on board the fishing vessel *Carrumeiro*. Initially given sentences of eight years for the job, the brothers were eventually acquitted. This was the beginning of their legendary status as lords of the Costa da Morte. 'Nothing moves in that area without their say-so,' says one retired *guardia*. 'They started out providing logistical support to the primary clans, but very quickly went out on their own, with Fernando at the head. I see them as the most efficient clan of all, and the most slippery. Very hard to crack open, very good at what they do.' The Lulús have always had a vast system of contacts across the Costa da Morte, one that has proved resistant to any infiltration attempts.

> They've got so many local lads on their books. For every drop-off they post a whole host of lookouts, and lots of local property owners let them hide the goods in their warehouses, or work for them as informers. If anyone wants to do anything around here, it has to go through them.

In October 1998 the Guardia Civil received a tip-off about a consignment that was headed for Os Muíños beach, near the heart of Lulú territory. But by the time the authorities arrived, all that remained were marks in the sand, a couple of bread sacks and some tins of fruit. They tracked Fernando García Gesto down a couple of days later, and flagged him down in his Golf GTI, but he just put his foot down. A chase ensued, the motorways of the Costa da Morte briefly became a rally-driving circuit, and shots were fired, but the young *capo* got away. Some 526 kilos of hashish were found the same day, hidden among some hay bales in a place called Dumbría. The property was owned by one José Manuel Franco Noya, a man who had never registered on the authorities' radar until that moment.

It would be another three years before justice caught up with García Gesto. Incredibly, under the protection of a group of locals, he hardly left Muxía in those three years. 'Between 30 and 40 of them, some friends and accomplices, some loyal comrades,' explains the same *guardia*. The authorities had staked out the area for months, with blocks on both the main roads and the forest paths, but, 'with a little help from his friends', García Gesto continually evaded them.

His status as a fugitive was no impediment to growing the business. That same year, 1998, the Lulús brought a 10-ton hashish consignment in at Nemiña beach, also in Muxía. 'They were doing jobs almost monthly,' recalls another *guardia*. 'They were beasts.' Around that time a crew from Televisión Española went to carry out a report on the clan, but didn't get very far. One of García Gesto brothers, cudgel in hand, hurled himself at the cameraman and the producer, and both ended up in the local Guardia Civil barracks. The whole Lulú clan then came and gathered outside. The journalists fled Muxía with a Guardia Civil escort that same night.

At the time of writing, Fernando is still at large, while his brother and right-hand man, Andrés, is in jail.

Alfredo Cordero

Alfredo Cordero, aka 'the Barrow', was no good at poker. His sessions at the table were legendary in Vilanova, and people still remember him losing over 11 million pesetas in a single night. Cordero was a veteran *capo* who operated throughout the 1990s in the shadows cast by the bright media lights trained on Oubiña et al. He had often worked for the Charlíns, and was charged alongside them as part of Operation Nécora. And, alongside them, he was acquitted. After that he set up on his own, and was caught in 1997 attempting to smuggle in 5,000 kilos of cocaine at a cove in Tapia de Casariego, Asturias. A local person saw the goings-on and called the police. The dangers of not working from home.

Cordero managed to get away. The authorities spent the following three years looking for him, though in fact he had not gone far; he was found hiding in a modest apartment in Vila de Cruces, a little way from Santiago de Compostela. He was given an 18-year sentence, though he was let out early. There-after he made a show of living the quiet life as the manager of a family bar in his native Vilanova. In March 2015 he demon-strated – once again – the propensity of Galician *capos* to always come back for more: he was arrested after information linked him to a 10-kilo shipment of heroin. He was acquitted, but the job ensured that the Barrow became a regular fixture from then on in any headlines concerning drug activities.

Falconetti

The last time Luis 'Falconetti' Falcón stood before a judge was in 2012. By now quite an old man, he was asked to explain the great wealth he had amassed in his life. The prosecution were less than convinced that it could be from hospitality, which was precisely Falconetti's claim: a snack bar on As Sinas beach, two restaurants and an American diner in Vilanova. He was eventually acquitted due to lack of evidence, and the prosecution did not appeal the decision. Now, at 73 years of age, he gives all the impressions of being a retiree.

Falconetti is another veteran of the tobacco era (it was him who placed a gun on the table in a meeting with an Arousa town councillor, telling him 'It only costs a million pesetas to bring a hitman over from Portugal these days'). He goes so far back that in the talking shops of the region some people claim it is him, and not Old Man Charlín, who holds the honour of bringing the first drug shipment into the *rías*.

A failed shipment in 1988 – Falconetti was caught unloading 1,200 kilos of hashish in Hondarribia, Guipúzcoa – was the reason he never gained the same renown as the likes of Oubiña and Miñanco. The 18-year sentence he was given in 1991 (of which he served six years) put him out of the equation when Operation Nécora came around. Many people think he returned to his former activities upon release. One police officer told me about an 8,000-kilo cocaine consignment on the Lugo coast that he was involved in shortly after leaving prison: 'We know he did it, but there was never sufficient evidence. He was smart.' Everyone was looking at Oubiña, Miñanco et al. in the 1990s, and Falconetti was another who undoubtedly made inroads in the meantime.

Franky Sanmillán

In 1994, Javier Martínez 'Franky' Sanmillán had his finger-prints erased and his appearance altered with some light cosmetic surgery to his face. The veteran *capo*, born in León but raised in Pontevedra, was charged as part of the Nécora proceedings, but a day before the sentence was due to be handed down (he faced a 12-year stretch), he disappeared. Unlike his Galician counterparts, Franky decided to go a little further away – though not that much further. He took himself off to Dénia in Alicante, where, installing himself in a 12,000 square metre villa, a raft of forged papers in hand, he assumed a new identity – and went on with his contrabandist activities. 'What we couldn't have imagined,' one police officer said on the day of Franky's arrest, 'was the changing of his finger-prints, because it hadn't been seen in Spain at that time. The only known cases were in Colombia and the US.' During his 14 years on the run, he became one of the country's 15 most-wanted criminals, and was involved in at least two large-scale cocaine operations – the *Tammsaare* job and another along-side Alfredo Cordero in 1997, in which the authorities believe

5,000 kilos of cocaine came ashore at Tapia de Casariego, Asturias. Franky was nearly caught that day, after a local raised the alarm, but just succeeded in dodging the authorities once more. 'Franky knew what he was up to,' one police officer told me. 'Some 20, 30 tons of cocaine must have reached these shores because of him, and every time, he managed to get away.' But in 2006 a *guardia* in Alicante happened to recognise Franky's face and approached him. They ended up taking him in for questioning, and the forensics team ascertained that his fingertips had been altered; they were then able to go about determining his true identity. In 2009 he was sentenced to 13 years in prison.

Jacinto Santos Viñas

Jacinto Santos Viñas transported drugs in his high-seas tugs, the *Pitea* and the *Clarinda H*. The former was docked in Vigo and the latter in the outlying Coruña port of Oza, and they alternated between the perfectly licit towing of freighters and bringing drugs ashore. Santos Viñas hit the headlines in 1996 when it occurred to him to try bringing 35,000 kilos of hashish up the River Pontevedra on board the shipping vessel *Volga I*. And he did manage to bring it ashore, at the port of Marín, but was arrested following the unloading, leading to a four-year sentence. No sooner was that complete than his tow boats set to work once more, plying the waters around Coruña and Ferrol in particular. He went on to sell the vessels in South Africa in 2004, but it seems that something went wrong with the deal and the Moroccan gangster for whom Santos Viñas worked gave information on him. The *Pitea* was boarded by the French navy as it came along the coast of Togo, and half a kilo of cocaine was found on board. The *Clarinda H* had been seized a year earlier off the coast of southern Portugal – also on her way from an African port, but closer to the final destination this time. Those two operations were enough to win the Galician *capo* a 12-year sentence.

His right-hand man, Eulogio Pérez Refojo, was convicted as part of the same proceedings; he had already served eight years as part of Operation Nécora. This time, given the recidivism, it was 19. Refojo had been in charge of maintaining the two boats. He began his career working for the Charlíns and is assumed to have taken part in the vengeance killing of Manuel 'O Caneo' Baúlo, the *capo* who had cooperated with Garzón and who was gunned down as he read the morning paper. Refojo rented the apartment in which the three Colombian hitmen had stayed.

Manuel Carballo

There was another casualty in the hit on Manuel Baúlo: Carmen Carballo, who ended up in a wheelchair. Carmen's brother was Manuel 'Sparrowhawk' Carballo, another smuggler from the tobacco days – and his move to drug trafficking proved costly. It would appear that he had been among those most resistant to the shift, and flying bullets would later prove his misgivings well-founded: Vilanova-born Sparrowhawk, whom we have also encountered before (when he pushed a *guardia* into the port at A Pobra do Caramiñal), as well as seeing his sister paralysed, lost a son, Danielito Carballo, and he nearly died himself in a shootout following a shipment with some less than trustworthy associates. Having been one of the 'smoke lords' in earlier days, he always made a show of remaining in that line of work. He was also among the fugitive *capos* who attended the meeting with the regional president in Portugal. It is said that Danielito had urged him to begin trafficking in hashish early on, but he was only convinced once he saw the money being made by his rivals. And then from hashish to cocaine: he was caught bringing 2,000 kilos into Cedeira in 1991, a joint effort with the narco lawyer Pablo Vioque. That job ended badly, though Carballo did manage to avoid justice by Colombian hands.

That consignment led, six years of enquiries later, to a 17-year sentence. A few days before it was due to be handed down, while on bail in 2003, he fled to Latin America. Local people in Vilanova say he returned to the town on a regular basis, and would go around in the streets quite openly. But by 2006 it seems he'd had enough: he handed himself in at A Lama prison. There he spent two years, after which he began experiencing heart problems. He died at home in 2009.

THE FALL OF THE OUBIÑA EMPIRE

'Want us to kill them, sir?'

If the struggle against drug trafficking was a war, then 8 January 1995 would have marked one of the most significant battles. This was the day when the Baión estate was seized by the authorities, the jewel in the crown of the Oubiña empire and great symbol of all the Galician *capos'* excesses.

Carlos Bueren, a magistrate, and Luis Rubí Blanc, a judicial administrator, arrived on the estate with a Guardia Civil escort. A large and rambunctious crowd of Érguete mothers had gathered at the entrance. The magistrate asked Esther Lago, Oubiña's wife, where the cash was hidden. She tried talking her way out of it, but finally gave in, telling them it was in the kennels.

'But inside the kennels were quite a lot of rottweilers,' said Luis Rubí Blanc the day I went to speak to him at the legal practice in Madrid where he now works, the hard years of drug work behind him. 'I looked at Esther Lago. "Yes, in there." I took another look at the dogs.' Then one of the agents came over and murmured in his ear: 'Want us to kill them, sir?'

'"No!" I said. "What do you mean, kill them?"'

And in the end they didn't need to – Lago went in and brought the dogs out. The agents spent a short while searching, but found nothing.

'Come on, Esther,' said Bueren. 'You're wasting our time. Where is it?'

Lago said nothing for a few moments. In the distance, the ongoing cries of the Érguete mothers continued at the gate. Finally she spoke, telling them to look in the roof beams. 'Which we did,' says Rubí. 'We went up, got inside the roof, prising it all open, a hell of a job. But again, nothing.'

Lago gave them two or three further places to look: the oven, a supposed *zulo* in the floor of one of the bedrooms, even a cistern. The *guardias*, the magistrate and Rubí lost patience. Finally Lago pointed at the dovecote: 'It's in there. I swear.' But it wasn't. They had seized the estate but not found the treasure. Bueren and Rubí left empty-handed. There was not a single peseta on the estate, or, if there was, it had been squir-relled away very effectively. Nor did it matter. Or not overly. The investigation had begun. The state had decided to confis-cate the Falcon Crest of the *rías*, whose grounds included the largest Albariño vineyard in Salnés county.

It marked a change of strategy. The disappointment of the Nécora acquittals had taught the authorities an important lesson: the near impossibility of catching the main *capos* in the act. The chances were slim at the time, and have become even more so over time. Tax avoidance has become the only viable route for prosecution. This was one of the reasons why a new money-laundering law was passed. The legislation had been altered in 1988, but 1995 saw further, more aggressive modifications that helped level the field. The situation was clearly summarised by the then chief of the Galician police, José García Losada: 'The important thing is to hit these organisations where it hurts. This is why we are going very specifically after the laundering of proceeds from drug trafficking. Big busts might seem to help the statistics, but they don't lead to anything substantive: bread today, hunger tomorrow, as we say.' That's even more true today. In Coruña, the chief of the Galician UDYCO, Félix García, puts it plainly. Walking ahead of me down one of the corridors in the UDYCO buildings, he pointed at the sign that read 'Department for Tax Crimes and Money Laundering'. 'These guys,' he said. 'These are the guys who can really get them.'

In the fight against tax fraud, the Customs Surveillance Service (SVA) are the infantry. As a branch of the Spanish treasury, the SVA is tasked with the investigation, discovery and prosecution of contraband violations. It has become a de facto police corps and its infrastructure is better for counter-drugs work than that of the Guardia Civil, including two long-distance patrol ships with a sailing range as far as Latin America. One of the early arguments used by the *capos'* lawyers was that the SVA was not a law enforcement authority. But this legal loophole was subsequently closed, allowing the Supreme Court to regulate the judicial functions of the SVA – on a legal level, at least. The story on the ground was, and remains, quite different. Brushes between *guardias* and the

SVA are well known. And the controversial lack of definition over the SVA's precise functions has yet to be fully resolved. Agents from the two bodies have frequently tangled. Once, after one seizure of a tobacco consignment in Tarifa, officers fell to blows.

'But it's calmed down now,' says Luis Rubí, who ran the SVA between 1996 and 1998. 'We did a significant job; we were pioneers. Those were the first ever initiatives of their kind, and to this day they are the biggest.' Rubí's proactive approach won him many admirers. He revitalised the fight against tax fraud and pushed SVA agents into more police-like tasks. But he was sacked in 1998, when close to concluding an investigation against Marcial Dorado.

> Dorado was the most respected and powerful of all the tobacco *capos*, and I believe he was protected. I think my sacking was political. There were some extremely signifi-cant business interests there, huge profits on the line; maybe, when we started making a nuisance of ourselves with Dorado, he asked for someone to step in. It's been a few years now, I'm not as upset as I was then, but I still think I was fired on that basis.

Rubí's dismissal – another suggestion of the huge sphere of the contrabandists' influence – meant the SVA stepping back from the front line. A breach into which the Policía Nacional stepped, in the form of the aforementioned Anti-Drugs and Organized Crime Unit, the UDYCO, which had been created in 1997. Even so, the different corps continued to collaborate

– and they still do – an approach whose wisdom is borne out by results.

The confiscation of the Baión estate was one such result. Although it belonged to Oubiña, his name appeared nowhere in connection with any of the deeds. The property – as we have seen – was registered in the name of a lady from Cáceres (the aunt of narco lawyer Pablo Vioque), whose monthly rent was 200 pesetas. The vineyards were registered to a cluster of interlinked Panamanian companies – one of which, when the treasury started pulling on the threads, turned out to be in Esther Lago's name. This was a start in unravelling the whole thing, and led directly to the decision to confiscate in January 1995.

The functioning of the vineyards was a long way down on Oubiña and Lago's list of priorities; they simply wanted to launder money through them, and, despite huge investments, the facilities languished. 'Their production capacities were incredible,' says Rubí. 'They could have processed all the grapes in Salnés. A huge amount of machinery, all the latest gizmos. But none of it used to make a profit. It was nothing but a sideshow, a smokescreen.' After the confiscation, Rubí suggested that the estate be nationalised. Until that time, state-seized assets would always be closed down (leading to job losses – in the case of Baión, 400 would have been lost) or sold at a cut-price rate, which enabled the narcos to buy them again through other smokescreen companies. (In reality, this still occurs, as we will see later on.)

It was the first time in Spanish history that the state had stepped in like this. Once the estate was in receivership, the

400 workers got their jobs back: 'We spoke to the workers,' says Rubí, 'explained that the business would carry on, and that they would be paid money they were owed. Two or three disappeared the moment we turned up. Their hands were dirty, in other words, and they decided to have nothing to do with us.'

Rubí, with no experience of the world of wine, suddenly had an enormous vineyard on his hands; he had to organise the harvest and bring the whole operation into profit.

> I had no idea what I was doing. But then again, I was later appointed administrator of day-to-day operations at Atlético Madrid, and that was a really tough job; I received threats, my family received threats. At Baión, and with the narcos, I had no problems. Give me narcos over football any day!

> The hard part was securing funding. Investors were not forthcoming. There was the payroll to deal with, the workers' social security to be arranged ahead of harvest, machinery to repair, fertilizers to buy … I had to make sure the grapes would actually be picked. It was obstacle after obstacle, but in the end we found a bank to give us a loan.

Rubí remembers when it came time to taste the yield: 'I had no idea, so I called Bueren, who told me to call Fraga, who said he'd bring me the best oenologist in Galicia. He showed up within a few hours, did a tasting, and said it was a very good crop.' Rubí was even involved in the marketing side of things.

'We wrote on the first labels that the estate was from a vineyard confiscated by the Audiencia Nacional,' he says with a smile. 'I believe it helped sales.'

A year later, in 1996, Freixenet, a large wine producer, rented the estate. In 2007, once appeals by Oubiña and his daughters had been put to bed (these went all the way to Strasbourg, though without success), the government put the estate up for auction. Restrictions were put in place to prevent other narcos from bidding – bidders had to show at least five years' experience in the wine sector. Condes de Albarei won the auction, the sale was formalised in 2008, and a celebration was held on the estate to mark the company's return to normality. Among those present – how could they not have been? – were the Érguete mothers. Serene, proud, beaming. The same women who, almost 10 years earlier, had all but torn down the entrance gate as Oubiña's bodyguards watched on, machine guns in hand.

Lago and Oubiña were also soon dealt with. Oubiña, after serving a short sentence for tax fraud in connection with the Nécora findings, was re-arrested in 1997 as part of Operation Amanecer – this was when he said to the agents as they handcuffed him, 'My wife's going to kill me.' The somewhat outdated domestic association of this phrase perhaps fails to cover its full meaning; Oubiña might have been lamenting having fouled up one of his wife's jobs. Everything the investigators found pointed to Lago as the true leader, responsible for both devising the tax avoidance schemes and organising shipments from the shadows. All of which came to a sudden end with her fatal car crash in 2001.

Oubiña spent nearly two years in prison awaiting conviction, and was then released in September 1999, a little under a month before his sentencing. He didn't waste any time: a fortnight later he was involved in an attempt to bring 15,000 kilos of hashish ashore in the ship *Regina Maris* (sailing under the name *San Andrés* to obscure its identity), which flew a Honduras flag and had come from St Louis, Mississippi via Cape Verde. The SVA boarded her in international waters and she was towed to port in Cadiz. This operation, ingeniously dubbed Ocaso (Sunset), completed the job begun two years before in Amanecer.

At the same time as this boarding, Esther Lago was arrested in Vilagarcía, while in Vilanova her son and heir to the business, David Pérez, was taken in for the first time. A further 15 people were apprehended, but not the *capo* himself. Oubiña was nowhere to be found; an arrest warrant was issued. It turned out that he had fled, and with three sentencings outstanding: one for the 1994 Martorell consignment, and one each from Operations Amanecer and Ocaso. Interpol went to work.

'He knew what was coming and bolted,' says one journalist I spoke to, who preferred to remain anonymous. Initially the Arousa *capo* went to Andalusia, to a small town in the interior. The only person he maintained contact with was his son, David Pérez, and through these communications the police came close to capturing the father after a few months. But again he got away. Enter Munzer Al Kassar, a Syrian weapons trafficker and one of these mysterious, seemingly mythical criminals who enjoy state protection by countries in need of arms. In theory, Al Kassar was wanted by the UK, France and the Netherlands, but in practice he entered and left those countries, using a variety of passports, with relative ease. His immunity might have been due to his importance to Western secret services as a source. *Time* magazine published an article in the early 1990s describing Al Kassar as providing arms in Iran, to the PLO and to anti-Sandinista guerrillas in Nicaragua. His connections made him the envy of many. And his name had come up as part of Operation Nécora in connection with Oubiña, to whom he had allegedly sold weapons.

Al Kassar's renown as a secret-service collaborator grew when Interpol asked him to set up a meeting with Oubiña, in exchange for easing off on their investigations into a period he had spent operating in Marbella. Al Kassar contacted Oubiña, offering to bring him in on a scrap-metal deal in Russia, and they arranged to meet on 31 October 2000, 13 months after the Galician *capo* had gone to ground. The appointed place was room 315 in the Hotel Pelagos on Eubea, the Greek island where, it transpired, Oubiña had been living under the false identity of Señor Romeu. When Oubiña, accompanied by David Pérez, knocked on the door, Interpol agents opened it. After a number of days in a Greek jail, he was extradited to Spain.

'Following the arrest,' says the journalist, 'some of us began to wonder if Al Kassar had been the facilitator. Garzón contacted us a few days later asking us not to publish anything to that effect.' Their suspicions were confirmed. It was Julio Fariñas who broke the story in *La Voz de Galicia*, paying heed to journalistic instinct rather than Garzón.

Oubiña spent the following 11 years behind bars. And when he got out, in June 2012, he felt the gentle winds of freedom for three short months; in September he was convicted for a further four years on a pending money-laundering charge. 'He was a scapegoat,' says Javier Zaragoza, recalling the Galician *capo*'s uncouth ways. 'He was the idiot with his name on all the receipts. They really went after him. He didn't know what he was doing and his lawyers constantly lied to him. Rather than joining his different convictions into a single sentence, he ended up serving all of them separately.'

Oubiña was the model inmate. He paid the legal fees for several penniless prisoners and contributed to the upkeep of the prisons themselves. Wing 3 of Alcalá Meco was repainted in 2004 – funded by him. In the same year he rented a house in Guadalajara for his daughters to stay in: he wanted to make it easier for them to visit, and for the girls not to have to drive all the way from Galicia every time. His wife's death is said still to weigh heavily on him. 'They've treated me worse than a terrorist,' he said in an interview with the journalist David López. 'Like the worst murderer or rapist. Terrorists have actually said to me I've been treated worse than any ETA guy. The worst was in Zuera prison in Zaragoza: I was beaten, and when I reported it, the report got shelved.'

The *capo* of the Baión estate, symbol of all the ostentation and impunity that once reigned in Galicia, was freed in 2016 at the age of 70, making him one of the prisoners to have served the most time since Spain's transition to democracy: 26 years.

IMITATING THE MAFIA

'Drop your weapon, Octopus, or we'll shoot you down!'
'Go for it.'

NARCOPOLITICS

On 5 May 1991, in a coastal village in Galicia, people got out of bed in the morning, looked out to sea and found a flotilla of cocaine bales in the bay. They had dropped over the side of the RIB boat belonging to José Manuel Vázquez Vázquez, aka 'O Piturro', as he attempted to bring them ashore during a storm the previous night.

O Piturro and his son-in-law Juan Carlos Sotelo had travelled from Colombia aboard the ship *Dobell*, bringing 2,000 kilos of Cali cocaine with them. Cartel merchandise always bore the emblem of its producers, and in this case the bales had been stamped with the Cali dollar sign. Evidence suggests that the *Dobell* had stopped off in Ribeira, where a portion of the merchandise had been handed over to a narco named Ildefonso Treus Castelo. What is certain is that when she reached her final destination, the Coruña port of Cedeira, a storm was raging and the operation was on the verge of being cancelled. The narcos hesitated but ultimately decided to press ahead, unloading the bales onto the RIB, end to end like a string of garlic heads. They began to fall away as soon as the RIB made for shore, and by the time it made landfall only 300 kilos of the original 2,000 remained. The rest greeted early-rising locals the next morning.

O Piturro went on to claim that, once they were ashore, they passed these 300 kilos over to 'three guys who weren't Galicians'. The goods were loaded into a car which then drove away.[1] Its destination was not his concern: on this particular operation, he was only providing transport services. In charge were Manuel Carballo and Pablo Vioque, the latter being the former PP member and lawyer, and the man whose task it then was to explain to the Cali cartel what had happened. But he decided to become creative with his explanations, and said the *whole* shipment had been lost, neglecting to mention the 300 kilos that had made it ashore. That, predictably, did not turn out well.

* * *

'The banks on Paseo de Gracia in Barcelona would open after hours if Pablo Vioque was coming to town. All that was missing was the red carpet,' blasts Félix García.

> If the well-established *capos* had had their heads screwed on, and had taken his advice, we really would be looking at a Sicily on the Atlantic now. One hundred per cent. He knew his way around all these different areas: the law, the criminal players, politics … Throw in his total lack of scruples, and if he had pitched up in Vilagarcía 20 years before, he'd have ended up running the place.

An opinion seconded by one veteran *guardia* I spoke to: 'Vioque was the only one with a brain. The rest only got their act together when he showed up.'

Pablo Vioque came to Arousa in 1975 from Extremadura, western Spain. His brother-in-law had promised him a job if he completed his law studies, which he financed himself by playing semi-professional basketball. The brother-in-law kept his word and provided introductions at the Vilagarcía Chamber of Commerce. His rise was astonishingly swift, and in a short number of years he was sharing the best Albariño wines and the finest seafood with the area's business elite – in this case a euphemism for tobacco smugglers. He was their perfect man: he could defend them in court and, as an added bonus, assist in laundering their money. Just nine years after his arrival, Vioque was made president of the Chamber, thanks to support from the PP, for whom in turn he guaranteed a healthy proportion of the local vote. He did not reach quite so high as Don Vicente with his gold party medallion, nor was he made mayor of anywhere, unlike José Ramón 'the Kid' Barral in neighbouring Ribadumia, but he wielded more power than either of them and was on excellent terms with all the party's top brass. 'He donated money to their campaigns, and helped economically on other fronts,' says one judge who preferred not to be named. 'All the right-leaning parties took his money: the PP, the PSOE, the Galician Nationalist Bloc (BNG) ... He paid off debts they had, he paid for everything.' In July 1997, when he was in Carabanchel prison, he told a journalist he wanted to come clean on all the Galician political parties he had helped to fund. He claimed he had evidence that would make uncomfortable reading for senior officials in the regional government – PP and PSOE politicians. The evidence, however, never came to light. His threats called to mind something Oubiña had said in an interview a number of years before:

> When the country was moving to the democracy people now say we live under, I gave money to the Alianza Popular, to Fraga, to the Unión de Centro Democrático, to Suárez. I wasn't the only contrabandist who did, either. And I'd just like to remind those politicians that I am still the same person I was back then.

'We've never really got to the bottom of things in Galicia,' says the judge. 'Narcos have held high office. Have, and still do. People just choose not to talk about it.'

Vioque became the closest thing Arousa has seen to a Sicilian mafioso. His wedding in 1987, held in a monastery in Armenteira, Pontevedra, was a star-studded affair, with leaders of the business community, contrabandists, high-ranking *guardias* and police in attendance. The journalist Elisa Lois pointed out later that some of the wedding guests were among those later to put Vioque in handcuffs.

'He turned the Chamber of Commerce into a mafia outpost,' in the words of the same judge.

> Clan meetings were organised from there, drop-offs, defensive manoeuvres for the *capos* … His goal was to create a narco syndicate whereby all the clans' activities

could be centrally organised: money laundering, kick-backs, drop-offs ... and each of the *capos* was a kind of spokesperson. It was the closest we have come to seeing full-blown mafia practices here in Galicia.

One police officer I spoke to had similar memories of the Chamber of Commerce becoming a site for events and parties: 'Fraga went there for drinks, Feijóo ... everyone. They'd all stop by.'

At the start of the 1990s Vioque was top of the pile. His firm represented the clans in court, taking inflated fees for their services, he was dominant among local business leaders, made sure politics in the region served his interests, and, on the side, was bringing speedboats full of cocaine in along the *rías*.

* * *

At the time of the failed Cedeira drop-off, Vioque was at the height of his powers. Perhaps this explains the daring (or stupid) decision to lie to the Cali cartel. It seems the Colombians were not entirely convinced, and Vioque hurried to dispose of the 300 kilos that had made it ashore.

This was when it all stopped going Vioque's way. The Guardia Civil seized the 300 kilos in Valencia, not the only eventuality Vioque had failed to foresee. They then invited the press down to take photos of the confiscated goods. Suddenly pictures of the 'missing' drugs, piled together like so many bricks, were all over the news. And guess who was watching? The Cali members in Spain would have immediately recognised their insignia on the bales. It was all the proof they needed: Vioque had lied.

The summons came from Bogotá. The lawyer-businessman-politician-narco managed to convince them to meet him on Spanish soil, in a place called Benavente, exactly halfway between the cartel headquarters in Madrid and the *rías* of Arousa. And in another unexpected (and cowardly) twist, Vioque sent two associates in his stead: the treasurer of the Chamber of Commerce, José Manuel Vilas Martínez, who was his right-hand man, and the businessman Luis Jueguen Vilas, who was his cousin, and – no, this isn't a film script – also a cousin of Manuel Carballo, who had collaborated on the Cedeira consignment. On 17 March 1992, these two men drove to Benavente in a Peugeot 505. They arrived in the early evening and went and sat in a park across from the La Mota hotel. Two Colombians walked up to them, and the conversation began. Unsurprisingly, the two parties were not of the same mind. The Colombians' solution to this impasse was to take out a gun and shoot Vilas Martínez, the treasurer, in the eye. The gun was then turned on Jueguen Vilas, but he ran off through the park as bullets flew – one leaving a hole in his blazer. He carried on running until he reached the local bus station, taking the first bus he could find to Galicia. Vioque met him in Santiago. He probably acted surprised. 'My husband was sent to a certain death,' said Vilas Martínez's widow in court a number of years later.

The dog's dinner of Cedeira led to Vioque's arrest – and that of 10 others – in 1995. This was the result of a tenacious, four-year-long Guardia Civil investigation. And only at that point did the Chamber of Commerce relieve him of his duties. The coup de grace would come two years later at the hand of O Piturro, who, fed up after seeing none of the proceeds, decided to come clean to Garzón. Vioque, who had been in pre-trial detention for three years, was released with the trial still pending. And, like any self-respecting *ría capo*, he attempted a job the second he was free, organising the transfer of 1,800 kilos of cocaine from Valencia to Madrid in a lumber truck. The merchandise was intercepted and he was given 18 years. Days before the sentencing, a number of his associates, including Luis Jueguen (the survivor from the Benavente shooting) and Manuel Carballo, fled to Latin America. Carballo, as we saw earlier, would return two years later and give himself up to the authorities before dying of cardiac problems. Jueguen is still a fugitive at the time of writing, believed to be residing in Argentina.

Pablo Vioque's Hollywood career was not quite over. Diagnosed with colon cancer before going into prison, he was intent on one last hurrah. A week after his incarceration at Soto del Real prison, he tasked a cellmate, the Colombian Diego León Cardona, with finding him a hitman: he wanted the head of Javier Zaragoza, the then head of the Anti-Drugs Office, later to become chief prosecutor at the Audiencia Nacional. Cardona made a call, and a connection of his in turn contracted an Ecuadorean hitman, who went on to receive the weapon, an advance on his fee and photos of Zaragoza. But the Ecuadorean also turned out to be an informer for the Guardia Civil. Although Vioque denied all knowledge, this further charge added a number of years to his sentence.

By 2009 his cancer was confirmed as terminal, and he requested leave to die at home. He died on 24 January that year, though many Guardia Civil joke that even in this he might have tricked everyone: 'He's still going. Working on the next job.' After three decades of his games, it seems understandable that they should be suspicious.

NARCO LAW, NARCO JUSTICE

One retired *guardia* told me that, for a time, the authorities in Madrid were prohibited from sharing any information whatsoever with their counterparts in Galicia. There were a number of years when the anti-drugs units in both the Guardia Civil and the Policía Nacional, as well as judges and public prosecutors, knew it wasn't safe to share information with those in the north-west. The clans had ears everywhere, from lawyers' offices to those of district mayors, from Guardia Civil barracks to local shops – and still do today, to an extent. Although the drug traffickers' power has diminished, the occasional story emerges of tip-offs and bribes.

In June 1991, a *guardia* got in touch with a local mayor asking for his assistance in bringing a 2,000-kilo consignment of cocaine into Galicia, in concert with a pair of narcos called Slapdash and José the Dog. It sounds like magical realism, which it is – all except for the magical part. At the start of the 1980s José Luis Orbáiz Picos had changed career path, giving up his day job as a traffic officer for the Guardia Civil and going into smuggling instead. After the occasional low-level job, he went on to become an associate of the Charlíns. It was he who made the journey to Valladolid in 1983 to seek out Celestino Suances, and was sent home with his tail between his legs after a beating from some local *guardias* there, and it was he who, along with Old Man Charlín, kidnapped Suances and held him in a cold storage room. He was also an associate of Pablo Vioque, whom he would end up betraying to Garzón in a plea bargain.

In June 1991 Orbáiz Picos offered his services to the Cali cartel, who had earmarked a 2,000-kilo consignment of cocaine for Spain. Alfredo Bea Gondar, mayor of O Grove between 1983 and 1991 and a member of the AP party, was the man who ended up helping him. He in turn asked Manuel González 'Slapdash' Crujeiras, an associate of Sito Miñanco, to come in on the job. It would be another 10 years before the trio were convicted.

The former *guardia* was arrested in 1996 when the SVA boarded the fishing vessel *Anita* in Vigo; she had 1,100 kilos of Colombian cocaine on board. 'Our most significant operation since the dismantling of Laureano Oubiña's network,' said the euphoric spokesperson of the National Drug Plan at the time, Gonzalo Robles. Robles presumably did not suspect that Oubiña's network, far from being dismantled, would go on to carry out various smuggling jobs in the future. The hazards of trying to write the next day's headlines.

When the trial came around, Orbáiz Picos was less than discreet. He told Garzón everything he knew about José the Dog, claiming he had gone in with the narcos undercover, at the behest of the Policía Nacional. But, he said, the police had then withdrawn their support, and by then he was in too deep and feared Colombian reprisals. The judge, unconvinced, handed down sentences of 20 years for both Orbáiz Picos and José the Dog. This did not deter Orbáiz Picos's son José Luis from following in his footsteps. In 2008 the police stopped him aboard the passenger ship *Armada*, which ran regular services between Colombia and Marín, and found 275 kilos of cocaine among his belongings. He was given a six-year sentence but, on Christmas Day 2014, when he was due to go into prison, he vanished. He remains a fugitive at the time of writing, as well as an orphan, after his father the turncoat *guardia* died from heart problems.

Orbáiz Picos was not the only one to switch sides. 'It's just the way it was,' says one *guardia* on the front line at the time. 'Galicia was riddled with corruption. Bear in mind how many of the agents were from the area they were supposed to be policing; it would be their own family and neighbours they were supposed to be putting behind bars. They couldn't bring themselves to do it.'

In 2002, four *guardias* from Sanxenxo were suspended after the SVA caught them setting up meetings with Sito Miñanco's gang in the cemetery of a small town called Meis. Five meetings were observed, one of which Sito attended personally. The *guardias* claimed the meetings were part of an investigation of their own. The judge, unable to establish the true nature of these encounters, reduced the suspensions to a year each. The military branch of the Supreme Court called the meetings 'gravely contrary to the integrity of the Guardia Civil'.

Nowadays the problem persists, though less overtly. A 2012 operation dubbed 'Espartana' (Spartan) led to the arrest of José Álvarez-Otero Lorenzo, a *guardia* for over a decade in Corcubión. Working with Cali cartel heirs the Vélez brothers, he had tried to bring some 108 bales of cocaine ashore on SV *Nikolay*, a 370-foot Bulgarian freighter. It was carrying cocaine and nothing else; no attempt had been made to hide the product among other goods. Such was Álvarez-Otero's confidence. He thought everything was 'under control' on his home territory, the Costa da Morte, from the SVA through to the Guardia Civil. Among the rank and file, rumours had been rife for a long time about the Corcubión sergeant, though they never amounted to any official complaints. He owned various properties along the coast, including a pub in a place called Cee that was a well-known crime hotspot. There was a widespread view that he offered protection to the clans, both passing them inside information and making sure the *rías* were clear for drop-offs. So nobody was surprised by the *Nikolay* capture. Or, probably, when his wife Rufina Palacín was arrested a few months later on money-laundering charges.

'From what I can tell, it's hardly a problem now,' says one young *guardia* working in the Rías Baixas. 'Corruption was a huge issue before, but things have improved. There will always be the occasional loose cannon. But I think that's the case everywhere. We aren't the only ones.'

Two such loose cannons were arrested in August 2013. Diego Fontán of O Grove and Javier López from the Pontevedra headquarters were accused of giving inside information. Suspicions were raised when a consignment the authorities had been tracking was abruptly cancelled; the narcos must have been warned about the surveillance. López went on to admit that he had sold the information to the highest bidder, and the Guardia Civil disciplinary body identified five other enquiries stymied by him. Fontán, on the other hand, was less forthcoming and, along with two other agents who were arrested in February 2014 for tipping off the narcos, his sentence remains pending.

The influence of the narcos, as well as touching officers and politicians, extended to the courts. In the 1980s, Judge José María Rodríguez Hermida of the Pontevedra Palace of Justice gained a reputation for being particularly soft on any defendants brought in on drug-trafficking charges. Local lawyers began referring to his cases as 'RH positive', and in 1984 he was struck off after taking a bribe from Antonio Bardellino, the boss of the Neapolitan Camorra, who had been imprisoned in Madrid. Hermida set a ludicrously low bail of 5 million pesetas, which Bardellino paid before promptly fleeing. He has evaded authorities in all national jurisdictions ever since.

Francisco Velasco Nieto of Vilagarcía worked in Vioque's law firm, representing Laureano Oubiña and Esther Lago for many years. He died of a heart attack in 2004, aged 52, and locals remember him for the wide-brimmed hats he always wore. Judges and other members of the bar have a less picturesque recollection of a man who frequently obstructed raids and interfered in police operations. Who, in other words, was doing his job. He was sent to prison in 2001 for laundering some of Oubiña's money.

Velasco Nieto was one of a group known as the 'narco lawyers', most of whom were part of Vioque's firm, accused of complicity in various contraband- and drug-trafficking activities. The journalist Perfecto Conde recalls a 1988 picture that is worth a thousand words. It features Velasco Nieto on the steps of the Corcubión courthouse, surrounded by sailors from the ship *Smith Lloyd* of Cairo, which had just been seized with Galicia-bound tobacco in the hold. The sailors crowd round as Velasco Nieto hands out wads of cash: their bail money.

Oubiña was represented at other times by Gerardo Gayoso Martínez, who would later go to prison on hashish-trafficking charges, and Ana Soler, who was tried alongside the *capo* in his last money-laundering defence.

'In general, the lawyers took them for all they were worth,' says one journalist. 'They charged them way more than the going rate. Oubiña once paid his lawyers 10 million pesetas [€60,000] to go to a hearing in Madrid where they didn't even have to speak.' There was more than enough narco money to go round. Just as, in general, there was more than enough narco culture.

NARCO VIOLENCE

We were out on a night in Cambados. In the town centre, at one of our favourite pubs. We came outside at one point and saw these girls looking in at a car window. They said something to us, we went over, and then we saw it: there was a dead guy in the driver's seat. His face was covered in blood, his mouth was open, and a shotgun on the passenger's seat. Suddenly a load of people were crowding around the car; everyone wanted to see the dead guy. 'It's a payback job,' someone said. The police showed up and cleared the scene – we went back inside the pub. We carried on drinking. Not that this was an everyday thing, but we were a bit like, if they want to go around killing each other, have a ball.

The speaker here is a Vilagarcía woman I am calling Veronica, and the dead body that of Antonio Chantada, aka Tucho Ferreiro. He had come to carry out a hit on Danielito Carballo, son of Manuel Carballo and Sito Miñanco's right-hand man. That much he managed: Danielito was out having a drink with

Rosalindo Aido in a pub called Museo de Vilagarcía, a regular haunt for the young narcos of Arousa, when in walked Tucho with a .38 Brazilian shotgun hidden down his trouser leg. He had just come out of prison, was depressed and suffering withdrawal symptoms, and Danielito owed him money. It didn't help matters that, while he had been inside, Danielito had gone off with his girlfriend. Without a word, and in front of a large crowd of pub-goers, he pulled out the firearm and blasted Sito's lieutenant in the throat. As he went to reload, with people screaming and pushing to get out of the premises, Rosalindo Aido fled. Some of the shot hit her in the arm, but she got away.

Tucho then got back in his car and drove to Corvillón, on the outskirts of Cambados. He parked outside a pizzeria and headed inside with the gun. Juan José Agra, a veteran narco, was sitting having a pizza with his three-year-old daughter. Tucho pointed the gun at Agra's chest and, as the girl's jaw dropped, pulled the trigger. His next target was Rafael 'the Ox' Bugallo, a narco he had worked for in the past. He went looking for him at the Cambados bar he was known to frequent and, failing to find him there, he went back to his car, put the gun in his mouth and, for the last time, pulled the trigger. Veronica and her friends found him a few minutes later.

Tucho and Danielito, who had grown up together on the same street, were buried on the same day. The funeral processions followed the same route and took place half an hour apart. Murderer and victim. The obituary notices were placed side by side at the Vilagarcía town hall. Only in Galicia.

Tucho's double murder and suicide sent shock waves through the region. More so than the Benavente hit on the treasurer of the Vilagarcía Chamber of Commerce. According to Enrique León, former head of the Galician UDYCO, 'Considering the amount of drugs there have been in the area, and all the clans based here, the level of violence has always been relatively low.' Félix García, the current head of UDYCO, concurs:

> Probably because they were so keen to avoid the notice of the authorities. They knew that every dead body would cost them millions, because we'd go in and they'd have to suspend operations for a time. It was like an unspoken rule: anything went, but don't go round shooting guys. Though, of course, sometimes it was broken.

The same line of reasoning explains why the clans never took the authorities on head to head: 'They didn't dare. They knew, and know, it wasn't a war they could win. We haven't had judges, agents or officers being killed around here. Which is why, in my view, when people talk about Galicia as quasi-Sicilian, I actually think it's overstating the case.'

'Also,' says Enrique León, 'the smaller clans were more prone to fighting among themselves. It never spilled out into society. And nobody had a perception of this as a violent place. I never met a single local person who described this area as violent.' Veronica agrees:

> It wasn't us they were interested in. It's true, you came across horrible things sometimes. Hard guys, short

tempers. I remember seeing a near car crash on a round-about coming into Illa de Arousa a couple of summers ago. Both cars stopped, insults started flying. One guy gets out a baseball bat, but he put it away again when he saw what the other one had – a gun.

Veronica smiles – a disdainful smile. 'But always among themselves. And if you weren't from around here, you'd never pick up on it. I have never personally felt threatened.'

From a statistical point of view, the 30 deaths connected with Galician drug trafficking since the beginning of the 1990s seems about the minimum one might expect from activities as unlawful as these, with Colombian cartels involved and huge profits on the line. Also considering the willingness of clan members, as we've seen, to turn one another in at the drop of a hat. But 30 dead people is still 30 dead people. And, in their way, they have changed the *rías*.

In 1993, a few months after Tucho Ferreiro's killing spree, the police found the bodies of Luis Otero and Eugenio Simón, two minor narcos from a place called Cangas do Morrazo: their bodies had been chopped up and placed in some septic tanks in the nearby town of Meis. Only Luis Otero's DNA could be matched with any records, which means Eugenio Simón is still officially considered lost. The septic tanks were part of some workshops belonging to a man named Antonio Silvestro, who went on to be accused of the crime. Allegedly, he owed 7 million pesetas to the narcos and, rather than pay up, decided to contract a couple of hitmen instead. But lack of evidence meant the police struggled to build a case, leading to his acquittal. The crime is still considered unsolved.

Two years later, in 1995, a body was found riddled with shot at the showers on A Lanzada beach. Later identified as Manuel Portas, the killer was found to be Andrés Miniño, in whose debt Portas had been, to the tune of 12 million pesetas. An associate of Portas, Carmelo Baúlo, got away with a small amount of buckshot lodged in his body as a souvenir. A few days later, the strangled body of one Ángel García Caeiro appeared in a forest in Vilagarcía. Some local firefighters found it while putting out a forest fire. García Caeiro had been lost, presumed missing, for several months, and it turned out he owed the clans 80 million pesetas. José Manuel Rodríguez Lamas, aka 'Octopus', was the protagonist in another vendetta story, which comes from 1997. At dawn one day he entered a hostel in Vilaboa, Pontevedra, screwed a silencer onto his pistol and shot three small-time narcos who had been staying the night. He was picked up a few days later in the Cabral *barrio* after a chase and exchanges of gunfire. 'Drop your weapon, Octopus, or we'll shoot you down!' said the officers before they took him in. 'Go for it,' came his response.

There were three further deaths that year, all members of smaller clans, and all with debt problems. Two women and one man were found dead on Cabanelas beach in Ribadumia. The women, later identified as Ángela Barreiro and Dolores Gómez, were unfortunate bystanders, while Francisco San Miguel was the intended target: the trio lost their lives after a heated discussion between San Miguel and a narco named Francisco Rey. A death occurred every 12 months for the following five years. This included that of a Lulú henchman, Juan Freire, who was found in a burned-out car in Cee.

'The reprisals between the clans never affected us in our day-to-day lives, but they did grab the headlines,' says Abel, a resident of Vilagarcía. 'Violence wasn't the problem, drugs were. But these are the things that get on TV, and then people start thinking Galicia is this terrible place.' In his earlier life, Abel did military service in Madrid, and talks about a friend he made from Albacete:

> I said why didn't he come and spend a few days in Galicia
> – he'd never been. Then, a few days before he was due to
> come, Danielito Carballo's killing at the pub was on the
> news. My friend got spooked. He said he didn't want to
> come, it sounded like Sicily or something. And nothing I
> could say would change his mind.

Recent years have seen continued, if sporadic, inter-clan violence. The clans have also faced other enemies, including, in the early 1990s, the Guerrilla Army of the Free Galician People (EGPGC), a separatist organisation that carried out a number of attacks on the clans and their assets. The EGPGC saw drug trafficking as a blight on the cause of Galician nationalism. They placed bombs in Cambados, Vilagarcía, Vilanova, Pontevedra and Coruña, none of which led to any deaths. One of their targets was the aforementioned Louzao dealership in Coruña, the one used by Colombian *capo* Matta Ballesteros to launder money.

But if you play with fire ... On 11 October 1990, the EGPGC placed a device in a Santiago disco called Clangor that, according to them, was used as part of the drug-trafficking networks. Not that their claims matter a great deal, considering how events unfolded. The bomb was supposed to go off when the disco was empty, but detonated while the terrorists were depositing it; the disco was full. The two EGPGC men died, along with a student, and 49 youngsters were left wounded. The EGPGC later said it was an 'unintentional error' and that they 'understood' people's pain.

ALL OUT

'I estimate that between 2001 and 2003, 150,000 kilos of cocaine came ashore in Galicia.'

2001–03: TRAFFICKING FRENZY

'Cocaine avalanche unchecked,' read a headline in *El País* on 5 July 2003:

> The day before yesterday, Guardia Civil and SVA agents seized close to 3,000 kilos of cocaine after boarding a fishing vessel in the mid-Atlantic. The ship had set sail from a port in Venezuela and was bound for the Arousa River in Pontevedra. The seizure, which is the sixth in the same area of international waters since 31 March, brings the quantity of confiscated cocaine to 20,000 kilos in six months. Over the course of 2002, 17,616 kilos were seized.

Two years before this article appeared, Mariano Rajoy, Spain's Home Secretary at the time, had referred to 2001 as 'Galician drug trafficking's *annus horribilis*'.

'It was a scary time,' says one *guardia* who served in those years. 'The most tumultuous period ever for Galician drug trafficking,' adds one specialist journalist. In 2001 the authorities confiscated 31 tons of cocaine handled by the clans. This was five times more than the previous year and a record, according to National Drug Plan figures. 'In total, 54,000 kilos of cocaine were confiscated in the three years,' says José Antonio Vázquez Taín, a local judge. 'I estimate that between 2001 and 2003, 150,000 kilos of cocaine came ashore in Galicia.'

The question is: why? And there is no scientific answer. We can point to certain factors in these three 'busy' years, reasons partially explaining why there were so many drop-offs, such quantities of drugs, and so many police operations. Why, that is, the struggle between the narcos and the authorities in Galicia suddenly hit a new level.

The primary factor was the new head of police operations: this was Taín, who went on to earn a reputation as a scourge of the Colombian cartels. Garzón had passed him the baton in 2001, at which point there was a wholesale strategic change. Taín made the battlefield larger and introduced new methods. No longer did the authorities target the clans in isolation: they went after everyone they were associated with, from low-level henchmen to lawyers, from consultants of any kind to speedboat repair mechanics; anyone who supplied goods, any petrol stations they used, any warehouses or companies whose vehicles they hired.

Taín was born in Allariz, Ourense, and Vilagarcía was his first posting. Within a space of six months he had led four operations against the clans. He didn't so much arrive as explode in Arousa. Not that those on his own side made it easy for him. The first sentence he handed down – jail time for six Galician narcos found guilty of transporting three tons of hashish on the sailboat *Chad Band* – was annulled by the Audiencia Nacional. A move described as 'astonishing' by chief prosecutor Javier Zaragoza. Eventually, the Supreme Court, which supersedes the Audiencia Nacional, reinstated the sentences. It was to be the first of many such over-rulings.

The judge signed an agreement so that, on maritime operations, not only would the SVA, the Guardia Civil and the police collaborate, but the navy as well. This huge deployment of force had a counterweight, a locomotive that was coming in the opposite direction, and just as fast: between 2001 and 2003 the Galician *rías* had seen their greatest ever proliferation of new clans. The fall of main players such as Oubiña, and the pressure being exerted on the likes of Miñanco and Marcial, left the way free for the consolidation of these smaller groups, until then feeding off scraps. The well-established powers were forced to look on as they were deposed. The nature of the competition changed in a new, headlong race to bring cocaine into Galicia.

Taín's more comprehensive approach combined with an upsurge in clan activities to usher in an unheard-of number of raids, ship boardings, arrests and seizures. The judge signed off 19 operations in these three years. 'Taín really pissed the cartels off,' says one *guardia*. 'Really messed with their heads. They were sure there had to be an informer, thought that was the only explanation. They reacted, sent guys to come and ask around in the *rías*. But there wasn't any informer.'

One more factor fed the trafficking frenzy: the laissez-faire attitude of Hugo Chávez's government towards drugs. While in Colombia the government had declared war on the cartels, across the border Venezuela became something of a safe haven. The narcos were allowed to cross unchecked into the neighbouring country and, similarly, could send their goods out from Venezuelan ports without any trouble. As a knock-on effect, *Chavismo* proved a blessing for Galician drug trafficking, though not an everlasting one. In 2014, the police forces in Colombia made a public statement praising the Venezuelan government for its help in fighting drug trafficking.

'And in the same period,' says Taín, 'the cartels extended their operations into Africa, places like Togo, Cape Verde, Senegal. They'd have a layover there on their way to Galicia.' It was not long before the Venezuela–Africa–Galicia route started being referred to by Spanish security forces as Route 6, and was abandoned with similar alacrity.

> The Africans were too corrupt, even by cartel standards. Everyone wanted their cut: the army, the police, local gangs … And if the cartels ever left anything on African soil, a ship or a jet plane, they'd find it weeks later as scrap. Working with the Africans made the cartels appreciate the efficiency and seriousness of the Galicians.

One other possible factor in these boom years was the relaxation of media interest. Not that the press stopped covering drug trafficking, but the zeal for the topic waned, which in turn generated the – entirely false – sensation among the Spanish populace that the worst of drug trafficking was behind them, that Operation Nécora and the fall of the principal *capos* had been an end to things. A less intense media focus on the secondary clans probably also gave them extra freedom to make gains.

* * *

In 2001, the SVA intercepted the freighter *Abrente*, while in a simultaneous operation the police arrested Manolo the Catalan, who was running the shipment.[1] This was the opening in a long series of hostilities between Taín and many different clans – including far too many manoeuvres by the authorities to allow for anything more than a summary here. In the same year, the yacht *Estrella Oceánica* sprung a leak and broke down mid-seas with 2,000 kilos of Cali cocaine aboard, and though the narcos involved managed to transfer the merchandise to another ship, both crews were arrested on arrival in Galicia. In the same year, Manuel González Crujeiras, aka Slapdash, agreed to work with the Cali cartel on a job to bring 1,800 kilos of cocaine ashore. The deal was organised face to face – Slapdash happened to be hiding out in Venezuela. He recruited some former colleagues, including the ex-*guardia* Gerardo 'Felipe' Núñez, who was also a direct contact of the cartel. The Spanish special forces ended up boarding the ship they used, the *Meniat*, after it had stopped off in Cape Verde.

Another of the significant busts around this time took place on Arbeyal beach, which served as the first appearance for the son of O Piturro – the narco who later skippered Vioque's RIB with its 'garlic string' of bales squandered in a storm. Juan Carlos Vázquez García, the son, had just turned 20 in December 2003 when he was caught unloading some 3,000 kilos of Colombian cocaine from a fishing vessel. O Piturro

Jr was given an 11-year sentence, though investigators were convinced he was put forward as a scapegoat. 'Too young to put together an operation like that,' in the view of one of the officers involved.

TAÍN'S FINAL BLOW: THE FALL OF MIÑANCO, CHARLÍN AND DORADO

A marquee moment in this busiest of periods came on 16 August 2001, with the arrest and imprisonment of Sito Miñanco. In policing terms, the move – run by Madrid-based judge Juan del Olmo – was quite brilliant. Sito himself couldn't understand how they had done it. 'But how did you get me?' he asked when he was taken in. 'You didn't know when to quit,' came the answer.

The Cambados *capo* had been caught in the act once again. On the previous occasion, in 1991, the special forces had found him poring over nautical charts in his Pozuelo de Alarcón safe-house. That won him a seven-year stretch in Alcalá Meco. All the agents I have spoken to agree that, if he had called it quits at that point, they probably would have done so too. But Sito, like most *ría* narcos, knew no other way. And so he went back for more – in reality, he had never stopped: as we have seen, it was from behind bars that he organised the shipment seized in Operation Amanecer. The villa he based himself at for this job was in a residential area called El Bosque, in the Villaviciosa de Odón suburb of Madrid. Once more, when the special forces arrived, there he was standing over his nautical charts, a satellite communications system and three phones near to hand. They say his jaw dropped when he heard the door being knocked down. As they led him away, he turned to one of the *guardias* he knew: 'Eloy,' he said, 'they're going to make you superintendent for this.' 'I'm already a superintendent, Sito.' 'Well then, a shitload of medals at least.'

Sito had been working on what in theory was his last job. The *Argios Constandino* was waiting 1,000 miles off the coat of French Guyana for the shipping vessel *Titiana* to come and collect the 5,000 kilos of cocaine she had on board. But the DEA showed up first, after a word from the Policía Nacional, and they met little resistance in boarding her. In a synchronised move, the Spanish special forces entered the villa. All in parallel, putting everything on a plate; the judge wouldn't have too much work to do. 'I'll find out who it was,' said Sito as he was led away, referring to a leak – which indeed there had been. Sito's gang itself was watertight, but the shipment had required contact with a Lebanese trafficker – who also happened to be a DEA informant. The Americans had shared the information with the Spanish three days before the *Argios Constandino* set sail, at which point they had identified Sito's whereabouts before making a move on him. Hence Sito's astonishment. He couldn't understand what had gone wrong.

His lieutenant, the Cali cartel man Quique Arango, went down too. 'Everybody was surprised about Sito, why he didn't just keep his nose clean,' says one police officer. 'We thought he'd done all the jobs he was going to do.' In the photos of this final arrest, Sito was not looking his best: overweight, hair unkempt, downcast. Compared with the Ría Escobar of yore, going around in his Ferrari with moustache gleaming, he looked positively hobo-esque. This time the sentence was 20 years. In April 2015 he was granted a work release from his Valladolid prison; he had to return each night and at weekends. He got a job with a construction company. He had originally put forward the idea of working as a mussel fisherman on the *rías*, an idea met with not much enthusiasm. In fact, the judge prohibited him from ever setting foot in Galicia. And yet Sito Miñanco's story was not over yet. Not by a long way.

Sito's arrest was the second blow against the main players. Seven months before, Josefa Charlín, the daughter of Old Man Charlín and heir to the throne, had gone down. She had been a fugitive since a 1994 arrest warrant, issued by Judge Garzón as part of Operation Nécora. With her father already behind bars, she fled to Portugal, where she assumed control of the clan. She became something of a myth during those years: while the authorities searched high and low, she continued to coordinate shipments and to run the clan with an iron fist. She was a well-known character in Arousa – particularly to the employees of La Carpa, the canning factory that, although a smokescreen business, was run tyrannically and with terrible working conditions. At one point the workers organised a rally, and she gave the order for them to be dispersed with riot hoses. Men in the clan never spoke back to her. 'La Charlína' is said to have used one of her daughters, while still a minor, to help launder money: an account in her name was found to contain 400 million pesetas (€2.4 million). The girl ended up testifying before the Audiencia Nacional.

Josefa is said to have attempted to smuggle ashore what would have been the largest ever shipment of cocaine in the history of Galician trafficking, but the boat containing that seven tons of cocaine sank off Morocco in 1997.

'The Godmother', as she was also known, was arrested on 15 December 2000. She had a passport with the name Ángela Acha on it, and apparently put up no resistance when the Portuguese authorities placed the handcuffs on her. In her years as a fugitive, while still running the clan, she had established a very profitable wine production company. She was extradited to Spain immediately and given a 12-year sentence.

The final blow came on 13 October 2003, and it also turned out to be Taín's goodbye. In Operation Retrofornos, which he personally coordinated, the Policía Nacional and the SVA seized the freezer ship *South Sea*. Hidden inside its double hull were 7,000 kilos of cocaine. The narcos responsible for this ambitious shipment were Carlos Somoza and Roberto Leiro; the former, from Vilanova, had worked for the Charlíns and was married to another of the Old Man's daughters, though by this time he ran his own outfit. But the most notable upshot was the consequent arrest of Marcial Dorado, who was found to have made arrangements for the ship with which the *South Sea* was supposed to be connecting, the *Nautillus*. Dorado always maintained that he had never moved out of tobacco smuggling. Some agents think the *Nautillus*, which Dorado built and then sold to Somoza and Leiro, was truly an isolated lapse, but there are just as many who think of Dorado as a narco like all the rest – only cannier. In any case, the foiled *South Sea/ Nautillus* job brought him a 10-year sentence, which, added to a later money-laundering sentence handed down in 2015, means he is still in jail at the time of writing. Somoza and Leiro fled the country with their trials pending.

The fall of Dorado in 2003, the last of the main players in Galicia's drug-trafficking golden age, brought proceedings to a brief halt. A small period of dead time in which the Galician clans regrouped, after a flurry of blows that left even the Colombians stunned. Following this apparent period of inactivity, the clans went back to work, but under a different guise. Their role was to change. With Dorado, Josefa Charlín and Miñanco gone, the landscape changed definitively. The end of one era, the beginning of another: the era of 'narco carriers'. The speedboat engines were fired up.

CHANGING OF THE GUARD

'The most incredible speedboat Galicia's ever seen.'

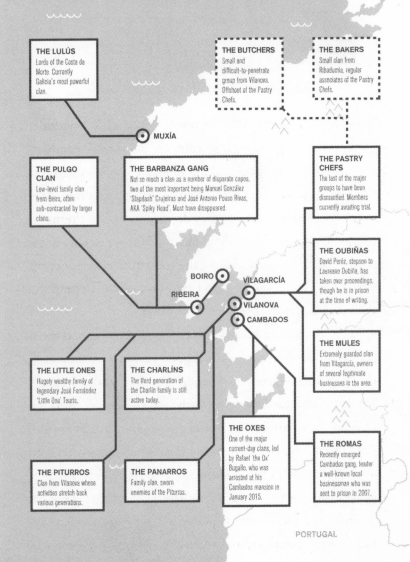

GALICIAN DRUG TRAFFICKING IN THE TWENTY-FIRST CENTURY

THE LULÚS
Lords of the Costa da Morte. Currently Galicia's most powerful clan.

THE BUTCHERS
Small and difficult-to-penetrate group from Vilanova. Offshoot of the Pastry Chefs.

THE BAKERS
Small clan from Ribadumia, regular associates of the Pastry Chefs.

MUXÍA

THE PULGO CLAN
Low-level family clan from Boiro, often sub-contracted by larger clans.

THE BARBANZA GANG
Not so much a clan as a number of disparate capos, two of the most important being Manuel González 'Slapdash' Crujeiras and José Antonio Pouso Rivas, AKA 'Spiky Head'. Most have disappeared.

THE PASTRY CHEFS
The last of the major groups to have been dismantled. Members currently awaiting trial.

THE OUBIÑAS
David Peréz, stepson to Laureano Oubiña, has taken over proceedings, though he is in prison at the time of writing.

BOIRO
VILAGARCÍA
RIBEIRA
VILANOVA
CAMBADOS

THE MULES
Extremely guarded clan from Vilagarcía, owners of several legitimate businesses in the area.

THE LITTLE ONES
Hugely wealthy family of legendary José Fernández 'Little One' Touris.

THE CHARLÍNS
The third generation of the Charlín family is still active today.

THE OXES
One of the major current-day clans, led by Rafael 'the Ox' Bugallo, who was arrested at his Cambados mansion in January 2015.

THE ROMAS
Recently emerged Cambados gang, leader a well-known local businessman who was sent to prison in 2007.

THE PITURROS
Clan from Vilanova whose activities stretch back various generations.

THE PANARROS
Family clan, sworn enemies of the Piturros.

PORTUGAL

NARCO CARRIERS LTD

There was a hangover after the revels of 2001–03. A period of reduced intensity and relative calm ensued. The Colombians spent a couple of years seeking out new business partners, though unsuccessfully. As one police officer told me: 'After Taín's moves against them, they decided to look at alternative routes. We'd done them some serious damage, so they began trying Africa, Bulgaria, Russia, the Netherlands ... But everywhere they tried, they weren't convinced. The Colombians need the Galicians.'

This pause was also a chance for the Galician clans to consider their options. Like all good companies, they made the most of the crisis to remodel the business and change strategy. The gap created by the departure of Miñanco, Oubiña, the Charlíns et al. would go on to be filled by smaller, specialist transport groups; the distribution work and any drug dealing that the Galicians might have become involved in were forgotten about. Here, the protagonists were the children and nieces and nephews of the main players, and their former associates and underlings; in general, those who had occupied the lower echelons of the now-dismantled clans. Youngsters – and some not so young – who had learned the lessons of the previous few years. They were more reserved and showed greater professionalism. All they gave away in magnitude, they made up for in discretion. It was no longer about owning boats, trucks, country estates, having your own team of lawyers, great arsenals of weapons, industrial facilities … From now on they were going to offer transport services only, and they would be charging cash. 'They transformed into a kind of transport union,' says Fernando Alonso, manager of the Galician Anti-Drug Trafficking Foundation. 'Small corporations who offered their services to the Colombians, and worked together. For each shipment, two or three different clans had to join forces.'

There were two levels within this new ecosystem: the organisations and the speedboat skippers. The former were the heirs to the clans and their contacts; they brought the cocaine as far as Galicia. The latter were the result of the speedboat drivers' decision to specialise: they applied themselves solely to bringing the merchandise ashore, and sold their services to the highest bidder among the Galician clans. Thus the pattern of these operations altered: the Colombian *capos* would contact the Galician clans about a shipment, and the clans would see to its safe arrival, subcontracting the drop-off work to the speedboat skippers.

There had also been a change of guard across the Atlantic. The Cali cartel had succumbed to pressure from the Colombian authorities, allowing new, also smaller-scale, groups to spring up – the likes of the Vélez brothers and the Saín Salazar brothers. These were to be the Galicians' new Latin American counterparts.

This new modus operandi in the transatlantic movement of illicit drugs in turn forced the police to change strategy. A new Policía Nacional division was formed, focused specifically on tackling gangs, organised crime and drug trafficking: the Organised Crime Special Response Unit (GRECO). This was to work in concert with the UDYCO, the Guardia Civil, the SVA and the departments dealing with fiscal offences. It had become all but impossible to catch the new breed of narcos in the act. Almost all of the prosecutions from now on would be on money-laundering charges.

THE SPEEDBOAT SKIPPERS

A speedboat chase – you can't imagine what it's like. You're fly along so fast it's like the waves are going to smash the boat to bits. You're soaking wet – it's like being under a waterfall – and you can't hear a thing for the roar of the engine and the spray. It's like going out in a thunderstorm. Plus the fact those bastards are not easy to catch.

So says one *guardia* – the last phrase with unmistakeable admiration in his voice – who took part in numerous such chases during his time working in counter-drugs teams. 'It's the worst part of the job. Madness, making us risk our lives like that at sea.' He casts his mind back to a morning a decade before when he and a colleague were out in a patrol boat, and they came upon a speedboat. Or what seemed to be a speedboat. 'This one was really flying. We began going after it – normally we didn't bother, you know you're never going to catch them. But that day we gave it a go.' The chase had begun on the River Arousa, and it carried on into a branch of the Muros, at which point the suspects veered off and began heading straight for a small cliff on the riverside. 'They were very fast, very good, but then I couldn't understand what they were up to. They were going to corner themselves.' Within feet of slamming into the cliff, the nose of the speedboat lifted into the air, like a motor-bike doing a wheelie. 'Up it started to come, till they were virtually vertical: our jaws dropped. And then, it's at about 90 degrees and does an about-turn, spin it round and come flying back past us. We'd never seen anything like it. Away they went, out to sea.' The agent couldn't conceal his captivation. 'Only Patoco could pull a stunt like that.'

Skippers of small, fast vessels had been a feature since the times of tobacco smuggling. Sito Miñanco himself had been one of the best at manoeuvring them. The change came with upgrades in the vessels, which were becoming faster and more powerful all the time, allied with the seasoned nature of those skippering them.

The shift to specialised narco carrying benefited the Galician speedboat skippers. They did not need to involve themselves in the logistical difficulties entailed by shipments, or try to raise finances, or charter fishing vessels for crossings to Colombia or Venezuela. All they needed to do was collect the cocaine from the supply ships, get it safely ashore and hand it over to the Colombians again. On occasion sailing as far as the Azores or Cape Verde for the pickup.

These narco carriers had plenty of 4x4s to move their speedboats on land if necessary, as well as cranes and backup skippers, and they had barns and sheds dotted along the coast – on the property of local accomplices – in which they could store the necessary petrol reserves and shelter the speedboats themselves. They would hide the vessels, as best they could, in workshops and warehouses, and as close to an inlet as possible, and preferably no more than a throttle-burst away from open waters. When the authorities moved against the skippers, it was not only cocaine they were interested in seizing, but motors, petrol and the boats themselves.

The clans began ordering the latest and highest-spec speed-boats from English and Italian shipyards: they were looking for the aquatic equivalent of rally cars. Semi-rigid vessels, 50-feet long and with motors ranging between 1,500 and 2,000 horsepower, all the components growing lighter and lighter with the increasing use of plastic resins. They needed to have compartments large enough to hold 20,000 litres of petrol and 10,000 kilos of drugs, rubber-cased for water protection. They could go up to 65mph, and, with five or six engines, could maintain such speeds for long periods. 'Arousa to the Canary Islands in 12 hours,' says Julio Fariñas. 'They packed them full of extra petrol, a bit of food and water, and away they went. They'd be gone and back inside a day.'

Not all the clans could afford their own speedboats, and not everyone had places to hide them. A 1987 royal decree had created regulations on the berthing and maximum engine size of these vessels, at the time the preserve of tobacco smug-glers. Only a few groups actually had their own, so the other clans leased from them.

Technological advances threw up some surprising episodes, including an attempt by one group to buy a subma-rine. A joint Guardia Civil–Policía Nacional operation in August 2006 led to the discovery of a 40-foot bathyscaphe in the River Vigo. It was empty when found, and the engines were running. It would seem that two or three of the clans, interested in exploring different means for bringing drugs across the Atlantic, had contracted a shipyard in Seville to make it. But something put them off – perhaps the fact no more than 30 kilos of cocaine would fit inside such a vessel.

In a world so prone to myth making, the speedboat skippers became kings, popular icons who generated breathtaking tales – such as the one at the beginning of this chapter. Indeed, the figure of the speedboat skipper took on such proportions that legions of Arousan teenagers wanted – and some still want – to follow in their footsteps. Drop-offs or chases with the authorities would be followed by bragging contests (and, doubtless, a good deal of untruth). To some sectors of Galician society, particularly those with smuggling in their backgrounds, the speedboat skippers were viewed as high-octane men of the seas, sporting fast cars, expensive sunglasses and weathered faces. The same *guardia* from before: 'I couldn't tell you if they're brave or just stupid. I've seen these guys catching waves in their boats to avoid radars – catching waves, like a surfboard. That's unbelievably foolish at such high speeds – one false move and you'd flip over.'

Among the most prominent narco carriers of this period were the Feijóo cousins, Ramón Prado (a cousin of Sito Miñanco), Ramón Fabeiro, José Vázquez 'Nando' Pereira, Gregorio 'Yoyo' García, Juan 'O Parido' Carlos Fernández, Baltasar 'O Saro' Vilar and, more than anyone, Manuel Abal Feijóo, aka 'Patoco'.

Patoco had worked as a speedboat skipper for the Charlíns in pre-Operation Nécora days. He was known as 'Little Patoco' then, and we have read about him before – it was him who had his photo taken by his girlfriend with a speedboat in Portugal. He went on to create an out-and-out monopoly for himself on the *rías*.

* * *

But there's no peace without war. Before Patoco's reign, a good deal of strife went on between new groups – young, impulsive men in the main – as they vied to fill the power vacuum. The tranquillity always sought by the former ruling *capos* was dashed as soon as there was money to be made again. An upsurge in vendetta killings ensued.

Ricardo Feijóo, his brother Juan Carlos, and their cousin José Ángel – all from Cambados – took the lead, but not to happy effect. They were among the locals who, as youngsters in the 1990s, had done the leg work for the main clans and thought themselves made after a couple of drop-off jobs. When they decided to take the step up and become bona fide narcos, it ended in tragedy.

First, in 2004, Juan Carlos disappeared after going out one day in the five-engine speedboat they kept in Catoria, at the mouth of the Umia River. He was headed for the Canary Islands, where a consignment from Colombia awaited. But something happened on the way there. Neither he nor his mate, another young Cambados man, came back. Their bodies were picked up by the Tenerife–Gran Canaria ferry three months later. Their wetsuits had their documentation stuffed inside.

Ricardo and José Ángel met similar ends. In 2005 they took on a job for José Manuel González Lacunza, who operated in the Basque Country. The details never became clear, but it would seem the cousins kept some of a consignment for themselves. One Galician journalist picks up the story: 'The speedboat skippers were constantly double-crossing each other. If treachery was rife in Charlín's and Oubiña's time, with this new crop it hit epic proportions. They had their hands in each other's pockets the whole time.' He tells a story about the head of one of the incoming clans who, after losing a colleague, rang four of his associates demanding they each buy a wreath as a sign of respect. 'He bought one and kept the rest of the money for himself.'

But in the case of the Feijóo cousins, they kept some cocaine that did not belong to them. And Lacunza was not happy. After issuing a number of warnings, the trafficker travelled to Catoira when they were away and set fire to the shelter where they kept their speedboat – speedboat inside. This pyromaniac decision – a common recourse for aggrieved narcos and skippers – proved to be an expensive lesson.

The fire was only the start. With Lacunza had travelled Patrice Louise Pierre, a German hitman raised in Hendaye. When the Feijóo cousins hurried back to Arousa, Lacunza kidnapped them both – in Ricardo's case, entering his home with his wife and 10-year-old son present, before bundling him into the back of a car. Lacunza and Pierre drove the pair to an old windmill in Serantellos, Cambados, and the hitman fired the shots that killed them. Lacunza emptied another round into the dead bodies for good measure, before setting fire to them. The windmill crime – as it came to be known locally – sent ripples through the region. Lacunza and Pierre were each given 40-year sentences. The hitman died in March 2005 in Botafuegos prison, Cadiz.

And, in May 2005, the trauma recurred. A pair of low-level narcos, Víctor González 'Sparrow' Silva and Santiago Mondragón Paz, were found dead on a forest path in a place called Silleda. The police went on to uncover €1.5 million in Sparrow's garage, seemingly stolen from another clan. On this occasion, some Colombian hitmen had been called in to punish the theft. In the same year, Ramón Outeda, also of Cambados, was gunned down in his doorway, again by some Colombian hitmen.

* * *

Manuel Abal 'Patoco' Feijóo was born in Cambados and first skippered a speedboat at the age of eight. He started out working for the Charlíns, and came through Operation Nécora without any convictions. It was in those years that his legend began to grow, with breath-taking manoeuvres and cinematic chases such as the one already described. And on 18 July 1996, his renown was sealed when a pair of speedboats went out into the fog, and, of the four men who set out aboard, he was the only one to come back alive. Manuel Durán 'Kubala' Somoza was one of those who died in that violent encounter; he had been considered the best skipper around, as well as being a mentor to Patoco.

Following the fall of the big clans, Patoco started to build up a fleet of his own. In 2008 he had a black speedboat made by a Milan shipyard that was going to be the most powerful in Arousa: '*Patoca*', as he dubbed her, had seven 2,100 horsepower engines, each with independent starter mechanisms, and a top speed of 80mph. In a fleet that would go on to be 12 vessels strong, it was always his darling. He paid nearly €100,000 for her. They say his intermediary in the deal, a businessman from the Balearics, constantly had to send him photos while she was under construction. Patoco had the navigation systems and the engines installed in Galicia (costing him a further €700,000). The Policía Nacional recorded a phone conversation between the mechanics, which Elisa Lois went on to publish in an *El País* article: 'The mafia guys were here yesterday for their engines. They came to check them out. They had a bag with 10 million pesetas in, and they sat there counting out the cash.'

'Patoco was quite the character,' says Enrique León. 'Even as a young man he said it: he was going to be the only guy running the transport side. He knew the business, and he didn't want for ambition.' Another police officer concurs: '*Patoca* was a way of thumbing his nose at us. She was a monster. The most incredible speedboat Galicia's ever seen.'

This jewel in the crown was kept in a pig shed. To the naked eye, the pig farm, which was situated at the mouth of the River Umia, was unremarkable. Look again and you would have seen dozens of CCTV cameras, reinforced doors, and other security measures possibly unjustified by the presence of livestock. The whereabouts of the farm was a closely guarded secret. Patoco's underlings were said to circulate every roundabout five times on their way there, and to pull up suddenly on pavements and tracks in case they were being followed, or just to drive along at 10mph. The people who worked with the pigs were said to be driven blindfolded to the site.

The speedboat skippers and their activities spawned a complicated support network of workshops, warehouses, cranes, trucks, tow boats and petrol stations, and numerous mechanics and shopkeepers were on the payroll. Patoco's lieutenant was José Ángel Vázquez Agra, nephew of the head of the Piturros clan. Next in the chain of command were Baltasar Vilar Durán, aka 'O Saro' and Gregorio García Tuñón, aka 'Yoyo', Patoco's brother-in-law. Each was assigned a role within the clearly demarcated organisational structure – much like the clans of old. O Saro coordinated the movements of one part of the speedboat fleet, and Yoyo another. Following Patoco's death, this internal division took on added importance, with the question of his legacy needing to be resolved.

Patoco ruled with an iron fist, and as he tried to assert sole ownership of the *rías*, skirmishes became commonplace. He gave the orders, and almost all the skippers worked for him. His organisation worked for the clans, and each drop-off was a €100,000 job. There was even the occasional direct assignment from the Colombians. The SVA detected speedboats belonging to Patoco in the mid-Atlantic a few times, waters it would take them 20 hours to reach. 'They were totally crazy to be that far out,' says one *guardia*.

And it was worth it to plan something like that in the middle of the ocean, but in the *rías* … There, they'd be swerving between *bateas* and rocks, at 100mph. They'd go out at night, in thick fog, anything. Madmen. But then again, since most of them had been skippering since they were boys, they knew the *rías* like the backs of their hands.

On 19 August 2008, Patoco and Nando set off for a pickup out at sea, but when they arrived at the prescribed coordinates, nobody was there. On returning to their hideout, they were surprised by a Guardia Civil patrol. The agents, however, merely cordoned off the speedboat and did not leave anyone to guard it. The narcos simply came back and moved her to a different location. The Policía Nacional were said to be less than pleased, having spent the best part of a year monitoring the hideout; now they had to start again from scratch. But that proved to be their last chance to take Patoco in, because he died in a car accident a week later. An elderly man stepped off the pavement in front of Patoco's onrushing motorbike, and both driver and pedestrian lost their lives in the collision.

The death of the leader left a void, and a succession struggled ensued. On one side, Yoyo and his men, and on the other, O Saro and his.

The face-off between Patoco's former cohorts proved to be the beginning of the end. It was open warfare, which made it easier to catch and arrest them, and the empire came tumbling down. The cracks were quick to show: in February 2009, the SVA found a speedboat abandoned in Muros. It had five 300 horsepower engines, with propellers coated with metal for additional stability; these details marked the vessel out as unquestionably belonging to Patoco's fleet. Two months later, on 15 April, another speedboat was found torched on Raeiros beach in O Grove. A shell fisherman came across it at dawn and alerted the Guardia Civil. These two abandoned vessels were most likely the upshot of vendettas between Patoco's men. Pointless quarrels, as it transpired. Rather than fighting among themselves, they would have been better off paying attention to moves being made by the authorities: Operation Tabaiba was underway.

OPERATION TABAIBA

In dismantling the network of speedboat skippers that had begun to gain a stranglehold on the *rías*, Tabaiba turned out to be as significant as Nécora. The philosophy underlying it differed to that of Garzón's undertaking: whereas in 1990 the authorities made a single, wide-ranging series of surprise raids, here the idea was to carry out long-term surveillance operations before picking off the speedboat operatives and their associates. This approach was ushered in by José Antonio Vázquez Taín and continued by Cambados judge Irene Roura. She handed out arrest warrants for everyone from mechanics to shipyard workers, petrol pump attendants, drivers, locals who leased garage space to the criminals, and anyone seen to be playing a supporting role, however minor or major. Gone were the days when one could sell an outboard motor to someone, 'no questions asked'; that would no longer fly. People couldn't just look the other way any more, and anyone found to be consorting with Patoco and his people went down. In total, after two phases of arrests, 26 people were prosecuted.

Tabaiba could be carried out with such precision partly because of the 2007 establishment of GRECO, which turned out to be the Galician clans' worst nightmare.

O Saro and O Parido were apprehended in the first phase of the operation, in January 2009. They had been en route to Muxía with Lulú member Andrés García Gesto, on their way to unload a 3,600-kilo cocaine consignment. The authorities intercepted them, and they had to get rid of the cocaine and abandon the speedboat. The actual arrests happened in the following days, though the trio were released pending trial. Yoyo, with the help of his cousins the Fabeiro brothers, took advantage of these developments to assume full control of Patoco's empire. But on 12 February a strange thing happened: Yoyo contrived to lose *Patoca*. The enormous speedboat was found, like the tragic corpse of an elephant, floating in the shallows of Area Fofa beach in Nigrán. One of the outboard motors was broken, and she had close to 20,000 litres of petrol on board, as well as mattresses and large quantities of food and water. In other words, all set for a long trip out to sea. Why, in that case, had she been abandoned? Was this part of another vendetta? It seems too self-destructive for that. The most likely explanation seems to be that the launcher engine failed, or that the skipper in some way failed to handle the size and sheer power of the vessel. This symbol of Patoco's organisation, once a slew of agents had come and taken as many fingerprints as they could, was towed away by the Guardia Civil. Nowadays *Patoca*, repainted in the colours of the Spanish navy, spends most of the time patrolling the Indian Ocean, specialising in escorting fishing vessels that pass through waters plagued by Somali pirates.

Some weeks after that traumatic incident, the second phase of arrests took place, and the Conexos – Yoyo's men – were taken in. 'This is the first time,' said an officer from the Policía Nacional, 'we've been able to bring charges against those who knowingly *provided support* to those transporting drugs.' In total, 26 individuals were brought to trial, and 12 speedboats were seized, along with two yachts, two fishing vessels, dozens of outboard motors, cranes, tractors that had been used to tow the speedboats on land, three trucks, two 4x4s, and €180,000 in cash. At the time of writing, the trials are ongoing in Madrid, with the attorney general requesting 23-year sentences for each of the accused. And all of them, doubtless, thinking of the absent main player, the man who initiated this new phase: Manuel Abal Feijóo, aka Patoco. The speedboat king of the *rías*.

THE ORGANISATIONS

David Pérez Lago and the long shadow of the Oubiñas

It goes more or less like this: Tania Varela and David Pérez Lago fell in love in 2005. Well, they started dating. Pérez Lago's renown as a *bon vivant* lady's man means the clarification needs making. Varela is a lawyer from Cambados, and Pérez Lago the stepson of Laureano Oubiña, Esther Lago's son, and by this point head of the Oubiña clan. A year later, in 2006, the police arrested the pair on drugs charges. They employed the services of Madrid lawyer Alfonso Díaz Moñux, who had defended Sito Miñanco and Oubiña Sr in the past, and he managed to have Varela released on bail. Then Varela and Díaz Moñux became an item, and she moved to Madrid to work at his firm. At that point Díaz Moñux began receiving threats – which he reported on numerous occasions to the Policía Nacional Kidnap and Extortion Unit. Then, on 18 December 2008, as he was getting into his car outside his home in the Madrid neighbourhood of Chamartín, a pair of hitmen came by and fired two shots into him. Varela was at his side and got away unscathed. The hitmen vanished.

It was then that the real soap opera commenced, with Pérez Lago as prime suspect. One theory, though it seems unlikely, is that he had contracted the hitmen to take down the man who stole his girl. Unlikely because, when Varela and Díaz Moñux went off together, he was already seeing other people – various other people, by all accounts. Another possibility is that the Colombian hitmen were sent because part of a consignment had gone astray. The third and most feasible option would make for quite the plot twist, and take the focus away from the Rías Baixas: at the time of his death, Díaz Moñux was also defending Zakhariy Kalashov, a Georgian mafia boss. The truth of the matter is yet to be determined, and Varela's disappearance in 2013 – she fled the country just as her sentence for working with Pérez Lago was due to be handed down – did not help matters. Interpol suspects that she might be in Iceland, but she has managed to evade all attempted arrests.

Pérez Lago was known as 'Davicito' – 'Little David' – during his days at private school in Santiago de Compostela. Even in adolescence it was clear what kind of man he was going to become: big cars, flashy ways, parties, girls. The standard narco's son – but with one difference: Davicito wasn't stupid. His head for business was evident early on – the business of trafficking drugs in particular. As far as the authorities are aware, his first job was in 1999, when he took part in an operation to smuggle 12 tons of hashish into Spain aboard the *Regina Maris*. This was the job that preceded Laureano Oubiña's flight to Greece, after which he was arrested on the Greek island of Eubea; his stepson, having already become his right-hand man, was present that day. So, following Esther Lago's death in a car crash in 2001, he assumed full control. And with considerable aplomb, according to the authorities.

Once he had reshaped the empire, he became the young *capo* of Galician drug trafficking. He divided his time between the *rías* and Madrid, built up a collection of fast cars, and owned three mansions and an array of different companies. He also became a fixture at all the jet-set Madrileño parties of the time.

The good times came to an abrupt end in April 2006, when, as part of Operation Roble (Oak), he was caught participating in a 2,000-kilo cocaine consignment at Corme on the Costa da Morte, the territory of habitual accomplices the Lulús. (Local people claim that some of the product from that intercepted job remains in yet-to-be identified *zulos*.) He was given a nine-year sentence and, upon his release in 2014, was brought to book on some separate money-laundering charges. A deal of some sort was made with the attorney general, however, and he accepted a three-year sentence – currently being served. Many believe his story is far from over. 'We're sure he's still running the business,' says one police officer. 'He is one of Galicia's main *capos*. And when he gets out, that's what he'll carry on being. No question.'

The situation could also be read another way. Etched into the hearts of Galician narcos is the idea that anyone who makes a deal with the attorney general must have given information in return. Many will now see him as a certain snitch. Suspicions will be rife when he gets out after just three years.

The Oxes: dodging death

The most powerful clan during this period were the Oxes, whose name came from the boss's alias: Rafael 'the Ox' Bugallo is a six-foot-tall bodybuilder from Cambados.

The Oxes started out providing transport services to the Charlíns in the days of tobacco smuggling. The Ox later made the leap all speedboat skippers in Arousa wanted to make, by getting a job on Sito Miñanco's boats. He took part in numerous operations and came close to death at least twice. On 5 October 1992, while he was making a call from a payphone, he felt a gun in his ribs: it was Tucho Ferreiro, come to claim a debt. Tucho drove him to a cemetery and forced him to dig his own grave. The Ox went so far as to climb in, before biting Tucho on the hand and running off, bullets whistling by. Only in Galicia. A year later, Tucho came looking for him once more; it was the same night he came for Danielito Carballo in the Museo de Vilagarcía pub and shot Juan José Agra dead in front of his daughter. Luckily for The Ox, he had chosen not to go to his usual pub that night.

The Ox was well connected, and in 2001 signed a deal directly with Carlos Castaño, leader of the United Self-Defence Forces (AUC) of Colombia, a paramilitary group that went on to rename themselves the Urabeños. But the operation this led to – 2,000 kilos of cocaine loaded onto the fishing vessel *Paul*, only to be seized by the DEA in Caribbean waters – prompted Judge Taín to issue an arrest warrant for the Ox. The Spanish authorities' investigations were carried out in tandem with their US counterparts, and at one point Daniel

J. Cassidy, then head of the DEA, paid a visit to Vilagarcía to personally investigate links between the Colombian paramilitaries and the Galician clans. He brought with him a number of DEA agents who went out on patrol. Perhaps the Ox had bitten off more than he could chew.

One journalist I spoke to, who preferred to remain anonymous, points out something remarkable about that deal: 'The Ox was actually working for someone bigger. It's just impossible that he would be negotiating directly with the paramilitaries.' But for whom? 'A top *capo* no one knows anything about, or, more accurately, no one's allowed to say anything about.' An insinuation we will return to later on.

What is beyond doubt is the fact that the Ox succeeded in fashioning the most powerful organisation in this new era. He fled to Portugal with Taín and his men close behind – not that this has stopped him from overseeing at least two further consignments to date. He was very nearly arrested in 2006 after he crossed the border for a brief visit to a place called Tui. The authorities surrounded him but he managed to steal a police car and get away. And in August 2008, on his return to the Iberian peninsula, having picked up 2,000 kilos of cocaine off the coast of Cape Verde, he came upon some SVA radars. With one patrol boat and a Policía Nacional helicopter in hot pursuit, the Ox throttled the engines and headed for shore, while the other narcos aboard jettisoned cocaine bales as fast as they could. (These washed ashore over the coming weeks.) The speedboat came in at A Lanzada beach, in Arousa, where a 4x4 awaited; quickly setting fire to the boat, away they drove, losing their pursuers a little way inland in the rugged mountain terrain. Local beachgoers were met with quite a sight the following morning: the charred hull of a 60-foot-long, 10-foot-wide powerboat, six 220 horsepower engines at the back. No drugs inside, but cans containing a further 1,000 litres of petrol. The Guardia Civil finally caught up with the Ox the following week and, along with his mate that day (and cousin of Sito Miñanco), Fernando Prado, took him in.

By 2012, out on parole, he went for another job. Or tried to. There was a plan to smuggle 1,700 kilos of cocaine ashore on board the mackerel-fishing vessel *Ratonero*. But the operation fell apart, almost the entire clan was arrested, and an arrest warrant was issued for the Ox, who went on the run for the following two years. 'On the run': incredibly, he spent that time hidden away in his Cambados mansion, where he had everything a narco could hope for: *zulos*, secret passageways, Olympic swimming pool, car park big enough for 12 cars, and all the rooms fitted with CCTV. The Ox had demolished a recently built villa 10 years before because it had not been precisely to his liking.

And it was from the mansion that he attempted what would turn out to be his final job, in January 2015: 49 bales of Colombian cocaine aboard the Venezuelan fishing vessel *Coral I*. But on 17 January, a GRECO unit stormed the mansion and found him huddled inside one of his *zulos*.

'You'll never keep me down,' were his apparent words as he was led away. 'Never ...'

The day after this arrest, one journalist went around speaking to the Ox's neighbours. 'Rafael is a good man,' said one. 'He's done nothing wrong.'

The Ox, having 'done nothing wrong', is currently in prison carrying out various consecutive sentences.

The Piturros: family first

There are strong parallels between the biographies of the Piturros clan and that of the Charlíns: almost every person with a blood tie to the family, from fathers to sons and uncles to nephews, was eventually found to have had some involvement in drug trafficking. We have already encountered the patriarch, José Manuel Vázquez Vázquez, who is now in his seventies: he worked with the narco lawyer Pablo Vioque, and ended up giving information on him to Judge Garzón because of a long-standing unpaid debt. And we also came across his son, Juan Carlos Vázquez García, earlier in the book: it was him whom Taín's men arrested at the age of 20 taking part in a drop-off on Arbeyal beach. There is José Ángel Vázquez Agra, lieutenant to Patoco, as well, but it is Manuel Díaz Vázquez who stands out among this tangle of Vilanova kith and kin. The patriarch's nephew, in 2012 he was given an 11-year sentence for attempting to smuggle a 2,200-kilo consignment of cocaine into Spain.

At the time of writing, almost every member of the clan is being investigated as part of Operation Cisne (Swan). They are accused of laundering €4 million – all of it allegedly proceeds from drug trafficking. The clan would have used this money in setting up their various businesses, including a shopping centre in Vilagarcía, a number of high-end clothes shops and a deep-sea fishing venture. Most of their assets have been frozen and their bank accounts shut down. Just about everybody in Vilanova knows which hotels, catering and commercial businesses belong to them, however, and it is plain to see that these have continued to run normally.

The Panarros: enemies of the Piturros

The next part of the story has twists and turns worthy of a mafia thriller. Keep a tight grip on the thread if you want to make it out of the following jumble of names.

On 19 February 2001, Manolo the Catalan and Joaquín 'Panarro' Agra worked together on a cocaine consignment using the fishing vessel *Abrente*. They were arrested, but eventually cleared.

The acquittal annoyed the Piturro clan, convinced as they were that Agra had won his freedom by giving information on them – information about another shipment. This betrayal (or suspected betrayal) was the starting gun on a memorable rivalry between the two clans. Both went on trial in 2009 and it was during this that their mutual dislike came to the surface most spectacularly.

The patriarch of the Piturros, José Manuel Vázquez, and the brother of Joaquín Agra, José, were in the dock, accused of transporting 3,000 kilos of cocaine aboard the fishing vessel *Pietertje* (boarded by special forces off Cadiz). In his statement, Vázquez (who had been bearing the stigma of snitching on Vioque) claimed that Joaquín Agra had run the operation. It was then José Agra's turn to testify, and he pulled no punches either: he said that he had nothing to do with this case, because his family never did business with Vázquez, whom he called a 'rat'. He went on to explain that, although they had been asked to come in on the job (at a dinner in 2006), José Agra had declined the offer, blaming heart problems. He had also been advised by Joaquín to avoid any dealings with Vázquez, a well-known police informant.[1]

The hostilities between the two clans ended in a draw – more or less: Vázquez was given 13 years and José Agra 11 years. And like all good Arousan clans, the Panarros are still going, in one form or another.

The Romas, the fortune teller and the X-rated website

The exception that proves the rule – or rather, an example of a less well-known rule. The Roma clan had avoided the attentions of the authorities entirely when, in October 2007, their boss Ramiro Vázquez Roma was arrested. His neighbours were surprised by the move, and it was almost news for the authorities too, which had not been monitoring his activities. Vázquez Roma's lack of history with the former main players, and the fact that he had no connection with drug trafficking in the 1990s, made him an outlier – or proof, perhaps, of another set of rules that had been in place all along. His example suggests that, while all the focus had been on the main players, others, novices included, had been making gains.

Vázquez Roma was a sailor from Cambados who had prospered in the recreational boating business, going so far as to set up his own shipyards, first in Cambados and later on in Viana do Castelo, Portugal.

He showed considerable acumen in establishing an empire that, among other things, included a hotel in Ribadumia, 10 properties, 20 country estates, vineyards, five boats and shares in shipyards in Vigo and Portugal. Many of his family members were supported by the proceeds from these businesses; in this respect, the Romas are a traditional clan. The *capo* had been working on an 80-foot speedboat in his Portuguese shipyard (larger than Patoco's famed specimen); the prospective buyer, the investigation found, was a group of Moroccan traffickers, long-standing clients of his.

The investigators also found that the Roma clan had worked for the Saín Salazar brothers, who were one of the Colombian groups to come in after the cartels of the 1980s and 1990s gave way.

'The case of the Romas was a classic one of a *ría* business being allowed in on one job, and it going well for them,' says one police commander. 'We assume they weren't the only ones. Their above-board business interests are very much active; this is just a bit of easy money on the side. Some of them get the bug, they can't leave it alone. Which is the case here.' The attorney general alleges that Vázquez Roma attempted to smuggle in a 4,000-kilo consignment of cocaine at O Morrazo in 2007. In 2013, with his trial still pending, his provisional custody period ran out; he then went in on an operation upon release. This time he was contracted by a Venezuelan *capo* called José Gregorio, and he worked alongside some established traffickers, including Francisco Javier Suárez Suárez, a smuggler active since the 1990s. The investigation has found (though the trial is yet to conclude) that the clan organised a shipment of 3,400 kilos of cocaine aboard a battered Senegalese fishing vessel called *Rippide*. It was due to connect with the yacht *Pisapo* on 26 May 2013, but something went wrong with the *Rippide*'s systems and it was unable to leave port. It was around this time that one of the deputies, the narco Manuel Rodríguez Camesella, rang a fortune teller 20 or so times to ask if the shipment would be a success. Although she assured him the auguries were good, they weren't: while the *Rippide* awaited the arrival of the yacht, the malfunction caused it to start spinning in the water, an unusual manoeuvre that drew the attention of the maritime authorities, who came to investigate and found the goods. According to another rumour, the authorities were able to locate the *Rippide* because one of the crew, an Indonesian sailor, had been watching pornography online, and his computer caught a virus that, in uncovering the computer's passwords and programmes, also gave away the ship's GPS location. The operation, which was dubbed Albatross, has come to be known in Arousa as the '€100 million tits' operation – the approximate worth of the confiscated goods.

The Charlíns never die

The most Sicilian of all the clans handed over the baton to itself. Their operations had been dismantled – not for the first time – in 2006's Operation Destello. Some people in Galicia – overly confident people – thought that marked the end for the Charlíns. Think again. In August that year José Benito Charlín Paz, a nephew of the Old Man, put together an operation in which a number of different clans participated: an attempt to bring 5,000 kilos of cocaine ashore on the luxury yacht *Zenith*. It was intercepted by the SVA on its way down from Coruña. Bales of cocaine were jettisoned on the open ocean – again – and, again, locals were to see them bobbing about offshore for months to come. The Cali cartel representative in Madrid at the time, Jorge Isaac Vélez, was not amused. The same group of smugglers worked together on another abortive operation in December, and this failed job paved the way for a series of busts later referred to by the Policía Nacional (with customary reserve) as 'the most important in Galicia this century'. As well as the Colombian *capo* and José Benito, a number of others with ties to well-established clans went down, including José Luis Oubiña Ozores, Laureano's cousin, and Manuel Baúlo's son, the Caneo man Daniel Baúlo (though he was eventually acquitted). It is quite something to see the Caneos and the Charlíns on a job together again, bearing in mind Manuel Baúlo's murder at the hands of Colombian hitmen most people assumed the Charlíns had hired.

In the Charlíns' latest appearance they again created waves with another revenge story. This was the 2004 disappearance of Fernando Caldas, a case that remains unsolved.

Caldas had previously worked for the Charlíns, both on drugs shipments and in a mobile phone shop they owned. 'He started out on a few odd jobs for them and, since they paid so well, he then tried to get all the work he could with them,' says a friend named Nerea. 'The problem with Caldas was that, every time he got paid, the whole world had to know. He had this car with all the mod cons, a TV screen in the back, white leather upholstery,' says Abel, another friend. 'He came into my shop one day and asked if we had any digital scales, and any money-counting machines. I said we had one left. He bought it and went away. The next day he came back and said he wanted 10 more.'

The clan was being run at this time by Jorge Durán Piñeiro, partner of the patriarch's niece Rosa María Charlín. (Durán Piñeiro was given a nine-year jail sentence in 2005 for drug trafficking and is currently awaiting trial on a number of charges.) Not liking Caldas' conspicuous ways, Durán Piñeiro gave him a rap on the knuckles. But it made no difference. On 16 July 2004, he did not show up to a dinner at his parents' house, and he wasn't picking up his phone. 'We started calling, and at first it did ring, but then it was off the whole time,' remembers Nerea. 'Right away I feared the worst, with the kind of people he'd been going around with …' Caldas never surfaced – the worst possible outcome. Investigations suggest that the Charlíns took him out because of his irremediably flashy ways. People in Arousa say his body is somewhere beneath one of the stanchions holding up the Milladoiro bridge, which was being built that year off the AP-9 motorway, near Santiago de Compostela. The only certainty is that he never came back and that, in the *rías*, his death is simply common knowledge.

The Barbanza gang: the 'disappeareds'

José Antonio Pouso Rivas, aka 'Spiky Head' (whose hair was in fact long and lank – the paths that lead to nicknames are many and winding), had six different children by five different (though all Brazilian) mothers. He used the women as fronts for his many businesses, and named the cafés he owned after the children.

As well as being a Don Juan, Spiky Head was one of the most well-known narcos in Barbanza, the county to the north of the Arousa River. He worked with Moroccan traffickers, mainly in hashish. Until something went wrong one day. By this point the reader will have come to understand that, in the world of drug trafficking, something always goes wrong – it is just a matter of time. Sometimes the narco goes to jail, some-times he or she is simply never heard of again – the latter being the case with Spiky Head after a ship containing a 4,000-kilo shipment of hashish sank off the coast from Lisbon – or, according to Spiky Head and his people, it sank. The Moroc-cans they were working with were unconvinced.

'He always used to say goodbye, and he always took luggage with him, but not this time,' says his girlfriend of the time, a Brazilian called Taisa da Silva. 'That's how I know something bad happened.' The authorities investigating the disappearance followed the trail to Morocco, Portugal and Brazil, but found it impossible to build a consistent story. The two options seem to be: a vendetta killing; or he skipped the country to avoid the money-laundering trial he was shortly due to face. The case was closed in 2014, though every month new evidence comes to light to tempt investigators to reopen it.

A kind of curse hangs over the narcos of Barbanza. Either that or they like going missing. The list is not short. First is Manuel González 'Slapdash' Crujeiras, a *capo* from earlier times – who came up earlier in our story when he worked on the 'magical realism' job, hand in hand with a *guardia* and a local mayor. Slapdash's life was full of such extraordinary moments. Locals in Ribeira remember him sitting at local café terraces openly discussing drug-trafficking ethics. He made no attempt to conceal his profession. When the discussions were over, he would pay for everyone's drinks. He always went around with a large bundle of cash.

Slapdash's smuggling CV goes on and on. The one he did least well out of was a shipment aboard the *Meniat*, a fishing vessel that was intercepted as part of Operation Candil (Oil Lamp) in 2002. Given a 13-year sentence, on his first temporary release from prison, he immediately fled the country – to Colombia, the authorities believe, although people in Ribeira said they still saw him around every now and then. He'd had practice as a fugitive already, having been on the run between 1994 and 1997, at the end of which he gave himself up. This second getaway did not end quite so well. Slapdash died in a Colombian prison in March 2014 after alleged overuse of the product he had been trafficking for so many years.

Three months earlier, the police had found Guillermo Falcón Fontán, aka 'the Myth', another Ribeiro narco, who at that point had been a fugitive for seven years. He had given the police the slip after his arrest as part of 2007's Operation Tejo (Tile), when they stopped him on a ship carrying 5,000 kilos of cocaine off the Azores. Astonishingly, when the police did eventually catch up with the Myth again, it was in his home town; he apparently had not set foot outside it for the entire time.

José Antonio Creo, who was spotted by one of the Guardia Civil's informants helping Marcial Dorado on a drop-off, is another to add to this inventory of absentees. He left his house one day, apparently bound for court, and was never seen again. And another is José Carlos Pombar, whom the authorities believe fled to Gambia to become a fisherman, leaving his life of crime behind. The most senior of these disappeared individuals is Santiago Garabal Fraga, another trafficker who was very active before the turn of the century and who, at the time of writing, has been gone – somewhere – for 20 years. And we will come back to Luis Fernández Tobío, the most recent Barbanza man to make himself scarce. His story, as a key witness who disappeared days before the trial of the Pastry Chef clan, is of Italian mafia proportions.

TRACKS IN THE SNOW

'You know the people who used to look the other way with the narcos? Nowadays they're looking the other way with the narcos' money.'

THE ETERNAL RETURN

There was a time when groups of journalists from all over Europe became a common sight in the Arousa area. German TV crews, French newspaper reporters, magazine journalists from the Netherlands … All trying to uncover the most recent operation: a photo of the latest consignment, with bales neatly stacked at the end of port gangways. All the Spanish newspapers had special correspondents in the region, and the Galician press had an obligatory reporter stationed in Vilagarcía. Nowadays, however, there are no journalists dedicated to covering the subject full-time. None. What this means is that Galician drug trafficking has ceased to exist in the collective imaginary. Which is simply a misrepresentation.

'The message coming down from the government is that there are eight or nine guys doing the occasional job,' says a specialist counter-drugs *guardia* I spoke to.

What I can tell you is that there are far more than that: there are still clans, and they are still well organised. More and more so, I would say. But the press have lost interest.

Say we've been on the case of a particular *capo* for a year and not got anything yet. The judge loses patience and shuts down the investigation. The lack of interest from the media has benefited them greatly. It's exactly what the criminals need.

Operation Tabaiba, which put an end to the activities of the speedboat skippers and weakened the next-generation clans, led to a second pause in proceedings in 2010 (the first being after the *anni horribiles* of 2001–03). And once more the Colombians tried to find new ways of getting their product onto the European mainland – and again had little success. 'They tried bringing it in through certain African countries, and through Andalusia, but the experiences were all chastening,' says a judge who preferred not to be named. 'A few years ago, FARC tried moving 20,000 kilos of cocaine through Africa, and had 20 per cent of their goods stolen along the way. They never had that in Galicia. Which is why, time and again, you see them coming back here.' Félix García agrees: 'It's true, there's a resurgence. Any chance they have, they are going to try to work with the Galician clans. They've built up a good understanding over all these years doing business together.' And the Andalusians? I put the question to one local *guardia*:

> Well, Andalusians are Andalusians … I spent a bit of time working down there, tracking some Andalusian narcos, and there's just no comparison. There you can be tailing someone for a hundred miles before they realise. Here, with the Galician *capos*, if you're on them for more than

10 minutes they clock you, they react. The Galicians are
the best around, there's just no comparison. That's what
makes the Colombians so keen to maintain ties.

'There is still this incredible production line of narcos in
Galicia,' says one journalist who specialises in Galician drug
trafficking. 'Of guys who will do the transporting, of speedboat skippers. Take one down, and another two pop up in
his place.' According to Guardia Civil statistics, of the boats
carrying 2,000 kilos of cocaine or more that have been seized
on their way to Europe since the year 2000, 80 per cent were
destined to come in through Galicia. 'Is that nothing then?'
says the *guardia*. 'So there is really nothing to see here? The last
10 boats containing two tons of cocaine or more that we have
intercepted were on their way to the Rías Baixas.' The numbers
are difficult to argue with, and clearly paint a picture of Galicia
as the continuing entry point for large consignments.

'There are busier periods, and less busy periods,' says
the journalist. 'But drug trafficking has always been a feature
in Galicia, and always will be. That is until the international
authorities get their acts together.' This call beyond Spanish
jurisdiction points to the fact that Galicia is only one link in
a chain that stretches from Colombia and Asia to the United
States and Europe, across dozens of countries and with many
different organisations implicated, the political class not
excluded. Any attempt to isolate the problem to Galicia is like
trying to change a car wheel while the vehicle is still in motion.

Colombia is still the source. The cartels of old have given
way to groups led by some of the same individuals for whom

Sito Miñanco, the Charlíns et al. worked. Their bases of operations are in Venezuela, and they have outposts in Spain. Their men coordinate the operations, take care of payments, and apply the law should anyone step out of line. 'There were three Colombians in A Guarda just recently,' says Félix García. 'Going around asking questions. So you just know something went wrong with a shipment.' People still get nervous if they hear a Colombian accent in the area.

Exclusivity clauses don't exist. Though not to the same degree as the cartels, the FARC guerrillas and the paramilitaries also use the Galicians. And the clans, in recent years, have begun working for another heavyweight group: the Camorra. In a 2010 interview with *Faro de Vigo*, Ricardo Toro, head of GRECO, said the Camorra were among a number of Italian criminal organisations using Galician carriers to smuggle drugs into Spain and beyond. 'The Camorra have links with the Galician clans, and in fact the local prosecutor tasked with tackling mafia groups has a number of investigations ongoing.' Alarm bells rang in February 2009 when the *Doña Fortuna*, a Neapolitan fishing vessel bound for Galicia, was apprehended with five tons of cocaine on board. The *capo*, known as 'President', José Manuel Vila Sieira, was the man responsible. The anti-drugs prosecutor in Pontevedra, Marcelo de Azcárragao, went on record a number of years ago about the indirect genesis of the Galicia–Napoli connection; to begin with, the Galicians acted as go-betweens for the Italians and the cartels.

The relationship came about when the Italians started wanting to import cocaine. There's the language barrier between them and the Colombians, and the fact the Galicians were already in touch. This made the Galicians the perfect intermediaries, and they have always tried to prevent any direct contact between the Colombians and the Italians, to make themselves indispensable. All the cocaine received by the Camorra comes via the clans.

All of this begs a question: what about the Mexican cartels? They have become the most powerful players in international drug trafficking, and yet there is no indication of Europe being one of their main importers, and even less of any Galician links. 'We know that the Mexicans did make offers, but these were rejected. What we don't know is why,' says one police commander. Mystery surrounds the issue, though there are suggestions that the Sinaloa cartel had something to do with the failed SV *Nikolay* shipment in 2012. Some of the Colombians arrested as part of that operation might have had connections with the Mexican cartel. The same sources suggest that the DEA warned the Spanish government about moves by Chapo Guzmán, the Sinaloa boss, to set up an outpost in Madrid. This remains speculation – either that or an attempt by the authorities to keep their cards close to their chest.

A number of Bulgarian criminal groups have also appeared on the scene – this is certain. Growing in strength, they have set their sights on control of the Galician *rías*. They mainly traffic heroin, which is cheap to manufacture and has burgeoning numbers of users. According to Félix García, 'They've been asking the clans to help bring heroin ashore. They're not to be trifled with. We know that José Calvo

Andrade had a relationship with them.' (Calvo Andrade is a clan leader currently serving a nine-year sentence for attempting to smuggle in a 3,000-kilo shipment of cocaine.) There was also Yolanda Charlín, niece of Old Man Charlín; we have already touched on her 2013 arrest in connection with a Turkish-run heroin lab in Madrid. 'But where we have to really watch out is with the Nigerians,' says García. 'They are the coming guys.'

The curious thing in this – the clans' umpteenth phoenix-from-the-ashes moment – is that they have not abandoned their traditional methods. 'Most of the drugs are brought in nowadays on container ships and yachts, but you still see smaller boats and the speedboats. Especially in Galicia,' says one *guardia*. The old ways continue, not out of nostalgia, but due to pure economics. The profits are greater when larger quantities of merchandise can be moved in a single go, and when the distribution is also faster. Not only this: the Galician narco carriers – or anyone able to transfer merchandise between ships at sea – can charge more. The very lucrativeness of these ventures guarantees their continuation. The profit-ability alone makes it worth the risk.

'Smaller shipments tend to come in through southern Spain, Andalusia in particular,' says Félix García.

They fill up container ships or they use yachts. Bear in mind that only 5 per cent of all container ships that enter Spanish ports are ever searched. Those aren't bad odds. But the Galicians, they tend to do their work out on the high seas, and they focus on high-volume shipments.

At the time of writing, the police estimate there to be 10 speedboats active in the *rías*, though fewer pickups at sea than in Patoco's day. 'The surveillance is heavy. We're pretty well on top of them.' Almost any time the current-day clans go anywhere, the authorities know about it. Just buying petrol for their vessels has become a mission in itself. They have to buy it on the black market and then transport it to wherever the speedboats are housed.

> If we hear that someone's just bought 600 litres of petrol in Vilanova, of course our ears prick up. It isn't like it used to be, when they were the lords and masters, and the petrol stations just part of their domain. Now, every step they take, we're on top of them. And they know it.

He seems only too happy for them to know.

If a speedboat has a fault, there are only three or four mechanics the clans can go to. The rest want nothing to do with them. They know the authorities are watching them too.

And almost all of today's *capos* keep money in accounts in Switzerland, Singapore or Hong Kong. Their great challenge is laundering it. The laws have grown stricter, and the Tax Fraud Office better equipped. The bursting of the Spanish property bubble also affected them badly. There was a time when the banks in Arousa would throw their doors wide for the likes of Esther Lago, coming in with rubbish bags full of dollars, florins and pesetas, but no longer. Gone are the days when a resident of Vilagarcía could take money out from a 4 million-peseta account, and the teller act as though he or she had seen nothing.

HOSTILE TERRITORY

'They're guarded. Very closed. And very, very sharp,' says one police officer – the same phrases that have been repeated, litany-like, over the last 30 years. 'It's very difficult to prise these organisations open. We still haven't fully untangled all of their business dealings, or, in any detail, how they really work.'

For both the police and the Guardia Civil, the Rías Baixas remain hostile territory. Enemy ground. 'It's quite something. Even the walls have ears,' says Félix García. Any time *guardias* or police officers come to the tolls at the entrance of the Rías Baixas, they pay their way, rather than showing the shields and being let through. 'And because of that, they already know we are on our way,' says one *guardia*. 'They've got people everywhere. We're obliged to use the electronic toll points, and if there are five of us, we go in five separate cars.' A few months before I came to write this book, the police arrested a man called Sanchez Picón who had been selling the registration numbers of police and Guardia Civil vehicles to the clans. 'He even went so far as to forge our insignia so it looked like an official document.' Which it wasn't, but, incredibly, all of the registration numbers were accurate. 'Sometimes we see people writing down our registration numbers when we drive by,' says one *guardia*. 'They've got the whole thing sewn up. Then again they more or less know which cars we drive by heart. We've started having to use hire cars. They smell us coming.'

If the *guardias* or the police go to a café or a petrol station in the area, they make sure the person ordering or paying is Galician, as an outside accent could also give them away.

Some places are effectively out of bounds for us, we just can't go there. If we show up in Vilagarcía in our civvies, they know who we are. Places like Vilanova or A Illa, the same. Their hackles go up. And as soon as that happens, we know we might as well call it a day.

One police officer told me about a drive he took one day to Cambados. 'I came into town and my phone rang. The guy at the other end of the line says, "Come to pay us a visit then?" It was one of the *capos*. And I was like, "How the hell did you know?"'

'In Cambados,' says Felíx García, 'all the bars have got CCTV. They see six strangers walk in and it's game over. They know you're there.' And this countersurveillance is always stepped up around the time of a shipment. In the preceding days they send one of their men to the Canary Islands and rent a room on the top floor of a hotel with views over the port, so they can phone home if any SVA patrol boats go out. The clan member in question will charge €500 a day to do this job. And in the *rías* it is the same: if any speedboat or helicopter belonging to the authorities makes any kind of move, the clans know about it. It is an underground war, a game not visible to the naked eye, let alone to the many tourists who come to the area in summer for the beaches and seafood.

The present-day *capos* very rarely attend meetings, having a plentiful supply of people they trust to act as gophers: drivers, speedboat skippers, warehouse owners, mechanics, lawyers … They tend to avoid using phones – though, according to one *guardia*, they are big fans of WhatsApp – and when there is no choice but to meet in person, the precautions they take are understandably paranoid. According to one *guardia*:

> In 2009 we got word of a meeting between the Costiñas and the Pastry Chef, in a bar in Carril. We went down there and one of my colleagues parked his car nearby, just to see if he could nab a vehicle registration, or get a few photos. When they were all inside the bar, Costiñas came back out, got on his motorbike and went along peering into all of the parked cars in the vicinity. My colleague lay back in his seat to try to hide himself, and Costiñas carried on by. Then, once he'd checked all the cars, he went back inside. A few minutes later, they all came back out and went on their various ways. No meeting.

Like the police in the first season of the US TV series *The Wire*, the drug authorities in Galicia today barely even have any photos of the criminals they are trying to prosecute. Apparently, in the current climate, even a picture taken in a rear-view mirror would be an accomplishment.

The Pastry Chef – one of the main *capos* – once changed cars five times in a period of five months. 'They've got them in the workshops constantly,' says one *guardia*. 'Adding new modifications, putting inhibitors on them.' This is the narcos' latest trick: they have been placing aluminium bars inside their cars that stop the authorities' locator devices from sticking.

> We were following one of our locator devices the other day, between Santiago and Santander. When we started getting close we saw that the device had been thrown in the trailer of a truck. They know what they're doing; they're nothing if not professional. One day one of them jumped in his car and, with us behind him, drove all the way to the Algarve without stopping.

The authorities know, for example, that in February 2002 Costiñas oversaw a 3,000-kilo hashish consignment at Burela. And that, in the winter of 2014, the Lulús smuggled in one very large consignment on the Costa da Morte. As one police officer says:

> It's normal for them to be wary, but the Lulús take it to another level. There's no way you are getting in there. On this 2014 job, they had 15 guys up on the hillside watching the local area. All with 'burners'. They all turn them on just before the drop-off happens, and then we pick up a load of phone activity. If they let it ring three times and hang up, that

means all clear. If any of the phones rings more than three times, the job's off, they ditch the phones and disappear.

Such precautions are the logical consequence of advances by the authorities. The constant struggle forces both sides to be creative. Which, as time goes on, keeps things in a kind of balance.

The possibility of catching the clans during a drop-off is far-fetched, a utopia for the authorities, and particularly without any informers. Of course, informers exist, in the pay of both the Policía Nacional and the Guardia Civil. The general rule is that any narco pleading guilty to a charge is immediately marked down as not to be trusted.

'They're paranoid, the lot of them – I really mean it, they're wrong in the heads,' says Félix García, without a drop of irony. I'm reminded of something a *guardia* once said to me: 'Every time they come to a roundabout, they circle it four times. Every time. And that's when they *don't* think anyone's following them.' The *capos* of former days, people's heroes with gold political party insignias, speaking at town rallies and getting the best tables in the best restaurants, are a far cry from what you see today: these are hermit-like individuals, watching their every step and unable to enjoy their money openly.

It used to be that, when they wanted to make plans for a drop-off, they'd get together in a restaurant, share a nice spread of *fruits de mer*. Nowadays, they have to drive to some isolated hillside, do 40 laps, before a couple of the guys get out and have a conversation under a tree.

This lack of ostentation, however, does not mean the money is not there. To outside eyes, they are very low key, but behind closed doors it is quite another thing. When the head of the Pastry Chef clan was arrested in December 2014, all his neighbours were astonished to find out that, on the inside, his villa had all the trappings of a luxury mansion.

'There is a very well-known *capo* from Arousa who owns the most incredible apartment in Dubai. They dress in the most expensive clothes, though they wouldn't know stylish if it hit them over the head. They're rich, don't you worry about it,' says Félix García. I was also told an anecdote about the casino in A Toxa being reserved one night for a private party. The lawyer of one of the clans apparently rang up and made the reservation. 'It's going to be pretty expensive to shut the place down,' said the person working the phones. 'Give me a price,' said the lawyer, 'and we'll pay it.'

'I do ask myself if it's worth it for them,' says one police officer. 'Yes, they get to be millionaires, but all that stress? No thanks.' But the answer is always the same: they know no other way of life.

Sometimes when we take one of them in, and they know we've got a cast-iron case, we just ask them, why did you do it? And it's always one of a few things: either they've done one job with the Colombians, and it's impossible to get out, or they've got debts to pay. But I still don't get it. You only need to do one drop-off, come away with €3 or €4 million, and you're away – just invest it. But they always want more. Greed, pure and simple.

And to get more they have to go back to the one thing they know. It's onto the next job. The next round of paranoia, the phones, circling the roundabouts. No chance to enjoy the money they've made. The cycle continues. Drug trafficking in Galicia continues. Sometimes busier, sometimes not so busy. But it hasn't gone away. Not in the slightest.

THE LORDS OF THE *RÍAS* TODAY

The baker – and his pastries

In March 2013, everything was in place for the trial meant to put Óscar Rial Iglesias, aka the Pastry Chef, behind bars; 'The most powerful *capo* in the *rías* today,' according to one *guardia*. He was accused of attempting to smuggle 3,000 kilos of cocaine into Spain aboard the Venezuelan shipping vessel *San Miguel*.

José Luis Fernández Tubío, a member of the Pastry Chef clan who took part in the shipment, must have had an attack of conscience, or perhaps just felt the burden of his coming conviction, and decided to give information: he gave the Pastry Chef and his clan to the authorities on a plate. In exchange, Tubío was granted indefinite police protection. He was given a 24-hour security team, in the hope that he might stay alive long enough to stand trial.

But four days before proceedings were due to begin, Tubío disappeared.

It would appear that he asked the security detail to leave him at a bar in Boiro – his home town – but he never came

315

back. What did reach the court were two letters, signed by him, claiming his previous allegations were untrue, and begging for the Pastry Chef's forgiveness. The Pastry Chef was acquitted and, a year on, the key witness resurfaced. Not in some faraway, exotic corner of the world, but breaking the speed limit in Zamora, a town in the Spanish interior. He was arrested, but has kept his silence so far.

Another person to resurface was José Isasis González, a Colombian narco with a Venezuelan passport. But when he did so, on 10 June 2014, it was inside a locked cold storage unit in Ponteareas, not far from Vigo, in the shape of a corpse with its legs chopped off. Isasis was a member of the San Miguel crew, and the only one to make an appearance at the trial against the Pastry Chef clan. Although investigators do not know for certain whether his death was linked to the clan, the signs seem fairly clear.

The events of the last few paragraphs did not take place in Sicily or the badlands of Mexico. They took place in Galicia, plain old Galicia, just a few months ago.

* * *

At the turn of the century Óscar Rial was a humble baker in Vilagarcía, baking bread rolls, sweet pastries and *empanadas*; he also had half the police corps watching his every move.

It was in 2007, with Operation Destello, that suspicions arose about his family. Although the Pastry Chef was found not guilty in those proceedings, it was then that the authorities began monitoring him. And they gradually came to find out that beyond the bakery lay apartments, sports cars, and an array of investments. His mansion on the outskirts of Vilagarcía was in the same mould as the residences of the former *ría* lords: statues, swimming pool complete with fountain, CCTV in every room.

The Pastry Chef was not involved in huge numbers of shipments, but those he did go in on were very well planned. 'They're extremely cautious, tie up all the loose ends,' says one *guardia* I spoke to. 'And if anything doesn't seem right to them – I mean, even the tiniest whiff – then the whole thing is off.' In 2008, some of the Pastry Chef's speedboats broke down on the way to pick up cocaine from a boat called the *San Miguel*, and the authorities moved in. To be on the safe side, the Pastry Chef and his men decided to sink the speedboats on the open sea and have the *San Miguel* collect the crew, but then the *San Miguel* ran into problems as well. By the time the special forces got to the vessel, the crew were suffering from malnourishment and dehydration.

Tubío was among the crew on the broken-down speedboats, as was José Constante Piñeiro Búa, aka Costiñas, right-hand man to the Pastry Chef (the same individual who came out of the clan meeting on his motorbike to check the nearby cars). 'These two are like brothers. They do everything together. They've even got a pair of Audi S3s with linked licence plates,' says one *guardia*. The third pillar of the organisation is José Andrés Bóveda Ozores, aka Charly. An anecdote told by this same *guardia* exemplifies the reach of the Pastry Chef's clan. 'We were running some checks on Charly the other day, and we rang up a car park he owns and asked for their insurance details. Straight afterwards, as in minutes later, we get a call from the provincial government asking why we'd been asking for that. I was gobsmacked.' He looks incredulous even telling me the story.

There were 40 people in the Pastry Chef clan. 'Without ever reaching the heights of the groups from the 1990s, they were formidable,' says one police officer. 'They were doing transport jobs, and some distribution too. They are the closest we've come to the power of the former main players.'

Some would go further. The *guardia* leading the investigations into the Pastry Chef clan is convinced they have backing from Sito Miñanco – him again: 'It is our view that he is the real boss. That he's running the Pastry Chefs from behind bars.' And there do seem to be grounds for the theory: in 2010 Sito was transferred to a prison in Huelva and a year later the head of the prison lost his job, apparently for having accepted gifts – a couple of high-end cars – from a trafficker then serving time in the facility. It was later discovered that Sito had been enjoying all manner of privileges in Huelva, from being allowed phones to getting day-release permits. Two years later, after being transferred to Algeciras prison, on his first release (this time an officially sanctioned one), he was allowed to go away for six days. And what did he do? He went to Galicia, of course, and there, with the Guardia Civil looking on from unmarked cars, he had a meeting with the Pastry Chef. 'We were amazed. Twelve years inside, and the first thing he goes and does is meet up with another *capo*.' It seems unsurprising, after episodes like this, that the Supreme Court should have decided, in 2015, to ban Sito from ever setting foot inside Galicia again.

But it wasn't after this meeting that the Pastry Chef was arrested. He went down in December 2014, and for the same thing almost all the Galician narcos would go down for: money laundering. A very thorough investigation had been carried out into his business dealings, until finally a loose thread emerged: the acquisition of a copper mine in Congo, a bank transfer that stood out like a neon sign. The investigation culminated in the winter of 2014 with a large-scale bust, featuring helicopters and dogs, that brought Vilagarcía to a standstill. No drugs were found in his house, but the authorities were – and for a long time had been – more interested in the numbers. So far it is known that the Pastry Chef held various companies in the names of retirees. Investigations are ongoing. He was released in 2015 after paying the €200,000 bail fee, and currently awaits trial. It remains to be seen whether another alleged heir to the drug-trafficking throne will fall foul of money-laundering enquiries. 'For now,' says the *guardia*, 'all we can do is keep an eye on him.'

Hand in hand with the Pastry Chef and his men come the Baker clan from Ribadumia; as far as investigators know, the alliance was formed quite recently. The Bakers are said to have entered the business in 2006 with some low-level jobs, smuggling small amounts of cocaine from Colombia. They lasted one year: in 2007, a 270-kilo consignment was seized in the port of Vigo. The men in charge, Francisco and Rafael Thomas Barreiro, were each given 10-year sentences. But the authorities believe that the rest of the clan remains active.

And they point to one more clan that has collaborated sporadically with the Pastry Chef, a small, murky group from Vilanova known as the Butchers.

The 'classics': the Lulús and the Charlíns

Two of the 'classic' groups, the Lulús and the Charlíns, have carried on operating alongside the more recently formed clans. The former, say the authorities, are in the best shape out of any of the groups, and have been posing the most problems.

The last time they made the news was on 5 December 2014. A meeting had been arranged between Bernardino Ferrío, a narco from Muxía and frequent accomplice of the Lulús, and a group interested in working on a consignment with them. Ferío, an old hand on the Galician trafficking scene who had already served a number of prison sentences, received them at his house in Aboi, a village on the Costa da Morte. There were a number of Colombians among the guests. What had been mooted as a get-together to agree details on a consignment swiftly turned into a robbery; the supposed narcos were a gang whose specialism turned out to be robbing traffickers. A risky line of work. And all the more so if your victim is someone like Ferío – not a man to be trifled with, in the view of the authorities. One of the Colombians shot him in the stomach, but he managed to raise his own shotgun and return fire. Four days later, a resident of Ribadeo, nationality Colombian, showed up at the hospital in Lugo with gunshot wounds in the leg. The police succeeded in arresting the hold-up artists a number of months later, and they are currently under prosecution.

And as for the ever-durable Charlíns, they now have a third generation at the helm. Old Man Charlín himself has apparently retired from business, spending his days going down to Villanova to enjoy a cup of coffee, where elderly gentlemen approach to pay their respects. His granddaughter's husband, Marcos Vigo, is the current boss. He was arrested as part of Operation Albatross in 2013 (when an Indonesian crew member allegedly led authorities to the consignments by frequenting X-rated websites). 'But we have to watch him, even if he's behind bars,' says one police officer. 'He's still got his fingers in pies. We know he has a mobile phone in prison. But we let him have it,' he says, half-laughing, 'that way we might get some leads.'

Vigo has had assistance from Jorge Durán Piñeiro, partner of Rosa María Charlín, the Old Man's nephew. He was given a nine-year sentence in 2005, and is currently awaiting trial on a different, and mounting, set of charges. The pair were investigated for their alleged involvement in the disappearance – and possible murder – of Fernando Caldas, the young Vilanova man whose body was found beneath one of the stanchions holding up the Milladoiro bridge.

Adding to the current Charlín ranks is José Luis Viñas Morgade, aka Little Apple, a veteran who shows no sign of retiring. Little Apple's first encounters with the Guardia Civil came as far back as the days of Operation Nécora, in 1990. He was involved in a car chase – he was driving a truck carrying 1,200 kilos of cocaine – at the end of which, cornered on the coast, he threw the goods into the sea and tried to swim away. His boss in those days, Manuel Rey Vila, another associate of the Charlíns, was with him, but rather than jumping into the sea he opted to shin up the side of a water tower and hide inside. When they found him he had half frozen to death.

Among those still in the pay of the Charlíns is Manuel Gómez Rey, aka Chanfainas, and Antonio Carballa Magdalena. The former went down as part of Operation Destello in 2007. He was arrested in Melilla, a regular haunt of his. It would appear that Chanfainas offered his services to some Moroccan gangs as a speedboat skipper – an art he learned under Sito Miñanco in the '*batea* Winston' days. As for Carballa Magdalena, he stands accused of money laundering and involvement in a recently established moneylending racket. Charging extortionate rates of interest for loans, inevitably.

Nor have other members of the clan been taking it easy, it would seem. Many have been investigated as part of Operation Repesca for money laundering. First-, second- and third-generation men in the clan – and they do tend to be men – are accused of moving enormous sums of money around. In 2009, the clan bid €800,000 at a state auction for an expropriated canning factory they had formerly owned. A circular metaphor that seems only too appropriate in the context of Galician drug trafficking.

The Little Ones

Also active as far back as Nécora was José Fernández Touris, a local who emigrated and then returned to Galicia in the 1980s, setting up a building company in Vilanova before moving into tobacco smuggling. He shifted to drugs in 1992 with an attempt to move two tons of cocaine ashore aboard an English yacht. His sons are now in charge of the clan known as the Little Ones, though an internal power struggle seems to be going on. In the summer of 2009, one of these sons was walking through Cambados when a pair of Romanians jumped out and gave him a beating. Specifically, one held him from behind while the other laid into him with punches; like in the movies, but in the middle of town, in broad daylight. The victim of the attack was very well built and managed both to throw off the man holding him and return some punches, before his attackers fled. That wasn't the end of it. 'Little' got in his car, a Mercedes 4x4, and went after the pair, who were driving a BMW. He rammed into them and both vehicles ended up in a wreck on the roadside, drawing a large group of gobsmacked locals. The Guardia Civil came and cleared the scene. By all accounts, the beating had been ordered by members of his own family after a dispute over assets inherited from the patriarch.

The Mules

Out of the Arousan groups that are currently active and under surveillance, and that do not have a long-standing history, a hermetic family clan from Vilagarcía known as the Mules stands out. It seems that the Mules have been active in trafficking since as far back as the 1990s, just not very active. For all their years of experience, they have not carried out a great number of operations – one or two a year, perhaps, and all very painstaking. The rest of their time and energy goes into investing the proceeds in a large range of different businesses. Some of these are fairly well known in the area, including a popular boating company. 'They have always been in the shadow of the big players,' says Félix García. 'They've always been very discreet. But they're big-time.'

The *capo* of the Mules had connections in politics. His name appeared in the press when the 2011 Campeón case broke, a political funding scandal that implicated some of the highest echelons of Galician public servants, and which is yet to be fully resolved.

The Pulgos

Another tightly knit, though lesser, family clan from Boira. The group's general approach has been to provide services to more powerful *capos*. In recent years they have worked for José Manuel Vila Sieira, the President, who is also a Boiro man and is a contact of the Camorra in the *rías*. Investigators are in fact looking into the possibility that the President is the current leader of the clan. Both he and his son were given 15-year prison sentences in 2009 for the previously discussed *Doña Fortuna* fishing vessel job – in which five tons of Italy-bound cocaine were intercepted.

The unknowns

The only place to go from here is the murky realm of speculation. One local journalist points to a number of powerful Galician impresarios who have previous as drug-trafficking *capos*. In fact, this is simply a badly kept secret. In a 2010 interview with a Vigo newspaper, the anti-drugs prosecutor in Pontevedra spoke with unwonted frankness: 'There are still a number of heavy-weight *capos* active locally whom I don't believe we will ever catch, not under current legislation. They have always managed to keep clear of the merchandise, and never have anything to do with operational logistics.' To this the journalist adds: 'They're businessmen, they keep their noses clean. The fact they delegate lots of responsibility makes it pretty much impossible to link them to any operations.' One of his colleagues in the press, Julio Fariñas, goes further: 'These are people who already have a lot of money and only get involved in the occasional job, and not in Galicia, but elsewhere in Spain. They pick a spot they know isn't under surveillance and come in and out, scot-free.' The view of the police is less categorical:

> There might be some individuals contributing funds to some operations, but they aren't what we would call *capos* as such. Any person who keeps on coming back for more, anywhere there is continued and sustained activity, it is easy for us to detect. In our view, there isn't some big-time *capo* who has managed to stay invisible to us. There is, however, a lot of talk.

Only time will tell if any of these purported *capos* exist. And then whether the authorities are able to get them. In any case, we will always know that, beyond the likes of Miñanco, the Oubiñas and the Charlíns, there have been others in Galicia who have done very well in this trade. Others whose identities will never be fully known, and whose stories will probably never be told in a book. If, that is, any idiot ever comes up with the idea of trying to write a book about drug trafficking in Galicia.

THE PLAGUE

Esther Lago's daughter had one of her girlfriends with her. 'Or one of her cousins, I'm not completely sure,' says Milagros, a Vilagarcía woman and the owner of the shop into which Lago and her relative went one afternoon, five years ago now. 'I recognised her straight away. I can't remember what she wanted to buy.' Wanted, says Milagros, because in the end she didn't buy anything. When she came to the till to pay, Milagros said her money wasn't good there, and ordered her to get out. 'She smiled, looked in her purse and brought out twice the amount of money …' At this point, Milagros – whose son Alfonso died 20 years ago after a battle with drug addiction – speaks with barely concealed anger. 'I took the coins and threw them into the street. They bounced against the shop window. And again I told her where to go.' Esther Lago's daughter gathered up the money, gave Milagros a look and left. 'I remember I was going to tell her she had blood on her hands. But the words wouldn't come.'

The line separating acceptable society and the activities of drug traffickers in the Rías Baixas, invisible in the 1980s and blurry in the 1990s, is far better defined nowadays. Anyone involved in the business is considered, with neither euphemism nor admiration, a criminal. And yet, after so many decades of gang culture, certain echoes remain. To re-quote Julio Fariñas: 'The tolerance had become entrenched. People had learned to live with activities that were manifestly illegal.' This kind of coexistence still exists, if less overtly. It's still something people don't want to hear about, and still less see committed to print.

The impunity with which the clans operated has gone, but not the mantle of silence. By no means. Local people still know things, and still say nothing. 'Because what can they personally do?' says Enrique León, former chief of police in Vilagarcía. This rhetorical question contains one of the keys to the whole phenomenon: how is one individual supposed to tackle something so widespread? Report someone to the police? Go to the press? What would the next day bring? The narco you've just been talking about is also your neighbour. The criminal knows who you are, where you live, where you work. And anyway, shouldn't the police be dealing with it? Isn't that *their* job? Such logic is perfectly reasonable, but still doesn't justify the resounding silence in the Rías Baixas – the 'not my problem' attitude is precisely what keeps people from lending their support to community anti-drug initiatives. Such silence is more marked in small places such as Vilanova than in larger, more modern towns like Vilagarcía and Cambados. The smaller or more isolated the village, the more difficult it is to combat drug trafficking. The government has some way to go before it penetrates the furthest reaches.

'People just prefer not to get involved,' says Milagros.

Because they're afraid, because they prefer to look the other way. Everyone said they hated them, but nobody did anything. It used to be that hundreds of us would go to the marches and meetings, people were up in arms ... Nowadays there will be 12 of us, the mothers, at most. Unless people have been personally affected, they don't get involved.

One local journalist agrees: 'People have the attitude now that it's always going to be like this; passivity has set in.'

Since the death of her son, Milagros and her husband Alfonso have been volunteering with Proyecto Hombre (the Man Project), which helps young drug addicts. 'It took us months to find somewhere to base ourselves: nobody wanted to rent to us. Everyone around here goes on about how they're against the narcos, but when it comes down to it, they don't lift a finger. There's only four of us left now kicking up a fuss.' People don't want trouble: this is the – perhaps understandable – *omertà* still in force in Galicia today.

Certain demographics in the *rías* are more open to drug trafficking than others. For the less well off, those with fewer life options, the chance to make money with an unloading job is sometimes irresistible. This tempting offer doesn't come out of the blue – it isn't as though a guy on the dole in Cuenca suddenly receives an invitation to carry cocaine up a beach. The opportunity is simply there, a presence, latent, and has been for decades. Say yes to this one easy job, and there's an immediate way out – one the licit labour market simply cannot provide. Drug trafficking remains a feasible alternative. 'This is a difficult aspect to guard against,' explains Fernando Alonso, manager of the Galician Anti-Drug Trafficking Foundation. 'You find a young guy, 20 years old, unemployed, family struggling, and no future to speak of, and then someone offers him €5,000 to drive a car to Madrid, leave it in a car park, and drive back in another one. How can you legislate for that?' I spoke to a young Vilanova man called Antonio who, as a teenager, was approached to take part in a drop-off. 'I said I didn't want anything to do with it, but a couple of my friends went and worked on the job. It was cocaine, and it was the last job either of them did, but they got €1,000 each – for a 20-minute job.' An anecdote that is far from isolated.

It would be reductive, though, to boil the whole phenomenon down to an exit strategy for the dispossessed. Stealing in order to eat. Very often those involved are not in financial difficulty, and sometimes they even come from affluent families. In the *rías*, drug trafficking is almost always a family business, something you are born into. You only need to look at the surnames of the drug traffickers from the early 1990s: no different, very often, from those of the individuals involved today. And if not blood ties, then ties of friendship: friends, neighbours, business partners … There is a looking inward, even to the point of inbreeding. Like a tradition, bales and powerboats are inherited. Like the shoe shop your great-grandfather set up – you become part of the setup by default.

To venture something of a social analysis: drug trafficking in Galicia today can mainly be divided into two levels –

the *capo*, and the *narquito* or mini-narco. The *capo* takes the lead in operations, is the head (or one head) of the clan, and, usually from humble origins, carries on in the poorly remunerated family business as a way of throwing the authorities off the scent: if the individual in question comes from a line of clam pickers, clams will continue to be picked, it's just that he will be driving home in an Audi. If the work has always been picking mussels from the *bateas*, that will carry on, but the handbag carried by the *capo*'s wife will be a Gucci. This is the aforementioned, specifically Galician kind of kitsch: seeing a woman making deep-fried calamari sandwiches in a beach hut, and then seeing the Rolex on her wrist. These details tell you everything you need to know in the Rías Baixas.

The other kind of *capo* is the successful impresario. Outwardly respectable men, hotel owners, shipyard owners, owners of shipping lines or estate agencies – meanwhile running consignments on the side and injecting the profits into their businesses. 'All the same, they stand out to us here,' says Pablo, a resident of Villanova. 'You can just tell. Something in their manner, the way they move, the way they even talk. It just screams narco.'

One rung down from the *capos* are their offspring. 'Daddy's boys', in the words of Veronica, a Vilagarcía resident. 'New money, and arrogant as you like.' You sometimes hear that one of them has 'gone to do a master's' – local code for an arrest. 'Around here,' says Pablo, laughing, 'it pretty much means just that. A master's degree: in other words, you're doing time.'

And on the bottom rung, the mini-narco, the young guy starting out in the trade, taking on the occasional odd job.

Gophers, speedboat skippers, lookouts ... An easily recognisable social group: showy souped-up car (failing this, showy souped-up motorbike), a propensity to buy rounds of drinks for everyone in the bar, designer clothes emblazoned with logos ... All of them 20 years old, and with no fixed job. 'In certain social circles,' says Pablo, 'it's cool to be one of the narcos' gophers. People aspire to it. You even get guys pretending that's what they do when it isn't actually the case.'

The risk one runs in analysing popular perceptions is that everyone can suddenly become a suspect. 'There is a fairly straightforward way of telling them apart,' says one Cambados man I spoke to:

> Especially the younger generation: a BMW comes by, enormous engine, and the guy in the driver's seat is about 22, and just has one of those faces. He's thick as a loaf of bread. To be honest, around here, that's all you need. Where's a guy like him going to get a car like that? You ask someone, and they say, 'Oh yeah, him, he's a mechanic in Vilaxoán.' All bets are off.

These are the kinds of young men who left school early and quickly got a taste, if fleetingly, of success. The words of Maria, a young lawyer from O Grove, are striking:

> During my law degree, I bumped into a guy I'd been at school with – a dropout. He was driving a convertible and he asked if I wanted to go for a drive. And always he'd have the same question for me: 'What's the point of your

degree, why bother?' And he wasn't making fun of me precisely, it was that he genuinely didn't understand: he and his pals had it all sorted already.

Maria has gone on to defend some of the same young men in court.

It's not only the mini-narcos who are viewed with such knee-jerk suspicion. In Arousa, an array of social signals automatically prompt misgivings. 'You see a big house around here, gilding, statues, extravagant tiles, and the first thing you think is ... well, you can imagine what people think,' says Veronica. Pablo adds: 'You go past a bar and there's three sports cars outside, and your first thought is, something's going on in there.' Another resident of Vilanova goes further:

> If you see a couple of more or less well-known, wealthy individuals eating together in a restaurant, you immediately wonder. What could those two possibly be chatting about?! Or if you see someone who you know to be mixed up in trafficking, and they're having a drink with some businessman or shop owner ... you have a pretty good idea of what the common ground might be.

The problem lies in the degree of overlap between the clans' activities and those of ordinary society. What they do, and what they have been doing for so long, has affected the entire region. 'It's insane,' says Vilagarcía man Abel. 'The sheer amount of drugs around, it's insane. Cocaine is the easiest one to get. Easier than hash.' In years gone by it wasn't uncommon to go into a bar in Vilagarcía and see lines ready to go on the edge of the pool table. In public toilets throughout Galicia you find peepholes in the doors so people can keep a lookout. 'I remember going out one night' – Abel again – 'and I went into the toilets and, washing my hands, I managed to get water on all these lines I hadn't noticed. Jesus, they were there, just ready to be snorted. Like it was just understood: nobody touch these. When I realised, I just ran.'

And the area's fame reaches beyond its regional borders: 'If you go to Madrid, or anywhere else in Spain for that matter, and say you're from Vilagarcía, you always get some joke, someone asking if you'll sell them some coke,' says Veronica. 'I've had it so many times I can't tell you. They only have to hear your accent.'

Such quantities of drugs in such a small area bring about other, despicable consequences. Milagros' son Alfonso lost the will to live in 1993, after a three-year-long struggle to kick addictions to cocaine and heroin. At the age of 25 he went to a hostel in Santiago de Compostela and hanged himself. Milagros describes him growing up, 'like all young people in Arousa', surrounded by drugs: 'And that was what killed him. The incredible thing was, out of all my kids, Alfonso was the least crazy, the one you always thought least likely to go off the rails. But ...' In the Rías Baixas, there's always a 'but'. 'For example, Alfonso joined the marching band at the naval school in Marín – we'd sent him there to get him away from all the problems around here. Then we find out that the lieutenant is pushing drugs.' At this point in the story, Milagros breaks down.

Her husband, Alfonso Sr, takes over: 'The bit I find hardest to believe is that parents are still involved. I know people from this area who have lost children to drugs, and they're still up to their necks in smuggling.' Narco-culture is not the most principled. 'Everybody around here has known kids of narcos who have also been junkies.' The experience of Milagros and Alfonso as part of Proyecto Hombre is an example of drug trafficking's flip side, the heavy, un-rose-tinted reality.

> I remember taking this one young guy home one day. He was really hooked, and that day he was in a bad way, lying there in the street. We got him in the car, and he told us the way to his house. We got there and his mother helped us get him inside. We got him into bed. The whole experience had destroyed her, she was in tears. Now, opposite the house were three mansions. With Mercs and 4x4s in the driveway, big gates. She pointed at them and said: 'Them, them and them.'

The people who had started her son down this path lived 30 metres away.

* * *

There remains a heavy covering of Spanish snow in the autonomous community of Galicia. The amount of drug money that has been – and is being – invested is incalculable. Hundreds of now-legal enterprises – from cafés to discos to shops – first opened on the back of proceeds from some consignment or other. José Vázquez, mayor of Vilanova in the 1980s, says as much: 'This is a serious thing: few and far between are the local companies that, at one time or another, have not had some kind of tie with the trafficking of narcotics. I find it difficult to say, it's very painful to me, but it is the truth.' In 2010, the SVA counted 100 businesses in Vilagarcía that were being used as dummy businesses through which to launder money. After the death of Patoco, 124 separate properties were seized by the state, all of them tied to this one individual. According to 1997 statistics from the Galician Anti-Drug Trafficking Platform, 80 per cent of hotels in Arousa then belonged to drug traffickers. As it happens, the man responsible for that study was a friend of Milagros and Alfonso. They said that when he came out of the press conference at which the study was announced, his tyres had been slashed. And they aren't joking.

In Vilanova, a place of some 10,500 inhabitants, there was a café where, during an audit, the owners told the authorities they were making 2,000 coffees every day. With completely straight faces.

'These people made their money in drugs,' says Milagros. 'We have to see them going around, big cars, huge houses, acting like they've made it as successful businesspeople.'

'Aren't you afraid to report them?'

'Afraid? I'm not afraid of them. When I lost my son, that was when I stopped being afraid.'

It isn't easy to be an upstanding citizen when the bricks that built 80 per cent of your local bars were bought with proceeds from illicit activities. 'I don't go in if I know it's one of theirs,' says Veronica. 'And there are a lot of people who think the same as me, but then also a lot of people who don't. They don't care. Sometimes it's a question of not being completely certain. Other times, you don't have a choice: it's the only shop there is.' Milagros agrees: 'I imagine I probably have bought things in shops belonging to narcos and not realised it. There isn't much around here they don't own. But I make an effort to find out who owns the businesses. It's all I can do …' And when people come into her shop, and they have a plastic bag from an establishment she knows to be connected with narcos, she takes it away and gives them a new bag instead. 'People don't care, they shop in those places anyway. Parents whose children are on the Proyecto Hombre programme, they're out there spending their cash in drug-money shops.' Then, in an afterthought, she seems to me to put her finger very precisely on the current predicament: 'You know the people who used to look the other way with the narcos? Nowadays they're looking the other way with the narcos' money.'

* * *

All assets seized from the clans are turned over to the Ministry of Health's national drugs plan, but there are problems with this procedure: by the time the prosecutions have been carried out, the assets have often depreciated massively. There are warehouses in Galicia full of the rusting hulks of ships in particular. This was the situation in the 1980s, and still nothing has been done about it.

Such assets may not be sold until the accused has been sentenced, and it is often many years before a sentence is handed down. The warehouse belonging to the Seized Assets

Fund in Coruña is full to the rafters with sports cars, yachts and outboard motors, all slowly turning to rust. Except, that is, when relatives of the *capos* come forward to claim them. 'The wives or children of the person under arrest get to carry on driving the BMW, or living in the expensive villa,' explains Fernando Alonso. 'This generates an impression of impunity. Which in turn disheartens those of us engaged in the struggle against these criminals.' The best example are Sito Miñanco's assets: to this day, his family continue to enjoy the fruits of his labours, from villas to top-of-the-range cars.

There is a way out of this, known as 'advance transfer of title', a recourse open to judges if they wish to seize assets before sentencing. The problem is that very few judges make use of it, because it entails certain risks. In the winter of 2013, Judge Fernando Grande-Marlaska acquitted the Pastry Chef and his clan after the key witness José Luis Fernández Tubío decided not to testify. The courts were then forced to undo all of the sanctions previously applied to their businesses and vehicles and to reactivate frozen bank accounts. This unleashed a behemoth of bureaucracy – one that is still grinding away now.

'The courts don't usually authorise advance transfer of title,' explains Javier Zaragoza, the chief prosecutor at the Audiencia Nacional. 'We see a general tendency to just hold the assets.' Which means around a third of those assets end up at the scrapyard.

'This is something that needs working on,' says Luis Rubí, the lawyer who worked on the seizure of the Baión estate, visibly annoyed.

Sito's family shouldn't be allowed to go on benefiting from his activities. The processes themselves need sharpening, because at the moment it can be 14 or 15 years before the administration process is complete. Assets lose value. It isn't good enough to say there aren't enough resources, there aren't enough people. There just should be.

Fernando Alonso puts it more strongly still: 'We want the goods to be embargoed sooner, and for that to be the norm. Not to have to ask a judge. We're asking for a shift in the entire innocent-until-proven-guilty presumption.'

A very difficult shift to bring about. The authorities have to presume that certain assets have been acquired using money from illegal activities. This then puts the onus on the proprietor to prove that the assets derive from licit activities. Should a judge consider it suspicious that a grocer from Vilagarcía is also the owner of three villas and five cars, an accusation may be made, and the grocer is then obliged to prove his innocence. This is a sort of presumption of guilt that does not sit well with the Spanish constitution, but which many people in the *rías* would support after so many years of impunity.

The outlook is not all negative. Two-thirds of the goods seized from narcos are successfully sold. The Vista Real estate, formerly owned by the Charlíns, is now open to the public (though in a somewhat run-down condition, truth be told), and a plaque in the gardens commemorates the victory over the Galician mafia, quoting Pablo Neruda: 'They may cut down all the flowers, but they may not prevent spring from coming.' It is dedicated to the memory of all the victims of drug trafficking in Galicia. Another example: when the regional government was choosing a company to redecorate and mend the interior of the Baión estate buildings, they stipulated that no reference should be made to drugs or drug trafficking. It was the one non-negotiable point.

Politics in Galicia also seems somewhat sanitised. In years gone by it paid, in terms of votes, to be on the side of the narcos. Even when Feijóo was photographed on Marcial Dorado's yacht, though it did not go down well, the scandal was eventually forgotten, and Feijóo kept his job. But once the traffickers could be figured as criminals, the politicians stopped getting into bed with them. Which did, however, have one negative side effect: by distancing themselves from the phenomenon, they could also stop doing anything about it. And, as has been the case across the board since the downturn of 2008, resources have been harder and harder to come by: the SVA patrol boat *Fulmar*, for instance, was relocated from Vigo to Cadiz in 2014. And both the police force and the Guardia Civil are less than happy. 'There have been cuts, and that only plays into the narcos' hands,' says one police officer. 'Everything is going into combating terrorism. Which I suppose you can't argue with, but still, it only makes things harder.'

And, as we have already seen, people in the media are also becoming less vigilant, which filters through into the attitude of many Galicians, who view drug trafficking as a memory, rather than a current reality. A memory of merchant vessels being stormed by pirates in centuries gone by, and of penicillin and scrap metal being brought across *a raia* from Portugal, and cans of petrol, and crates of cigarettes, and – the great leap

– bales of cocaine washing up on the shores. Nowadays, new niches are still being sought into which cocaine can be stowed, and new businesses opened as a way of passing off the profits. From Celso Lorenzo Villa and Don Vicente to the Pastry Chef and Patoco. From Sito to third-generation Charlíns. From rowing boats to powerboats with 1,000-horsepower motors.

It isn't over, and therefore mustn't be forgotten.

NOTES

INTRODUCTION

1 'The frontier' or 'the strip' in both Portuguese and the Galician language. The area under discussion is along the Spain–Portugal border, where these languages have always historically mixed.

BY LAND, SEA AND *RÍA*

1 The Spanish would be 'Costa de Muerte' – another linguistic marker of Galicia as a between place.

SMOKE

1 *Paradors* are castles, monasteries and other historic buildings that have been adapted into state-run hotels and luxury accommodation.
2 Together they were known as 'the Ferrazos' and they later formed their own gang. According to Spanish public prosecutors, between 1982 and 1983 they were responsible for bringing in over 3.5 million crates of cigarettes, each of which would sell for 30,000 pesetas (€180).
3 An icon in smuggling circles, Prado López was arrested in 2012 for a 3,200-kilo consignment of cocaine intended to be brought in at Corcubión, on the Costa da Morte.

GALICIAN MAFIA

1   A play on words with Operacion Nécora: '*nécora*' is a crab.

THE *CAPOS*

1   Sintasol is a floor-cleaning chemical.

WHITE TIDE

1   Figures from Galician Health Board.

OPERATION NÉCORA

1   The Grupos Antiterroristas de Liberación were death squads established illegally by officials of the Spanish government to fight ETA, the principal Basque separatist militant group. They were active between 1983 and 1987, and it was later proven at trial that they were financed by important officials within the Spanish Interior Ministry.

THE STRUGGLE CONTINUES

1   A kind of razor clam.

IMITATING THE MAFIA

1   The car belonged to Alfredo Bea Gondar, the mayor of O Grove and a PP member who was accused in 2001 of smuggling two tons of cocaine ashore. Gondar was found not guilty by the Supreme Court.

ALL OUT

1   The *Abrente* was purportedly a fishing vessel – specialising in swordfish and shark and fishing the waters south of the Canary Islands. On its return to Camariñas, however, it would hardly have any haul at all, and yet its captain, Manuel Martínez, never seemed worried.

Nor were his crew. And not without reason: if the job proposed by Manolo the Catalan came off, they would not have to look at a swordfish again for the rest of their lives. In reality, they could have left the *Abrente* docked in port until the day of the operation, but it was also important to make a show of being an active vessel (almost all part-time drug vessels continue going out with the fleet). On 19 February 2001, the *Abrente*, by this point two days' sailing away from the Canaries, loaded up with the cocaine. A matter of hours later, on its journey to Galicia, it was boarded by officers from the *Petrel*, an SVA patrol boat. The crew jettisoned the merchandise, but the *Petrel* was equipped with a flotation system that prevented the cocaine from sinking. Times had changed. At the same time, on land the authorities arrested Manolo the Catalan and O Panarro (who would again be arrested two years later, as part of the South Sea bust). The pair were finally acquitted after the judge refused to allow recorded phone conversations to be submitted as evidence. The conversations included a line by the ship's captain warning his interlocutor that the *Petrel* had launched: 'Maruja has come out of hospital,' were his words.

CHANGING OF THE GUARD

1 The patriarch of the Panarros, Joaquín Agra, after evading justice in 2008, was spotted two years later coming out of a café in Pontevedra. He now had a beard, had put on weight and was wearing a cap and sunglasses. GRECO agents swooped, and he was given a 20-year sentence. The authorities have continued monitoring his offspring, including Jorge Agra, who was murdered in Paraguay in 2004, after – all indications suggest – having fled with the family's money.

BIBLIOGRAPHY

Antón, Santo and Luis Manuel García Mañá, *O lume* [The Fire], Edicións Xerais, 1997.

Carré, Héctor, *Febre* [Fever], Edicions Xerais, 2011.

Conde, Perfecto, *La conexión gallega. Del tabaco a la cocaine* [The Galician Connection: From Tobacco to Cocaine], Ediciones B, 1991.

Escobar, Juan Pablo, *Pablo Escobar. Mi padre* [Pablo Escobar: My Father], Planeta, 2015.

González Martínez, Praxíteles, *Yo también fui contrabandista en el estuario del Miño* [I Too Was a Smuggler on the Miño Estuary], O Rosal, 2013.

Lema, Rafael, *Costa da morte, un país de sueños y naufragios* [Costa da Morte: Country of Dreams and Shipwrecks], Grupo de Acción Costeira da Costa da Morte, 2011.

Portabales Jr, Ricardo and Julián Fernández Cruz, *El diario de mi padre. Testigo protegido* [Diary of My Father in a Witness Protection Programme], self-published, 2015.

Rivas, Manuel, *Todo é silencio* [*All is Silence*], Alfaguara, 2010.

Rodríguez Mondragón, Fernando, *El hijo del ajedrecista* [The Chess Player's Son], Editorial Oveja Negra, 2007.

Suárez, Felipe, *La Operación Nécora +* [Operation Nécora +], self-published, 1997.

Trigo, José Manuel and Ramón Trigo, *O burato do inferno* [A Hole in Hell], Faktoría K de Libros, 2010.

Urbano, Pilar. Garzón, *El hombre que veía amanecer* [The Man Who Saw the Sun Rise], Plaza & Janés Editores, 2000.

ZED

Zed is a platform for marginalised voices across the globe.

It is the world's largest publishing collective and a world leading example of alternative, non-hierarchical business practice.

It has no CEO, no MD and no bosses and is owned and managed by its workers who are all on equal pay.

It makes its content available in as many languages as possible.

It publishes content critical of oppressive power structures and regimes.

It publishes content that changes its readers' thinking.

It publishes content that other publishers won't and that the establishment finds threatening.

It has been subject to repeated acts of censorship by states and corporations.

It fights all forms of censorship.

It is financially and ideologically independent of any party, corporation, state or individual.

Its books are shared all over the world.

www.zedbooks.net
@ZedBooks